SOUTH ASIA AND CHINA

This book brings together new perspectives on China's engagement with South Asian countries. It examines emerging trends in the ties between China and South Asia in the geo-political, geo-strategic and geo-economics context and looks at opportunities for collaboration and connectivity between them.

Drawing on extensive case studies, this volume discusses issues such as China's overarching Belt Road Initiative (BRI), regional responses and alternatives to BRI, the new politico-economic drivers in the region, India's China puzzle, the Wuhan informal summit, Nepal and its security dilemma in the region and China's role in peace and stability in Afghanistan. It presents analysis, debates and the way forward for a comprehensive South Asian regional understanding in the wake of the advancing Chinese presence in South Asia.

An important contribution in the study of the developing pan China–South Asia vision, this book will be of interest to scholars and researchers of international relations, Chinese studies, Asian studies, defence and strategic studies, regional cooperation, foreign policy, geopolitics, comparative politics and political studies.

Adluri Subramanyam Raju is Dean of International Relations, Professor and former Head of the UNESCO Madanjeet Singh Institute of South Asia Regional Cooperation (UMISARC) and Centre for South Asian Studies and coordinator of the UGC Centre for Maritime Studies, Pondicherry University, India. He is the recipient of the *Mahbub Ul Haq Award* (Regional Centre for Strategic Studies (RCSS, Colombo, Sri Lanka), the *Scholar of Peace Award* (WISCOMP, New Delhi, 2002) and the *Kodikara Award* (RCSS, Colombo, 1998). He was also a Salzburg Seminar Fellow (2006). He received the National Best Teacher Award (C.V.S. Krishnamurthy Theja Charities, Tirupati, 2017) and Best Teacher Award twice (Pondicherry University, 2013 and 2018). He is a member of the Third Task Force on Blue Economy, FICCI, New Delhi, India. He was previously a visiting fellow at the Bandaranaike Centre for International Studies, Colombo, Sri Lanka. He has published 22 books and seven books are forthcoming.

Routledge Critical Perspectives on India and China

India and China together are home to more than one-third of the world's population. Two of the fastest growing economies today, these two nations will be key to the world's future.

This unique collaborative series between the Routledge India and China publishing programmes aims to bring cutting-edge, interdisciplinary research from and on these two global powers. The books in this series will focus on topical and emergent issues in contemporary India and China, presenting new perspectives on politics, society, economy, environment and culture.

China and South Asia
Changing Regional Dynamics, Development and Power Play
Edited by Rajiv Ranjan and Guo Changgang

The Chinese Shadow on India's Eastward Engagement
The Energy Security Dimension
Edited by Sanjay K. Bhardwaj

The Rise of India and China
Social, Economic and Environmental Impacts
Edited by Kala S Sridhar and Li Jingfeng

India and China
Economics and Soft Power Diplomacy
Edited by Geeta Kochhar and Snehal Ajit Ulman

South Asia and China
Engagement in the Twenty-First Century
Edited by Adluri Subramanyam Raju

For more information about this series, please visit: www.routledge.com/Routledge-Critical-Perspectives-on-India-and-China/book-series/RCPIC

SOUTH ASIA AND CHINA

Engagement in the Twenty-First Century

Edited by Adluri Subramanyam Raju

LONDON AND NEW YORK

First published 2022
by Routledge

2 Park Square, Milton Park, Abingdon, Oxon OX14 4RN

and by Routledge
605 Third Avenue, New York, NY 10158

Routledge is an imprint of the Taylor & Francis Group, an informa business

© 2022 selection and editorial matter, Adluri Subramanyam Raju; individual chapters, the contributors

The right of Adluri Subramanyam Raju to be identified as the author of the editorial material, and of the authors for their individual chapters, has been asserted in accordance with sections 77 and 78 of the Copyright, Designs and Patents Act 1988.

All rights reserved. No part of this book may be reprinted or reproduced or utilised in any form or by any electronic, mechanical, or other means, now known or hereafter invented, including photocopying and recording, or in any information storage or retrieval system, without permission in writing from the publishers.

Trademark notice: Product or corporate names may be trademarks or registered trademarks, and are used only for identification and explanation without intent to infringe.

British Library Cataloguing-in-Publication Data
A catalogue record for this book is available from the British Library

Library of Congress Cataloging-in-Publication Data
A catalog record has been requested for this book

ISBN: 978-0-367-61287-0 (hbk)
ISBN: 978-0-367-70424-7 (pbk)
ISBN: 978-1-003-14622-3 (ebk)

DOI: 10.4324/9781003146223

Typeset in Bembo
by Deanta Global Publishing Services, Chennai, India

Dedicated to
UNESCO Goodwill Ambassador (Late) Dr. Madanjeet Singh
Philosopher, Diplomat, Philanthropist, Writer, Artist
Founder, South Asia Foundation, New Delhi, India

CONTENTS

List of illustration ix
List of contributors xi
Acknowledgements xiii

Introduction 1
Adluri Subramanyam Raju

PART I
South Asia and China: Opportunities 9

1 China–South Asia: New Drivers 11
  Srikanth Kondapalli

2 China and South Asia: Future scenario 28
  Adluri Subramanyam Raju

PART II
South Asia and China: Connectivity 39

3 BRI, Neo-Tribute System and international financial
  assistance: Perspectives for South Asia 41
  R. Srinivasan

4 China's overarching Belt and Road Initiative vis-à-vis India's
  predicament 58
  Y. Yagama Reddy

5 BRI: Regional responses and alternatives   72
   Ashminder Singh Bahal

6 BRI and BBIN: Asian economic growth engines   84
   Ujjwal Upadhyay

PART III
South Asian Countries and China   **95**

7 India and China in South Asia: Towards trans-regional politics   97
   Anindya Jyoti Majumdar

8 India–China trade linkages in the context of an emerging
   uncertain world trading environment   111
   Indra Nath Mukherji

9 China's regional role: Should India be worried?   127
   Smruti S Pattanaik

10 Indian media's perception of China: A montage of national
   and regional dailies   143
   Rakhahari Chatterji and Anasua Basu Ray Chaudhury

11 Pearl in the string: Sri Lanka–China relations in the twenty-
   first century   160
   N. Manoharan

12 China's deepening engagement with Bangladesh   171
   Sreeradha Datta

13 China's engagement and managing security dilemma in
   South Asia: A Nepali perspective   185
   Kosh Raj Koirala

14 The Dragon's embrace: The contours of China–Pakistan
   strategic relations   198
   Reena Marwah

15 Peace and stability in Afghanistan: China's role   211
   Sadaf Mohmand

Index   223

ILLUSTRATION

Figures

8.1	India China Trade (US $ billion)	112
8.2	India's monthly trade with China June-November 2018 (US $ billion)	113
10.1	Perception by intensity in national newspapers, 2012–2014	150
10.2	Perception by intensity in regional newspapers (2012–2014)	151

Charts

8.1a	India's exports to China by basic economic categories-2010	114
8.1b	India's exports to China by basic economic categories-2017	114
8.2a	India's imports from China by basic economic categories-2010	115
8.2b	India's imports from China by basic economic categories-2017	115

Tables

1.1	China's investments in South Asia 2005–2019	20
1.2	China's Confucius institutes or centres in South Asia	22
8.1	India's average exports to China of top ten major product groups: 2015–2017 (Average value US$10.33 billion)	116
8.2	India's average imports from China of top ten major product groups: 2015–2017 (Average value US$646.86 billion)	116
8.3	India top ten potential exports to China (US$ million)	117

8.4   India's Additional Market Access Frontier (AMAF) with
      China and possible substitution of US exports in Chinese
      market (USD Thousand: 2017)   119
10.1 Attention score of national dailies   145
10.2 Attention score of regional dailies   146
10.3 Editorials by themes by national newspaper (2012–2014)   147
10.4 Editorials by themes by regional newspaper   148
10.5 Perception by national newspapers, 2012–2014 (percentages
      in brackets)   149
10.6 Editorial perception by intensity by regional newspaper
      (2012–2014)   150

CONTRIBUTORS

Rakhahari Chatterji is Retired Professor, Former Dean, Faculty of Arts, University of Calcutta and Honorary Distinguished Fellow, Observer Research Foundation, Kolkata, India.

Sreeradha Datta is Centre Head, Neighbourhood Studies and Senior Fellow, Vivekananda International Foundation, New Delhi, India.

Anindya Jyoti Majumdar is Professor, Department of International Relations, Jadavpur University, Kolkata, India.

Srikanth Kondapalli is Professor in Chinese Studies, Centre for East Asian Studies, Jawaharlal Nehru University, New Delhi, India.

N. Manoharan is Associate Professor, Department of International Studies, Political Science and History, CHRIST (Deemed to be University), Bangalore, India.

Reena Marwah is Associate Professor, Jesus and Mary College, University of Delhi, New Delhi, India.

Sadaf Mohmand is Site Auditor, International Narcotics Law (INL)/FIAT, Kabul, Afghanistan.

Indra Nath Mukherji is Retired Professor and Former Dean, School of International Studies, Jawaharlal Nehru University, New Delhi, India.

Smruti S. Pattnaik is Research Fellow, Manohar Parrikar Institute for Defence Studies and Analyses (MP-IDSA), New Delhi, India.

Kosh Raj Koirala is Special Correspondent, Republica National Daily, Kathmandu, Nepal.

Anasua Basu Ray Chaudhury is Senior Fellow, Observer Research Foundation, Kolkata, India.

Ashminder Singh Bahal is Air Commodore, Dean, Centre of Excellence, Institute of Chartered Accounts of India, Hyderabad, India.

R. Srinivasan is retired from Air Force; Independent Researcher and Editor in Chief, *Electronic Journal of Social and Strategic Studies* (EJSSS), Coimbatore, India.

Ujjwal Upadhyay is a consultant, Development, Environment, Livelihood, Kathmandu, Nepal.

Y. Yagama Reddy is Retired Professor and Former Director, Centre for Southeast Asian and Pacific Studies, Sri Venkateswara University, Tirupati, India.

ACKNOWLEDGEMENTS

I express my gratitude to the South Asia Foundation (SAF), New Delhi, for financial support to carryout academic activities at the UNESCO Madanjeet Singh Institute for South Asia Regional Cooperation (UMISARC) and the Centre for South Asian Studies, Pondicherry University. I also express my gratitude to Prof.Gurmeet Singh, Vice Chancellor, Pondicherry University, for his constant encouragement and support to carryout academic activities at the institute and the centre. I also take this opportunity to thank all the authors sincerely for contributing their valuable chapters to this volume. It would be impossible to produce a volume of this nature without editorial and administrative support, and so I thank all, particularly Prof. P.V. Rao, Dr. S.I. Humayun, Dr. R. Srinivasan and Ms. Udita Banerjee for supporting me in this regard.

Adluri Subramanyam Raju

INTRODUCTION

Adluri Subramanyam Raju

Contemporary Asian diplomacy is guided by two broad objectives: first, the search for alternatives to contain a rising China, which is poised to transform the existing regional and global power structure; and second, the maximisation of benefits out of this arc of prosperity. If the first premise sounds laden with strategic overload, the second one embodies the growth rationale. But both are and should not be mutually exclusive and the pursuit of one objective is closely laced with the other. Ever since the epoch of Asian tiger economies began, all the countries of the region built a deeply interwoven network of economic relations. Strategic considerations often weigh less in relation to economic stakes, or to put it otherwise, economic interests are loaded into security discourse. All the powers involved in the Asia-Pacific therefore are busy devising the means to attain the above twin objectives. But central to all their bilateral and multilateral strategies is China, *cause belli* of regional security worries. Unlike the classical era of the balance of power and bipolarity of the Cold War era, modern geopolitical dynamics of Asia denies its players, small and stronger, simplicity of choices. Multilateralism is the most professed strategy by the plural world of Asia-Pacific powers though the myriad chinks apparent in their regional forums like ASEAN Regional Forum (ARF), East Asia Summit (EAS), Regional Comprehensive Economic Partnership (RCEP), Trans-Pacific Partnership (TPP) and the like. Consensus eludes finding a common strategy to meet the China threat, the inability of ASEAN as a group to take a firm stand on the Chinese adverse positions in the South China Sea and find a common strategy for resolving the threat common to all displayed its impotency. Quad and trilateral dialogue of which India is a constituent are the more recent multilateral initiatives.

The anthology of twenty-first-century Asian strategic terms is couched in overlapping acronyms suggesting rapid convergence of great power interests across the Indian and Pacific Oceans. Inconsistency and imprecision are the hallmark of the chosen acronyms – Asia-Pacific, Indo-Pacific, Asia-Indo-Pacific, Broader Asia. Each maritime power invented its slogan to give vent to these terms: India's "mausum," Japan's "confluence of seas," China's "Maritime Silk Road" and the US "two ocean" doctrine are the manifestations of the trans-oceanic convergence. Asian maritime geographies therefore are redrawn to suit the strategic imperatives of the Asian century.

Chinese Belt and Road Initiative (BRI) attempts to integrate the continental and maritime spaces into a common politico-economic domain. Whatever be the choice of terms, Asian continental and littoral powers are embracing new political geographies. The Indian Ocean thus faces the imminence of losing its specificity but also gaining a spatial elasticity. Trilateral dialogues and forums converging like-minded states is another form of response by those worried about China-triggered regional insecurity climate. Such forums were visible at the official and non-official level. So, if the India–Japan–US dialogue is an official one, India–Japan–Taiwan is a non-official annual trilateral dialogue beginning with 2005. Their compositions vary, though hardly any substantial difference in the contents of their dialogues and each of these is simultaneously engaged with others in a different arrangement. Each apparently is carrying their experiences from one concentric circle to another triangular or quadrangular.

South Asia is attracting global attention today for its political and economic dynamics. It is one of the fastest-growing economic regions in the world (6% growth rate per year). It is trying to integrate with other regions of Asia, which are expected to play a vital role in the global arena. The South Asian Association for Regional Cooperation (SAARC) has expanded its membership from seven to eight (Afghanistan joined in 2007 as the eighth member), and nine external and major states joined as observers, and China is one of them.

A resurgent South Asia could either align its domestic policies with international concerns over China and therefore add to the Sino-phobia or put its acts together to give a considered direction to its policies to create environments conducive for mutual benefit.

China shares border with five countries in South Asia. Whereas India shares border with all the South Asian countries except Afghanistan, and no other South Asian country shares border with more than two countries in the region. China is rapidly connecting itself to almost every South Asian country.

India and China are the two largest countries (in terms of population) in the world. They are simultaneously rising as economic powers in Asia/world. They are seen as engines of global economic growth in the twenty-first century. When the world is shifting from geopolitics to geo-economics, it is as important for China and India to concentrate on economic relations. India and China can join together in strengthening their economic ties through cooperation. On the other hand, both of them have apprehensions over each other as a threat. India feels uncomfortable about the expansion of China in the Indian Ocean region, whereas China has reservations over India's presence in the Pacific Ocean.

Among the South Asian nations, Pakistan has established long-standing politico-military relations with China. Ceding the northern reaches of Aksai Chin and considerable territories of occupied Kashmir to China has facilitated the road connectivity between the countries. Apart from the obvious strategic implications to India, coupled with Chinese investments to develop Gwadar port, this road could serve as the southern perimeter of the BRI networks. The port could serve as a sentinel on the maritime part of the BRI. Sri Lankan connectivity through Hambantota port has already given a foothold over the Maritime Silk Road in the Indian Ocean region. These initiatives appear to be guided by China's intention to become the largest and most influential power in the world.

In the geopolitical context of South Asia, a composite understanding of China vis-à-vis South Asia is a must. First, one must attempt at knowing China as it is, for in the millennia that have gone by, China has changed but little of its resolute attachment to its own interests. It has made little concession to the interests of other nations, unless such a concession itself is in its interest. Second, we must explore the geopolitical interests of countries in South Asia, with a little historical perspective. This would be essential since none of the countries in their present form, except perhaps Bhutan, existed through two or three millennia that China has existed. The purpose, therefore, would be to define these nascent nations' geopolitical interest vis-à-vis that of China. When such a common ground is obtained, it would serve as the foundation for developing a pan China-South Asia vision.

UNESCO Madanjeet Singh Institute of South Asia Regional Cooperation & Centre for South Asian Studies, Pondicherry University, organised the international seminar on *South Asia and China: Emerging Trends* from 5 to 6 March 2019. The seminar discussed relations between South Asian countries and China in the geopolitical, geo-strategic and geo-economic context.

This volume consists of 3 parts and 15 chapters.

Part I: South Asia and China: opportunities

This part sets the tone for the volume by looking into the geopolitical arena of South Asia and China. Drawing on the developments with the increased Chinese presence in South Asia, the two chapters in this part create a template of future scenarios, in which multifarious factors discussed therein could impact South Asian nations.

In Chapter 1, "China-South Asia: new drivers," Srikanth Kondapalli describes how China has embarked on a multipronged approach to rejuvenate itself in South Asia despite South Asia being a region of uneven economic development, ethnic strife, terrorism afflicted and nuclear-armed. China supported Pakistan and launched its BRI in 2013, encompassing the South Asian region, continental as well as maritime. The author explores China's efforts to become the power centre in the region in recent times as well as countermeasures that the other countries are adopting.

In Chapter 2, "China and South Asia: a future scenario,"Adluri Subramanyam Raju analyses the relationship between the South Asian countries and China. Though it is not a part of South Asia, China is more connected and politically attracted to the South Asian countries except India. Further, South Asian security cannot be understood without taking China into consideration. China has penetrated in the region through investment and infrastructural development. Further, the author discusses China's relations with other South Asian countries, which in his view are cordial. China's presence in the region is affecting stronger regional cooperation in South Asia.In view of these developments, the author constructs a future scenario with regard to relations between China and South Asia.

Part II: South Asia and China: connectivity

In Part II, four chapters deal with historical and interregional connectivity dimensions that have a bearing on the South Asian region in the context of developments concerning the BRI. Collaborative networks such as CPEC, ASEAN, Indo-US, SAARC and BBIN and the possible directions that these networks could take are discussed, and the alternatives needed to correct imbalances created through the BRI are presented.

In Chapter 3, "BRI, neo-tribute system and international financial assistance: perspective for South Asia," R. Srinivasan explains China's efforts to include more and more countries into its fold across South Asia. The author stresses that South Asia remains most affected by the developments that aid or detract the BRI because this region sits at the junction that connects the Middle East with China. He looks at the BRI by drawing lessons from a Chinese historical perspective, suggesting therefrom newer policy avenues for South Asian neighbours in dealing with the compelling attractions of the BRI.

In Chapter 4, "China's overarching Belt and Road Initiative vis-à-vis India's predicament," Y. Yagama Reddy gives a brief introduction of the Belt and Road Initiative. Reddy explains that although the initiative is the biggest triumph of China, some countries have expressed their apprehensions. India has expressed its concerns and has opposed it on the ground that it passes through PoK. Although on many forums India and China are on the same page, China has been overtly seeking India's support for the BRI. The changing geopolitic realities demand that India should reconcile both cooperation and competition with China in areas of energy security and economic ties, but should avoid confrontation given China's overall advantage in surplus capital India needs to explore the potential prospect of Act East Policy and Indo-Pacific system.

In Chapter 5, "BRI: regional responses and alternatives," Ashwinder Singh Bahal explains the merits and vulnerabilities of the BRI project and especially focuses on the debt trap by smaller countries. Bahal suggests that alternatives need to be searched to counter Chinese influence, whereas he relies on India for two reasons: (1) India–US collaboration, which will move beyond defence cooperation, could be taken further towards enhancing trade and developing infrastructural facilities; (2) India has improved its ties with ASEAN in its Act East Policy. Bahal further suggests that India needs to strengthen its cooperation among SAARC countries. India needs to help those countries that have a debt from China. Further, he suggests that India should link Afghanistan and CAR through Chabahar port, which will enhance trade and provide an alternative route bypassing Pakistan. Moreover, Chabahar port is likely to benefit from the international North–South corridor project, which was initiated by Russia, India and Iran in 2000.

In Chapter 6, "BRI and BBIN: Asian economic growth engines," Ujjwal Uphadyay explains the importance of connectivity to overcome the economic inefficiency and constraints to the available market linkages. The BRI and BBIN act as means of connectivity to connect both big and small nations across South Asia and Eurasia. Uphadyay further explains that as China is prepared to construct a railway line to the northern boundary of Nepal, it also presents India with a reasonable opportunity where India should think of reasonable trade-offs. He also stresses that the BBIN can greatly benefit Bhutan, Bangladesh, Nepal and India through small ship navigation, ensuring better connectivity. He mainly highlights how the ideas of the BRI and BBIN can be best capitalised, where both China and India can go further, ensuring mutual benefits to each other along with other nations located around them.

Part III: South Asian countries and China

Part III presents, in four chapters, perspectives specific to India–China relationships in the context of the BRI. The scholarly analysis in the first three chapters in this aspect gets supplemented by an interesting view from grassroots viz., popular media perception vis-à-vis China in the North-Eastern part of India, which is geographically the closest to China. The remaining five chapters deal with country-specific analysis and developments from Sri Lanka, Bangladesh, Nepal, Pakistan and Afghanistan. Together, this part presents analysis, debates and a way forward from a comprehensive South Asian regional understanding in the wake of advancing Chinese presence in South Asia.

In Chapter 7, "India and China in South Asia: towards trans-regional politics," Anandiya Jyoti Majumdar discusses the form of rebalancing China's growing foothold in the South Asian region. Majumdar discusses irritants in India and China relationship ranging from border dispute, resource sharing, divergent political perceptions and consequent policy posturing. Nevertheless, the relations between the two are increasingly becoming pragmatic, which includes cooperation in some areas and competition based on cost–benefit calculus. Majumdar further discusses that the rise of China makes the South Asian region of strategic importance. The feeling of being encircled by China compels India to adopt measures to protect and promote its interests by rebalancing China.

In Chapter 8, "India–China trade linkages in the context of an emerging uncertain world trading environment," Indra Nath Mukherji maintains that India has substantial trade linkages with China and also considerable trade linkages with the United States. China's trade linkages with the United States are even more significant. When the United States imposes tariffs on Chinese imports, it will try to substitute such imports from other supplying countries. Similarly, when as a countermove China puts similar restrictions on US imports, it seeks alternative sources of imports. To that extent could India take advantage of this? Looked at from another angle, the United States would like to seek alternative markets for its exports to China, and likewise, China would like to seek alternative markets for its exports to the United States. What are the implications for India in case such products enter the Indian market in large quantities? Is India prepared to face these opportunities and challenges? These are some of the questions this chapter addresses.

In Chapter 9, "China's regional role: should India be worried," Smruti S. Pattnaik discusses the competing role of China and India to expand their market and scout for resources to build their economy. Both countries are locked in a situation of conflict as well as engagement. Although there is a border dispute, they are still engaged intrade. Pattnaik explains that China is relatively superior to India in completing infrastructural projects and that India suffers from a delivery deficit. In this connection, she raises five questions: what is the nature of China's role in the region?;to what extent China impinges on India's geo-strategic role in the region?; what are the likely consequences of Chinese investment?; what is India's approach to the neighbourhood; and finally, should India be worried about China' s regional role?

In Chapter 10, "Indian media's perception of China: a montage of national and regional dailies," Rakhahari Chatterji and Anasua Basu Ray Chaudhury make an attempt to analyse the Indian media's perception of China. They describe two aims of their study: the study attempts to explore the national and regional print media's perception of China, and it makes a comprehensive assessment of perception at the national and regional levels. They have chosen the time frame as three years extending from 2012 to 2014,during which India and China both witnessed leadership change and important policy changes as China's BRI and India's Look East Policy into Act East Policy.

In Chapter 11, "Pearl in the string: Sri Lanka–China relations in the twenty-first century," N. Manoharan explains how China has become one of the major players in Sri Lanka and the latter's role to become a key pearl in the string of Chinese involvement in South Asia. Manoharan traces the relations between the two countries since 1957. He discusses Chinese involvement in Sri Lanka: infrastructure development, economic aid, investments, trade and support during Eelam War IV. The chapter also discusses the repercussion on India's economic and strategic interest in South Asia because of the relationship between Sri Lanka and China.

In Chapter 12, "China's deepening engagement with Bangladesh," Sreeradha Datta explains how China, which was reluctant to recognise Bangladesh as a state initially, has improved its relation with the latter over a period of time and emerged as the largest trading partner. Datta analyses how China does not interfere in the internal affairs and maintains relations with main political parties in Bangladesh and thus avoids criticism from opposition parties, while involving in various projects in Bangladesh. Further, the chapter explains the defence and strategic cooperation between the two countries. Datta narrates how Bangladesh can be seen by China as a critical factor in its expansion in South Asia and in Indo-Pacific.

In Chapter 13, "China's engagement and managing security dilemma in South Asia: A Nepali perspective," Kosh Raj Koirala discusses how Beijing's engagement with Kathmandu has increased manifold after major political changes in Nepal. While China has begun to invest in mega infrastructures such as roadways, railways, industrial parks and port cities but at the same time this has equally invited security concerns to some of the countries in the region. Koirala suggests how the brewing security dilemma can be managed between various countries vis-à-vis China.

In Chapter 14, "The dragon's embrace: the contours of China–Pakistan strategic relations," Reena Marwah explains the relationship between China and Pakistan. The chapter focuses on how the bilateral relations between them have an impact on India's sovereignty. It explains in detail how the cordial relations between them have changed the status quo between India and Pakistan. Marwah argues that Pakistan has been used as a pawn in China's strategy, including in CPEC and BRI projects, to expand its presence in the global arena.

In Chapter 15, "Peace and stability in Afghanistan: China's role," Sadaf Mohammad discusses the changing role of China in post-9/11 scenario. Sadaf argues that Afghanistan's natural resources and geopolitical positions are important for China to initiate its BRI in Asia. Afghanistan being a gate to Central Asia is much more important for the connectivity of China's projects. Therefore, a stable and terror-free Afghanistan can be beneficial for China. She evaluates China's economic relations and its role in bringing security and stability to Afghanistan.

PART I
South Asia and China
Opportunities

1
CHINA–SOUTH ASIA
New Drivers

Srikanth Kondapalli

Introduction

China's relations with South Asia, as with other regions, have been exhibiting a new flavour in the past few years.[1] These flow from the Communist Party National Congress that lay down the policies to be pursued in the next five years. In the past decade, two-party congresses in 2012 and 2017 have been relatively ambitious with larger goals. Specifically, the 19th Party Congress in October 2017 has been a major break in the history of the communist party in laying down a long-term plan for China till 2050. All the policies, projections and programmes that were evolved at the Party Congress are to be implemented by the foreign and other relevant ministries and bureaus in China. These act as guidelines for the respective institutions, think tanks and policy-making bodies in China.

In October 2017, China's Communist Party (CCP) held its 19th National Congress and advocated building a "community of common destiny" and fulfil its "dream" of rejuvenating the country.[2] The Party's constitution has also been amended to include the 2013 launch of the Belt and Road Initiative (BRI). It had also advocated ushering the country into the "centre stage" in global and regional orders. Instead of a "new type of major power relations," as mentioned in 2013, the 19th Party Congress suggested a larger role for China in international politics. A new road map for China was evolved with 2020 being the deadline for building a "well-off society," by 2035 a "well-off society with socialism" and by 2050 completing the tasks of "socialist modernisation." By this period, China intends to complete "two centennials" that of the hundredth anniversary of the Communist Party in 2021 and the People's Republic by 2049. Under the "Xi Jinping Thought of Socialism with Chinese Characteristics in New Era," "14 Upholds" were outlined that included providing holistic security;

emphasis on cyberspace; military modernisation to make it into "world-class" forces; observing the rule of law and emphasis on "One country, two systems." It reiterated Five Principles of Peaceful Co-existence evolved since 1954. China reiterated an independent foreign policy as it is gaining strength, emphasised on "Good Neighbourhood" of securing its peripheries, suggested that multipolarity is "rapidly accelerating," suggesting the relevance of institutions like Russia–India–China trilateral and the BRICS formation. The Party Congress stated "6 nos," that is "anyone, any organization, any political party, at any time or in any form, to separate any part of Chinese territory from China"; "maintain sufficient ability to defeat any form of Taiwan independence" – a clear signal for those countries or institutions to keep away from Taiwan issue. Moreover, with such vague formulation, this could also be applied to all issues under the Chinese "One China" policy and nudge the neighbours on Tibet, Xinjiang, South China Sea or Senkaku Islands, with likely application to "southern Tibet," the area of Arunachal Pradesh that China since 2005 started mentioning. Also of relevance is that China has decided to make its state-owned enterprises "globally competitive world-class firms." The Party Congress made a resolve as well to push of participation in global governance, such as International Monetary Fund, etc., for which coordination with India and other countries is a requirement. While the previous drivers in China's policies towards South Asia include balancing a rising India, countering terrorism, expanding trade and others, the above new drivers are visible in China's overtures towards South Asia. Of these, the most important one is the BRI, the success of which to a large extent could trigger the application of other drivers such as "community of common destiny," building a "world class" military, multipolarity or projecting China's model abroad. While many of these new drivers are vague and could be adapted by China in the coming years, the BRI is more visible and concrete in its "five connectivities." Hence, a major portion of the text below is focused on the BRI in South Asia, although other drivers are also mentioned for contextual reference. Another caveat is that many infrastructure projects launched prior to 2013 are also subsumed in the Chinese literature as a part of the BRI. It is argued here that the new drivers are intended to make China as the predominant power in the region.

In the background of these new drivers, China's policies towards South Asia, as with the other regions, will be affected gradually. Already, many of these changes are impacting the region. However, while China had advocated these, it is not clear what exactly these phrases connote for the South Asian region. For instance, China stated that it wants to build a "Community of common/shared destiny." In general, a few decades ago, Deng Xiaoping ruled out any military alliances or pacts, or stationing its troops abroad. However, today China's international and regional footprints have increased manifold, necessitating a change in policy for "partnerships" at the moment. South Asia is a fertile ground for such experimentation in the near future as already China has been active in the region suggesting these links. Secondly, as the BRI made it into the party constitution, China's interactions with South Asia are showing signs of Beijing being obsessed with this initiative. The BRI emphasises five connectivities (policy coordination, connectivity, trade promotion, currency integration, people-to-people contacts) although it is not stated what China intends to do after fulfilling these connectivity projects. In all these areas, Beijing is enticing many South Asian regions to join its initiative, albeit selectively. For instance, while China promised US$62 billion in China–Pakistan Economic Corridor projects, it pledged a paltry US$100 million for Afghanistan. All in all, China's investments in infrastructure projects are increasing substantially.[3] Below is a brief account of the impact of some of the policies adopted by China in recent times. Of these, the BRI and its connectivities are more explicit in its impact.

Afghanistan

China borders Afghanistan; it settled the territorial dispute in 1960s, although currently it is concerned about the spread of political violence into Xinjiang province. Since September 11, 2001, China had blocked its borders with Afghanistan. Nevertheless, after the Taliban was displaced, China has been involved in infrastructure projects and reconstruction aid work. It had extended assistance to Afghanistan, which increased from US$4 million to US$150 million. In 2014, China sent a special envoy from Sun Yuxi to Kabul, hoping to elevate ties. In October 2014, China hosted the Heart of Asia Istanbul Process meeting in Beijing for finding a solution to the Afghanistan issue. Beijing advocates "Afghan-owned and Afghan-led" solution with reconciliation of various ethnic groups, including the Taliban. China had contacts with the Taliban prior to the September 11 events and today maintains contacts with the Hekmatyar group as well. In 2014, a Taliban delegation led by Qari Din Muhammad from Doha visited China. Another Taliban delegation secretly visited Beijing in 2016, triggering speculations on support for the BRI projects.[4] The newly elected president of Afghanistan first visited Beijing. In 2016, China and Afghanistan signed a MoU on the BRI. The MoU signed by the foreign ministers stated

> [T]he two sides shall jointly promote cooperation on the One Belt One Road Initiative in a bid to realize the goal of common development and translate the advantages of solid political ties, economic complementarities and people-to-people exchanges into pragmatic cooperation in an effort to promote increasing economic growth.[5]

In May 2017, at the Beijing meeting of the BRI, Afghanistan participated in the discussions, although at a ministerial level. In the light of difficulties faced in the execution of projects in Pakistan and to broad base the BRI, in December 2017, Foreign Minister Wang Yi stated that China–Pakistan Economic Corridor could be extended to include Afghanistan.[6]

China has been involved in several projects in Afghanistan prior to the launch of the BRI. It had extended finance for the construction of Republic Hospital of

Kabul, Parwan water and irrigation project, iron ore, dams, railways and roads and began constructing a road through Wakhajir Corridor and tunnel under the Pamirs. In 2007, Chinese companies signed a deal for the Aynak copper mine for US$4.4 billion and a total of US$10 billion for affiliated projects. In 2011, China National Petroleum Corporation signed a deal for exploiting energy reserves in Amu Darya Basin with over US$2.5 billion in investments.[7] Many of these projects have now been incorporated into the BRI. However, the most symbolic of the BRI initiative was exhibited when in August 2016 a train began from Xinjiang to Afghanistan via Kazakhstan and Uzbekistan to the land port of Hairatan in September covering over 7300 km and importing US$4 million in goods.[8]

Joining the BRI could provide an opportunity for Afghanistan to export its copper and iron ore, besides providing stability, although China's commitment to Afghanistan is a paltry US$100 million for connectivity projects.[9] However, according to a study on mutual perceptions as reflected in the media, it was suggested that the mutual interests of these two nations differ.[10] The details of specific Chinese companies investing in Afghanistan are provided in the Annexure.

With the talks between the Taliban, United States, Russia and others intensifying, China sees strategic opportunities in Afghanistan. However, Beijing's minimalist policies are to keep at bay the Al Qaeda-Uighur connection and its spillover effect on Xinjiang.

Bangladesh

Although opposed to the creation of Bangladesh and indeed threatened to use its recently acquired veto power in 1971, China's relations with Bangladesh today have improved, including in the economic field. Since 2005, both have evolved "strategic" relations, with Beijing supplying high-end arms, including submarines. As mentioned earlier, trade is increasing between the two nations, although trade imbalance is also growing in favour of Beijing. Bilateral trade increased from US$1.2 billion in 2002 to US$4 billion 2008 to US$5 billion 2010 to US$6.4 billion 2012 and to over US$15 billion now. China made investments in Shahjalal Fertilizer Factory (of over US$800 million), constructed over six friendship bridges across Ganga river and Mukhterpur Bridge over the river Dhaleswari in 2008, built the Bangladesh–China Friendship Conference Center at Dhaka, a multi-lane tunnel under the river Karnaphuli, made efforts at tapping potential 60 trillion ft^3 of natural gas, involved in a coal-based power plant in Barapukuria, Pagla Water Treatment Plant in Narayanganj (of over US$226 million), bid for the Sonadia deep-sea port and Dohazari-Cox Bazar railway link, built nearly 500 Chinese shops at Kanchpur built at a cost of about US$6 million and its Exim Bank extended bank loans of US$200 million for upgrading the telecom network. Bangladesh was represented at the BRI meeting, and its foreign minister announced that the country will benefit from the connectivity projects of the BRI. While there is no direct link between the two, BCIM EC provides an opportunity to expand the BRI in the region, in addition to a plan to extend the energy pipeline in Myanmar to Chittagong. China's investments in Bangladesh in energy and infrastructure increased in 2019 by over US$600 million. Over 400 Chinese companies have been operating in the country in several projects – with 200 big and the rest small and medium enterprises. In the energy field, China intends to spend US$7 billion in thermal power projects for about 14 GW of capacity in Bangladesh, out of a total capacity layout of 102 GW in 23 countries. Such power stations are located in Chittagong, Patuakali, Cox's Bazar and others. In addition, China plans to spend US$10 billion on infrastructure projects, including the Chinese Economic and Industrial Zone, the 8th China–Bangladesh Friendship Bridge and the International Exhibition Centre.[11] The details of specific Chinese companies investing in Bangladesh are provided in the Annexure.

India

China has had good relations with India since 1949 but has marred in the run-up to and after the 1962 border clashes. Bilateral trade increased after Prime Minister Rajiv Gandhi's visit to China in 1988 when both decided to set aside the territorial dispute and enhance relations in other fields, including economic relations. Nevertheless, non-resolution of the territorial dispute – despite nearly three decades of talks on the issue – affects one of the core aspects of the recent BRI project, viz. connectivity. Connectivity could be possible through non-disputed areas like Sikkim, but here as well after the Doklam incident in June–August 2017, bilateral relations were affected. Both nations conduct extensive "strategic communications" between the two leaderships, and engagement is reflected in the institutional interactions at special representative, foreign secretary (strategic dialogue), defence ministry (annual defence dialogues and hand-in-hand army-to-army joint counterterrorism operations), home (counterterrorism), human resources (cultural exchanges), finance (financial dialogues) and the like. China–India trade is the largest among all other South Asian countries put together – increasing from a few hundred million to more than US$90 billion, although the goal of reaching US$100 billion by 2015 was not met.

India joined the Asian Infrastructure Investment Bank as the second-largest investor (after China) for infrastructure projects. It also agreed to pursue the BCIM (Bangladesh–China–India–Myanmar) initiative during the May 2013 visit of Premier Li Keqiang. Three meetings of the joint study group on BCIM at the official level were held by 2017, although India appears to be upgrading other initiatives such as BIMSTEC and BBIN, as China began preparations for China–Myanmar Economic Corridor. Also, of concern for India is the CPEC projects that pass through the Pakistan-occupied Kashmir region. The Indian leadership time and again has stated that sovereignty issues should be respected by China. China invited India to join the BRI.[12]

China's trade with India has been the largest among all the South Asian countries – at above $94 billion in 2018, although a 2015 deadline for crossing US$100 billion has not yet been met. The bilateral trade deficit is high in favour of China, with India losing about US$64 billion a year recently. India's suggestion to China to rectify trade imbalance has not yet been realised, although President

Xi Jinping during his visit to India in September 2014 promised to invest US$20 billion for the next five years. Cumulatively by 2019, China's investments in India are about US$8 billion.[13] The details of specific Chinese companies investing in India are provided in the Annexure.

Maldives

China evolved relations with the Maldives since 1990s but opened its embassy in Male a few years ago. President Xi Jinping's visit to South Asia began with the Maldives in September 2014, suggesting the renewed thrust in the region. China had built the Ministry of Foreign Affairs building, National Museum, 1000 Housing Units Project, renewable energy unit, hotels and invested in telecommunications. President Xi's visit resulted in infrastructure projects at Havan, Hulhule Bridge and other projects. In December 2017, the Maldives signed a Free Trade Area with China, although it was reportedly rushed without much discussion in the parliament.[14] TrinaBESS, a Chinese company was chosen by the Maldivian Ministry of Environment and Energy to provide micro-grids to the atolls of the island state, moving away from the current diesel power plants to the solar electricity grid and achieve carbon neutral by 2020.[15] The Maldives plans to attract more tourists from China from the current 350,000. As a part of the BRI, the Maldives intends to attract a million Chinese tourists in the next few years.[16] China's investments in the Maldives as a part of the BRI projects are having an impact on the geopolitics of the Indian Ocean, specifically on India.[17] Former president Mohamed Nasheed stated that China is "buying up our lands, buying up our key infrastructure and effectively buying up our sovereignty."[18] China's intention is to be a part of the Indian Ocean region.[19] With the change in government in Male in 2019, Nasheed's criticism of China increased. It needs to be seen whether China's projects will be affected by this change. The details of specific Chinese companies investing in the Maldives are provided in the Annexure.

Nepal

China's relations with Nepal remain cordial, and after the 1960s border dispute resolution, it provided conditions to improve further bilateral relations. China intends to be a part of Nepal's external power structure by keeping Kathmandu leadership away from India. It had supplied US$200 million worth of arms in 1987 to Nepal and offered alternative energy supplies to the landlocked nation when Madhesi agitation took place a few years ago. Beijing's efforts in Nepal is to wean away Kathmandu from Delhi's influence.

China's trade with Nepal increased from US$67 million in 1997 to US$220 million in 1999 to US$1.2 billion in 2012 to US$2.6 billion in 2013 to a reduced figure of above US$1 billion recently. The balance of payments position is in China's favour. Six border trade posts were constructed: Kodari-Nyalam, Rasua-Kerung, Yari (Humla)-Purang, Olangchunggola-RIYO and

Kimathanka-RiwoNechung (Mustang)-Legze, and today over 20 Chinese joint venture companies (out of 399 foreign-funded ventures) are functioning in Nepal.

Way back in 1967, China constructed the Araniko Highway of 104 km. Later, the 174 km Prithvi Highway, 36 km Narayanghat-Mugling road, 65 km Pokhara-Baglungroad, 27 km Kathmandu ring road, Dry port at Nepal–China border of Larcha and airport at Pokhara. It is planning to extend Golmud-Lhasa railway; made Lumbini investment of US$3 billion; involved in the US$43 million project of ZTE for four data centres in Biratnagar, Kathmandu, Hetauda and Pokhara; and, in February 2012, made a contract with Three Gorges International Corp for 750 MW West Seti dam at a cost of US$1.6 billion to be completed by 2019. China is also involved in the Trishuli hydroelectricity project.

Nepal signed the framework agreement on the BRI with Beijing in May 2017.[20] Many specific details of the projects to be undertaken under the BRI in Nepal are still not clear.[21] Some have also become controversial. For instance, on 3 May 2017, Nepal signed a contract with China Gezhouba Group Corporation to build a storage-type 1200 MW project at Budhi Gandaki in central Nepal under the engineering, procurement, construction and finance model estimated to be over US$2.5 billion. The height of the dam is to be over 263 m.[22] This Chinese company is already building the 30 MW Chameliya and 60 MW Upper Trishuli projects.[23] In June 2017, a MoU was signed. Given the scale and significance of the project, in September 2017, China included the Budhi Gandaki project as a part of the BRI.[24] However, over 20,000 people will be displaced during the construction process. This has generated controversy and former prime minister Baburam Bhattarai demanded the scrapping of the project and argued for self-financing and other measures.[25] Finally, the agreement was scrapped on 13 November 2017, citing financial irregularities by the Chinese company. Gezhouba company protested the Nepali decision.[26] Other hydroelectricity projects as well are behind schedule, including the West Seti and Kulekhani three projects.[27] During President Xi Jinping's visit to Nepal in October 2019, a slew of agreements was signed for tunnel construction, revamping the roads and possibly the feasibility studies for railway connect from Kathmandu to Lhasa in future. Xi was more concerned about the Tibetans in Nepal during this visit. The details of specific Chinese companies investing in Nepal are provided in the Annexure.

Pakistan

China has good relations with Pakistan since the 1950s, but has acquired more strategic depth after the India–China border skirmishes in 1962.[28] Relations between the two flowered in all dimensions, with Islamabad receiving the maximum aid from Beijing among all South Asian countries. Arms sales to Islamabad are also the maximum compared to other South Asian states, including nuclear and ballistic missiles or related technologies. The "all-weather" relations between the two have provided much resonance in the BRI initiative. Indeed, the CPEC projects have been outlined as "flagship" programmes by Premier Li Keqiang and as a "game changer" by Pakistan prime minister, suggesting the centrality of this project in the BRI.[29] China–Pakistan trade increased from US$7 billion in 2009 to US$8.6 billion in 2010 to US$18 billion in 2015, but reduced to US$15 billion in 2016. Much of this is in favour of China. China's *renminbi* is to replace the United States in the coming years as a part of the China–Pakistan trade.[30]

Prior to the launch of the CPEC, China was involved in many infrastructure projects in Pakistan, including the Karakoram Highway built in the 1980s. The CPEC includes widening of the Karakoram Highway, construction of hydro-electric projects, highways, railroads (including the Havelian-Kashi 1059 km), 820 km of fibre optics, Gwadhar port and others.[31] However, the CPEC projects face a number of challenges, including high costs, labour displacements, debts, derailing of projects due to political violence and terrorist incidents, environmental degradation and the like. Much of the controversy began with the financing of the projects and Pakistan's ability to repay for the projects. While one group argued that these projects could trigger economic growth rates, the other was concerned about China's role. For instance, the Planning and Development Committee of the Pakistan Senate suggested that in the CPEC projects, "only Chinese investors would be allowed to invest in the proposed special economic zones being created under the corridor umbrella. No assurances could be given that Pakistani labour would be recruited to work in the Chinese projects, or that the country would see a revenue windfall."[32]

Further, the Chairman of the Senate Committee Col Syed Tahir Hussain Mashhadi suggested that the CPEC projects are not transparent about the taxes, loans and usage rights.[33] On the remarks of Sartaz Aziz that the CPEC loans will be paid at 2% interest over a period of 20–25 years, Khurram Hussain argued that the actual annual net outflow from Pakistan will be about US$3.546 billion per year once commercial operations begin.[34] In 2017, Pakistan's external debt and liabilities have increased by more than 12% to the previous year to US$85 billion.[35] Also, in May 2017, two Chinese were killed by the ISIS after they were taken away in Quetta.[36] According to James Dorsey, the CPEC provides China with economic domination and surveillance and allows China to shape the media landscape in Pakistan.[37] Given these apprehensions, CPEC progress has been uneven with a recent report suggesting to stalling of the CPEC's three roadways financing citing corruption charges.[38] The details of specific Chinese companies investing in Pakistan are provided in the Annexure.

Sri Lanka

China began relations quite early and the Rubber-Rice Pact of the 1950s with Sri Lanka was cited for overcoming the US trade embargoes on China. Bilateral trade with Sri Lanka is in favour of Beijing and has grown from US$458 million in 2000 to US$3.14 billion in 2011 to US$3.62 billion in 2013 and to US$4.55 billion in 2016. Both nations began discussions about free trade area, which is at an advanced stage. China invested in Hambantota port (nearly US$1.5 billion) and in Colombo South Harbor.[39] There are also other plans, including the Norochcholai power plant – 900 MW of thermal power (US$1.3 billion) to meet 45% of the total demand of the nation's power grid. There are also Palai-Kankasanthurai railway link; Colombo-Katunayake Expressway; Jaffna Housing complex for the army personnel; the special economic zone at Mirigama (being developed by China's Huichen Investment with $28 million investment); and developing 1000 acre Tapioca farm. China had invested US$250 million in 2004, which increased to US$12 billion by 2019. It intends to invest US$50 billion in the next 15 years. There are over 30,000 Chinese workers in Sri Lanka in various projects, triggering criticism about the lack of skill transfers to the locals. On the other hand, in 2014, the Board of Investment of Sri Lanka suggested that in the 14 projects of Chinese companies registered in the country, they have generated more than 2500 local jobs. China was also involved in November 2012 in launching a communications satellite for Sri Lanka.

Prime Minister Ranil Wickremesinghe attended the BRI Forum in May 2017. In December 2017, Sri Lanka handed over Hambantota Port to China Merchant Ports Holdings on a 99-year lease arrangement with the intention of transforming from "transshipment port" to that of a "total logistics hub."[40] The lease was necessitated after Sri Lanka was unable to repay debt and converted the deal into equity. Under this arrangement, China will spend US$1.12 billion in lieu of 70% stake in the port.[41] China is also investing in a deep-water terminal port, the Colombo International Container Terminal in 270 hectares with an investment of US$1.5 billion. The details of specific Chinese companies investing in Sri Lanka are provided in the Annexure.

Comprehensive engagement

The case studies above in brief suggest that under the rubric of the BRI, China had expanded its links to the South Asian regions, as with the other regions of the world. To summarise the whole South Asian region, the following observations can be made, which suggest that the current phase of engagement with the region is comprehensive in nature in many fields so as to make China a predominant power in the region. China is enhancing its hard power and soft power in South Asia through trade, investments, organising trade expos at Kunming and arms sales on the one hand, while also increasing its soft power through Confucius Institutes and Confucius Classrooms in the region.[42]

Firstly, China's trade with South Asia is increasing step by step. While compared to the rest of the world, South Asia figured marginally in trade, connectivity and investments in infrastructure projects, and free trade mechanism could possibly expand such linkages. China had signed a Free Trade Area with Pakistan in 2006, hurriedly with the Maldives in 2017, and conducted negotiations with Sri Lanka on this issue. The total trade of China with the South Asian countries was about US$107 billion in 2016 – some with large nations (for instance with

India at US$70 billion, Pakistan US$15 billion, Bangladesh at US$15 billion), and with Bhutan it was US$15 million.[43] By 2019, China's trade with India grew to $93 billion. Many South Asian countries have expressed serious concern about the growing trade deficit with China and for the past decade they have urged China to invest in the region. China's BRI comes in this background. In order to further promote trade and business linkages and make the southwestern regions of China a magnate for the South Asian region, China has been organising Kunming trade fairs since 2013. From 12 to 17 June 2015, India was the country of honour at the China–South Asia Expo at Kunming, inaugurated by Vice President Li Yuanchao. In June 2018, the fifth Expo stated:

> With the purpose of promoting China–South Asia comprehensive cooperation and development, the main thread of promoting the "the Belt and Road Initiative" … it strives to create a high level and comprehensive exhibition of commodity trade, service trade, investment cooperation, tourism cooperation and cultural exchange, and become an important bridge of mutual benefit and cooperation between China and the South Asian countries and an important platform for China and South Asian countries to expand economic and trade exchanges with other countries.[44]

In June 2019, Sri Lanka was the country of honour with over 104 exhibitors. The 2019 Expo, combined with the Southeast Asian countries, saw the participation of over 3000 enterprises even as trade with South Asia in 2018 increased by over 10%.[45] While such expos are useful, blowing winds of recession in China and lack of major orders have been dampening such exercises.

Secondly, China's investments in South Asia are increasing gradually. The American Enterprise Institute suggests that while China had invested over US$2 trillion abroad, its investments in South Asia amount to over US$137 billion, nearly half of which is made in Pakistan, as Table 1.1 indicates. Some of the

TABLE 1.1 China's investments in South Asia 2005–2019

Country	Total investment ($ billions)
Afghanistan	3.48
Bangladesh	26.65
Bhutan	0
Maldives	1.42
Pakistan	58.46
Nepal	4.92
Sri Lanka	13.44
India	29.03

Source: American Enterprise Institute, https://www.aei.org/china-global-investment-tracker

investments were outlined in the section on the BRI above, and the Annexure below has the details of investments and the Chinese companies involved.

Thirdly, as a part of its hard power drive, China has been expanding its military contacts with the South Asian region both in the continental and maritime dimensions. According to the Stockholm-based SIPRI, China's arms supply to the South Asian region, specifically to Pakistan, has been a major driver for decades. This has only intensified in recent times. Pakistan received as much as 35% of Chinese arms between 2013 and 2017, followed by 19% to Bangladesh.[46]

Fourthly, in order to expand its appeal to the South Asians, China is establishing a number of Confucius Institutes and classrooms in the region. China had set up over 540 Confucius Institutes and over 1000 Confucius Centres across the globe in over 140 countries to enhance its soft power abroad and provide a positive image of the BRI projects and China's rise in the international system.[47] The Confucius Institutes impart Chinese language training to the locals and intend to enhance China's cultural appeal.[48] While many of these were established in the United States, Europe, Southeast Asia and Africa, some have become prominent in the South Asian region as well. Nepal, Pakistan and Sri Lanka today have vibrant Confucius Institutes. The Confucius Institute in Nepal was established in Kathmandu in 2007 with the purpose of enhancing "mutual understanding" between the two countries.[49] Table 1.2 presents details on such centres.

Conclusion

Cumulatively, as a result of the hard and soft power thrust in the South Asian region, China today is in a predominant position at a time when the United States has been exhibiting signs of withdrawal. On the other hand, Indian efforts to consider "neighbourhood first" have not yielded spectacular results. While the power structure in the South Asian region is still in overall favour of India, China has made major inroads in the last decade, with the BRI standing out as the major conduit. China is able to consolidate its position in Pakistan, while making inroads into Afghanistan, Sri Lanka and Nepal. It faced reverses in the Maldives, and relations with Bangladesh are on even keel. Beijing has no diplomatic relations with Bhutan, and the Doklam border incident in 2017 only resulted in further straining of relations with Thimphu. There is an increasing realisation that the BRI is leading to debts, environmental degradation and opaqueness in transactions. Yet several smaller countries in South Asia are finding the BRI tempting. Since the 19th Communist Party Congress, China's comprehensive engagement with the South Asian countries has increased, although it is not without its own set of problems. This is then the new driver in China's South Asian policies. The above analyses also point to the ability of China to expand its outreach in the South Asian region, despite a number of hurdles, mainly caused by opposing forces in India, the United States and others. China did make a dent in the structural power of the region as various

TABLE 1.2 China's Confucius institutes or centres in South Asia

Country	Partner institutions	Remarks
Afghanistan	Kabul University and Taiyuan University of Technology	Established on 9 January 2008
Pakistan	National University of Modern Languages, Islamabad and Beijing Language and Culture University	Established on 4 April 2004. On 14 April 2017, PM Nawaz Sharif presented the Urdu version of *Xi Jinping: The Governance of China* to the Institute
Pakistan	The University of Karachi and Sichuan Normal University	Established on 22 May 2013
Pakistan	The University of Agriculture Faisalabad and Xinjiang Agricultural University	Established on 19 February 2014
Pakistan	The University of the Punjab and Jiangxi University Science and Technology	Established on 17 June 2015. On 26 May 2019 Vice President Wang Qishan inaugurated this Institute. This institute is "to facilitate China–Pakistan Economic Corridor"
Bangladesh	North South University, Dhaka and Yunnan University	Established on 2 June 2005. Vice Premier Liu Yandong visited on 26 May 2015 and stated "we should develop a closer comprehensive cooperative partnership, enhancing political mutual trust."
Bangladesh	The University of Dhaka and Yunnan University	Established on 5 November 2015. On 5 April 2017 Chen Changzhi, Vice Chairman of the Standing Committee of the National People's Congress visited the Institute
Nepal	Kathmandu University and Hebei University of Economics and Business	Established on 5 February 2007
Sri Lanka	The University of Kelaniya and Chongqing Normal University	Established on 15 November 2006
Sri Lanka	Colombo University and Beijing Foreign Studies University; Honghe University	Established on 16 September 2014
India	The University of Mumbai and Tianjin University of Technology	Established on 16 December 2012
India	Vellore Institute of Technology and Zhengzhou University	Established on 19 April 2007

(*Continued*)

TABLE 1.2 (*Continued*)

Country	Partner institutions	Remarks
India	Lovely Professional University, Phagwara and Yichun University	Established on 5 December 2018
India	O.P. Jindal Global University and Shanghai University of Political Science and Law	Established on 5 December 2018
India	Confucius Classroom at The School of Chinese Language in Kolkata and Yunnan Normal University	Established on 31 May 2016
India	Confucius Classroom at Bharathiar University and CRI	Established on 15 May 2015

Source: Hanban website, http://english.hanban.org/node_10971.htm.

indicators above suggested, although again several barriers constrain China's further expansion.

Notes

1 Srikanth Kondapalli, "China's Interactions with South Asia: New Beginnings", in T. Nirmala Devi and Adluri Subramanyam Raju (eds), *Envisioning a New South Asia*, New Delhi: Shipra Publications, 2009, pp. 203–19. The current chapter focuses on most recent events, including changes in China's policies due to the 18th and 19th Communist Party Congresses (in 2012 and 2017, respectively). While previously China's policies in South Asia are seen as a "balancer" in the region against India, the current policies go beyond and intend to make China a predominant power in the region.
2 Timothy Heath, "The China Dream: Never Closer, yet Never More Elusive", RAND Corp, 1 October 2019, www.rand.org/blog/2019/10/the-china-dream-never-closer-yet-never-more-elusive.html, accessed 12 December 2019. For the long-term plans of China, see Hu Angang, *China in 2020 — A New Type of Superpower*, Washington, DC: Brookings Institution Press, 2011, and Hu Angang, Yan Yilong, and Wei Xing, *China 2030*, Heidelberg: Springer, 2014.
3 Penelope Marbler and Lea Shan, "Chinese Investments in Infrastructure Worldwide", *Asia Focus*, no. 36, June 2017, www.iris-france.org/wp-content/uploads/2017/06/Asia-Focus-36.pdf, accessed 13 December 2019.
4 Fu Yu, "China's Belt and Road Meets Trump's Afghanistan Plan", *The Diplomat*, 21 December 2017, https://thediplomat.com/2017/12/chinas-belt-and-road-meets-trumps-afghanistan-plan/, accessed 14 December 2019.
5 Afghanistan Ministry of Foreign Affairs, "Belt and Road Initiative and Afghanistan", http://recca.af/?page_id=2077, accessed 13 December 2019.
6 "China Wants Afghanistan's Ancient Trade Routes to Be Part of New 'Silk Road'", 26 December 2017, www.rt.com/business/414253-china-pakistan-afghanistan-economy-corridor/, accessed 14 December 2019.
7 Wang Jin, "The US Withdrawal and One Belt One Road: Chinese Concerns and Challenges in Afghanistan", *Strategic Assessment*, vol. 19, no. 3, October 2016, www.inss.org.il/he/wp-content/uploads/sites/2/systemfiles/SystemFiles/adkan19-3ENG_3_Wang%20Jin.pdf, accessed 12 December 2019.
8 See n. 5.

9 Meena Singh Roy, "Afghanistan and the Belt and Road Initiative: Hope, Scope, and Challenges", *Asia Policy*, no. 24, July 2017, pp. 103–109, https://muse.jhu.edu/article/666560/pdf, accessed 14 December 2019. Roy argued that China's assistance to Afghanistan for its reconstruction efforts remain US$250 million since 2001 (although it pledged another US$327 million to be spent in 2015--2017) compared to US$110 billion by the United States and US$2 billion by India.
10 Azeta Hatef and Luwei Rose Luqiu, "Where Does Afghanistan Fit in China's Grand Project? A Content Analysis of Afghan and Chinese News Coverage of the One Belt, One Road Initiative", *International Communication Gazette*, 13 December 2017.
11 This is based on "Infrastructure and Energy Bind Bangladesh to China", 13 May 2019, www.thethirdpole.net/en/2019/05/13/infrastructure-and-energy-bind-bangladesh-to-china/, accessed 16 May 2019.
12 Ma Jiali, ""一「一路"「想符合中印「「根本利益", 19 June 2015, http://news.163.com/15/0619/10/ASFDKTB7000146BE.html, accessed 14 December 2020. See also Shyam Saran, "India Must Join China's Silk Route Initiative", *The Hindustan Times*, 18 March 2015, www.hindustantimes.com/analysis/india-must-join-china-s-silk-route-initiative/article1-1327985.aspx, accessed 2 December 2019; Suman Bery, "How India Should Respond to China's Belt and Road", *The Diplomat*, 6 July 2017, https://thediplomat.com/2017/07/how-india-should-respond-to-chinas-belt-and-road/, accessed 2 December 2019; Saibal Dasgupta, "China Says Silk Road is Taking Shape Despite India's Reluctance to Join", *The Times of India*, 13 December 2014, http://timesofindia.indiatimes.com/world/china/China-says-Silk-Road-is-taking-shape-despite-Indias-reluctance-to-join/articleshow/45506242.cms, accessed 12 January 2015; "China Eyes Consensus with India on Building New Silk Road", *China Daily*, 18 September 2014, www.chinadaily.com.cn/world/2014xisco/2014-09/18/content_18623473.htm, accessed 3 October 2014; Ananth Krishnan, "China Wants India to Play Key Role in 'Silk Road' Plan", *The Hindu*, 10 August 2014, www.thehindu.com/news/international/world/china-wants-india-to-play-key-role-in-silk-road-plan/article6301227.ece, accessed 2 September 2014; Ananth Krishnan, "China Asks India to Put aside 'Maritime Silk Road' Concerns", *India Today*, 12 February 2015, http://indiatoday.intoday.in/story/china-india-asean-sushma-swaraj-maritime-silk-road-concerns/1/418576.html, accessed 2 March 2015.
13 On this subject see Amit Bhandari, Blaise Fernandes and Aashna Agarwal, "Chinese Investments in India", *Gateway House*, 1 February 2020, www.gatewayhouse.in/wp-content/uploads/2020/03/Chinese-Investments-in-India-Report_2020_Final.pdf, accessed 3 February 2020.
14 "Maldives Signed Off on China Trade Deal with Just an Hour's Debate over 1,000-Page Agreement", *Reuters*, 9 December 2017, www.scmp.com/news/china/diplomacy-defence/article/2123601/maldives-signed-china-trade-deal-just-hours-debate-over, accessed 14 December 2017. A 1000-page agreement was signed in 1 hour of discussion at Maldivian parliament.
15 "Trina BESS Successfully Completed the First Shipment in Its 'Belt and Road Initiative' Project", 29 January 2018, www.pv-magazine.com/press-releases/trina-bess-successfully-completed-the-first-shipment-in-its-belt-and-road-initiative-project/, accessed 3 February 2018.
16 "Maldives Aims to Attract 1 million Chinese Tourists via Belt & Road Initiative", 9 May 2017, www.travelandtourworld.com/news/article/maldives-aims-to-attract-1-million-chinese-tourists-via-belt-road-initiative/, accessed 14 May 2017.
17 Jhinuk Choudhury, "Can China's Inroads into the Maldives Displace India? Can China's Inroads into the Maldives Displace India?", *Huffington Post*, 18 December 2015, www.huffingtonpost.in/jhinuk-chowdhury/maldives-helping-china-co_b_8695656.html, accessed 24 December 2015.
18 "Belt & Road with Bumps, Maldives Ex-Leader Says Chinese Projects Akin to Land Grab", *South China Morning Post*, 23 January 2018, https://macaudailytimes.com.mo

/belt-road-bumps-maldives-ex-leader-says-chinese-projects-akin-land-grab.html, accessed 26 January 2018.
19 Shyam Sharan cites a Chinese naval document in this regard as "Select locations meticulously, make deployments discreetly, give priority to cooperative activities and penetrate gradually", see "Enter the Dragon", *India Today*, 15 February 2018, www.indiatoday.in/magazine/up-front/story/20180226-india-china-maldives-abdulla-yameen-male-mohamed-nasheed-1170909-2018-02-15, accessed 22 February 2018.
20 "Nepal Joins China's 'One Belt, One Road' Initiative, Possibly Alarming India", *South China Morning Post*, 12 May 2017, www.scmp.com/news/asia/diplomacy/article/2094091/nepal-joins-chinas-one-belt-one-road-initiative-possibly, accessed 18 May 2017.
21 According to the Chinese Ambassador to Nepal Yu Hong, Nepal should be able to specify these projects quickly, while Nepal's foreign secretary suggested that "a solid political commitment of a stable government, solid policy framework and cooperation measures in the future will take the relations of the two countries to newer heights". See "Nepal Urged to Finalise Projects under Belt and Road Initiative", *Himalayan News Service*, 13 February 2018, https://thehimalayantimes.com/business/nepal-urged-finalise-projects-belt-road-initiative/, accessed 16 February 2018.
22 "China Gezhouba Wins Nepal Hydropower Project Contract", *Nepal Energy Forum*, 31 May 2017, www.nepalenergyforum.com/china-gezhouba-wins-nepal-hydropower-project-contract/, accessed 4 June 2017. This report suggests that the Budhi Gandak project could overcome the 600 MW shortage that the country is facing. Nepal also has plans to generate 10,000 MW of electricity from the current 760 MW by 2025.
23 "China's Gezhouba Lands Budhi Gandaki Contract", *Nepal Energy Forum*, 24 May 2017, www.nepalenergyforum.com/chinas-gezhouba-lands-budhi-gandaki-contract/, accessed 4 June 2017.
24 "Budhi Gandaki Listed as Component of BRI", *Nepal Energy Forum*, 5 September 2017, www.nepalenergyforum.com/budhi-gandaki-listed-as-component-of-bri/, accessed 9 September 2017.
25 "Scrap Budhi Gandaki Deal with Chinese Firm: Ex-PM to Nepal Govt", *Nepal Energy Forum* 13 July 2017, www.nepalenergyforum.com/daily-news-analysis-scrap-budhi-gandaki-deal-with-chinese-firmex-pm-to-nepal-govt/, accessed 18 July 2017.
26 "Chinese State Firm Criticises Nepal over Decision to Scrap US$2.5bn Dam Contract", *South China Morning Post*, 1 December 2017, www.scmp.com/news/china/diplomacy-defence/article/2122475/chinese-state-firm-criticises-nepal-over-decision-scrap, accessed 4 December 2017.
27 "Chinese Infrastructure Projects in Nepal Running Way Behind Schedule", *Republic World*, 31 August 2017, www.republicworld.com/s/6070/chinese-infrastructure-projects-in-nepal-running-way-behind-schedule, accessed 4 September 2017.
28 See Andrew Small, *The China-Pakistan Axis-Asia's New Geopolitics*, London: Random House, 2015; Ghulam Ali, *China-Pakistan Relations – A Historical Analysis*, Oxford: Oxford University Press, 2017, pp. 203–209.
29 Ma Jiali, "建好"中巴""走廊", "出""一""路""一步", [*Dragon Dance Silk Road Website*] 19 December 2016, www.long546.com/?r=post/view&id=1153, accessed 24 December 2016.
30 "Pakistani Central Bank Allows Chinese Currency for Bilateral Trade", *Xinhua*, 3 January 2018, www.xinhuanet.com/english/2018-01/03/c_136868830.htm, accessed 6 January 2018.
31 S. Akbar Zaidi, "A Road through Pakistan, and What This Means for India", *Strategic Analysis*, vol. 43, no. 3, 2019.
32 The Chairman of the Committee was cited at "CPEC Claims and Doubts", *Dawn*, 2 March 2017, www.dawn.com/news/1317784/cpec-claims-and-doubts, accessed 6 March 2017.

33 See "Senate Panel Wants Pakistan's Interests Fully Protected under CPEC", *Dawn*, 1 March 2017, www.dawn.com/news/1317736/senate-panel-wants-pakistans-interests-fully-protected-under-cpec, accessed 6 March 2017.
34 "CPEC Cost Build-Up", *Dawn*, 15 December 2016, www.dawn.com/news/1302328/cpec-cost-build-up, accessed 21 December 2016.
35 Shahbaz Rana, "Pakistan's External Debt, Liabilities Increase 12.3% to $85 billion", *The Express Tribune*, 16 December 2017, https://tribune.com.pk/story/1585327/2-pakistans-external-debt-liabilities-increase-12-3-85b/, accessed 22 December 2017.
36 Ahmed Rashid, "The Stakes Are High for China in Pakistan and Afghanistan", *Financial Times*, 21 July 2017, www.ft.com/content/3a779394-66e5-11e7-9a66-93fb352ba1fe, accessed 26 July 2017.
37 James Dorsey, "One Belt, One Road: A Plan for Chinese Dominance and Authoritarianism", *The Turbulent World of Middle East Soccer blog*, 18 May 2017, https://mideastsoccer.blogspot.in/2017/05/one-belt-one-road-plan-for-chinese.html accessed 22 May 2017.
38 In December 2017, China temporarily stopped funding for three road projects due to the levelling of corruption charges. See "China Stops Funding CPEC Road Projects over Graft Issue, Pakistan 'Stunned': Report", *Times of India*, 5 December 2017, https://timesofindia.indiatimes.com/world/pakistan/china-stops-funding-cpec-road-projects-over-graft-issue-pakistan-stunned-report/articleshow/61929677.cms, accessed 14 December 2019.
39 Nilanthi Samaranayake, "China's Engagement with Smaller South Asian Countries", *USIP*, 10 April 2019, www.usip.org/publications/2019/04/chinas-engagement-smaller-south-asian-countries, accessed 14 April 2019.
40 "Sri Lanka Joins China's Belt and Road with Operations of Hambantota Port: PM", *Xinhua*, 9 December 2017, www.xinhuanet.com/english/2017-12/09/c_136813766.htm, accessed 14 December 2017.
41 Sri Lanka has been facing acute debt repayments issue with over 95% of government revenue going towards debt servicing. See Patrick Mendis and Joey Wang, "Belt and Road, or a Chinese Dream for the Return of Tributary States? Sri Lanka Offers a Cautionary Tale", *South China Morning Post*, 9 January 2018, www.scmp.com/comment/insight-opinion/article/2127415/belt-and-road-or-chinese-dream-return-tributary-states-sri, accessed 4 January 2018.
42 See Romi Jain, "China's Economic Expansion in South Asia: Strengths, Challenges and Opportunities", *Indian Journal of Asian Affairs*, vol. 31, nos. ½, June–December 2018, pp. 21–36; Smruti S. Pattanaik, "India's Policy Response to China's Investment and Aid to Nepal, Sri Lanka and Maldives: Challenges and Prospects", *Strategic Analysis*, vol. 43, no. 3, 2019.
43 These trade statistics are from United Nations Statistics Division UN Comtrade, see https://comtrade.un.org accessed on 14 December 2019.
44 "The Fifth China-South Asia Expo", http://ynoroph.com/exhibitions/fifth-china-south-asia-expo/, accessed 14 December 2019.
45 "Commodity Expo to Promote Trade with South Asian Nations", *Xinhua*, 25 June 2019, www.chinadailyhk.com/articles/2/146/211/1561438912084.html, accessed 27 June 2019.
46 "Trends in International Arms Transfers, 2017", *SIPRI*, March 2018, p. 5, www.sipri.org/sites/default/files/2018-03/fssipri_at2017_0.pdf, accessed 14 April 2018.
47 P. K. Balachandran, "China's 'Soft Power Instruments' Funded Confucius Institutes Change Goals to Suit Local Needs", *The Citizen*, 1 July 2018, www.thecitizen.in/index.php/en/newsdetail/index/6/14251/chinas-soft-power-instruments-funded-confucius-institutes-change-goals-to-suit-local-needs, accessed 4 July 2018.
48 Some Confucius Institutes became controversial in the United States, Australia and other countries and have to be closed. See Pratik Jakhar, "Confucius Institutes: The Growth of China's Controversial Cultural Branch", *BBC*, 7 September 2019, www

.bbc.com/news/world-asia-china-49511231, accessed 14 September 2019. On the problems related to these institutes, see Ren Zhe, "Confucius Institutes: China's Soft Power?", *Sigur Center for Asian Studies, Policy Commentary*, June 2010, www.risingpowersinitiative.org/wp-content/uploads/policycommentary_jun2010_confuciusinstitute.pdf, accessed 19 December 2019.

49 "Confucius Institute at Kathmandu University", http://english.hanban.org/confuciousinstitutes/node_10781.htm, accessed 19 December 2019.

2
CHINA AND SOUTH ASIA
Future scenario

Adluri Subramanyam Raju

Introduction

China is one of the most populous countries in the world. Having risen as an economic power in the world, its economy may surpass that of the United States by 2040.[1] It is also seen as an engine of global economic growth in the twenty-first century. Anticipating the shift across the world from geopolitics to geo-economics, China is strengthening its economic ties with other countries through multilateral cooperation/engagement across the world.

Economic globalisation has benefited China enormously. It is, therefore, essential for China to cooperate with the international system. To facilitate the peaceful rise with rapid economic growth and deeper international integration, China has adopted the use of soft power. China's focus over the years has been to further integrate itself into the globalised economy to pursue its interests. For instance, the Belt and Road Initiative (BRI) is to connect Eurasia with China. The project would cost US$1 trillion and covers 60 countries.

Further, China appears to have strategic and geopolitical calculations towards the neighbouring countries, regions and the world at large. Yet, these strategic calculations have not taken concrete form. China's presence in the South China Sea, its role in different parts of the world, China–Pakistan Economic Cooperation (CPEC), BRI and others provide scope for concern over its ambition and strategic calculations. Although experiencing a rise in economic growth, China suffers from a shortage of resources, environmental degradation and faces internal crises in the form of increasing social and ethnic tensions.

There is an intense discourse on the rise of China over the years. Some scholars argue that China is well integrated with the international economic system and has not exhibited aggressiveness towards others. Therefore, China's rise is peaceful. The advocates of this view are mostly liberal scholars of international relations. On the other hand, some argue that rising China is likely to challenge the existing global order by means of its huge economic strength and military expansion and therefore is a threat to international security. They advocate that necessary measures should be taken to counter future China.

South Asia represents one-fourth of the world's population with a low gross domestic product, low per capita income and low literacy rate coupled with high birth and high death rates. The region is afflicted by a number of social, political and economic problems. Disputes, mutual distrust, misunderstanding and suspicion remain in the region. The absence of collective identity and a lack of sense of belonging prevail in the region. Conflicts and disputes have pushed the region into backwardness. Further, though cultural linkages between the countries are common and strong, but they cannot influence them to come closer.

However, South Asia is viewed as an important region in the world, and it is gaining identity across the globe. South Asia is one of the fastest growing economic regions in the world (6% growth rate per year). It is trying to integrate with other regions of Asia, which are expected to play a vital role in the global arena.

China and South Asia are neighbours. China shares borders with five South Asian countries, while India with six countries. Other South Asian countries do not share borders with more than two countries in the region. While China is not part of South Asia, it has an observer status in SAARC. It is politically more attractive than India for most of the South Asian countries. Chinese investment and trade with South Asian countries is remarkable.

South Asian security, particularly the nuclear dimension, cannot be seen without China. China and South Asia together host three nuclear powers. China has contributed to nuclear proliferation in South Asia. India became nuclear power because of China's nuclear programme and India became a factor in Pakistan's nuclear programme. China has conducted series of nuclear tests since 1964, leading India to explore nuclear option. China's alleged supply of nuclear weapons and designs to Pakistan brought a different dimension to the security of South Asia. Though not a part of South Asia, China is a force to reckon with in the regional security dimension. After the Sino-Indian war of 1962, the nuclear threat from China looms large with a possibility of India being blackmailed in future. This was further buttressed by the fact that China warned India in India–Pakistan war of 1965 that it must bear the responsibility for all the consequences of its criminal and extended aggression on the Sino-Indian border in Sikkim.[2] Further in 1971, China declared that it would firmly support the Pakistani government to safeguard its sovereignty and national independence.[3] Further, whenever the situation arises, China never hesitated to announce its support to Pakistan.

India was a factor in Pakistan's nuclear programme. Pakistan felt the need to develop its nuclear capability for two reasons: to retain the lost prestige consequent to the 1965 and 1971 conflict with India and to neutralise India's military power and pose a deterrent for future conflicts with India. Pakistan linked its nuclear policy with India's approach towards nuclear proliferation. It tried to illegally obtain material for its nuclear weapon programme. It regarded India's nuclear development and its tests as a threat to its security. It involved in an armed conflict with India three times in 1948, 1965 and 1971 and felt that India could attack in future.

For Pakistan, "China's involvement (in South Asia) is a long-term counterweight to India."[4] It was not averse to China expanding its influence in the region. On 2 March 1963, it entered into an agreement with China over the 300-mile frontier between China's Sinkiang Province and the Pakistani controlled section of Kashmir, which is also claimed by India.[5] India questioned the agreement on the ground that China had no right to have a frontier treaty with a country with which it did not possess a common boundary.[6]

The relationship between China and Pakistan caused a sense of unease in India. China reportedly supplied arms and transferred nuclear weapon designs to Pakistan. Thus, Pakistan was instrumental in drawing China into the region in a big way with military linkages. After China acquired the atom bomb in 1964, India considered it a threat. Both the countries are yet to resolve their territorial borders. China has been a factor in determining relations between India and other South Asian countries.

China has cordial relations with South Asian countries, particularly with Pakistan, Sri Lanka, Maldives, Nepal and Bangladesh. China's relations with them is also seen by India as a threat to it, since China has expanded its influence in terms of investment, infrastructure or trade in the region. Its presence in the region is also perceived as an impediment to regional cooperation as the member countries, arguably though, use either China card or India card to fulfil their interests.

Weaving through the new dimensions that prevail or have emerged in South Asia as mentioned, seven probable future scenarios with regard to relations between China and South Asia are described below, with their potential implications.

Future scenario-building

Scenario 1: geography as a factor in China and South Asia relations

The geographic location of a country determines its relationship with other countries. Geography determines strategy. It influences a country's foreign policy with its neighbours. Geographical proximity has become one of the factors for China and South Asian countries to come closer. It plays a significant role in determining relations between the neighbouring countries. China has successfully improved its relations with most of the countries in South Asia at different levels. Its relation with Pakistan has been very cordial. However, the relation between China and India has been strained for a long time since 1962.

India and China maintained cordial relations since the latter emerged as an independent country on 1 October 1949. China raised the border dispute for the first time in January 1959. In a letter, on 23 January 1959, the Chinese Premier Chou En Lai wrote to the Prime Minister of India Jawaharlal Nehru that China had right over large chunks of Indian claim over Indian territory in different sectors of the Himalayas.[7] However, the border question was not raised in 1954 when negotiations were held between Peking and New Delhi for the agreement on Trade and Commerce.[8] On 22 October 1962, the Chinese troops attacked Tawang and Khinzemane in NEFA.[9] Chou En Lai sent a letter to Nehru urging a peaceful settlement of the dispute.[10] India rejected the proposal. On 26 October, 10,000 Chinese moved from Tawang in NEFA towards Tezpur in Assam. Till 19 November they continued to seize the main posts of India. At the same time, it asked India to respond to its proposal for peaceful negotiations to allow Chinese forces about 100 km deep inside Indian territory in the western sector, eastern sector and central sector, which India felt would jeopardise Indian position.[11] India rejected the proposal. Finally, China unilaterally decided on a ceasefire on 21 November.

China to show its superiority and its vision to expand its territory is evident when China had attacked India in 1962, despite its agreement on Panchsheel. If there was no war in 1962 between India and China, the situation between the two countries would have been cordial. Both failed to use geographical proximity as a stimulator to improve their relations. As long as the territorial dispute exists between the two countries, they would continue to remain as adversaries.

The past has been accounted for most appropriately. It can be extended to how geography has maintained and even accentuated geopolitical rivalry between the two emerging powers. A possible future scenario could be India increasing its footprint in the South China Sea, which China considers as its own backyard, and China, which has already indulged in influence accumulation in the Indian Ocean region, could surpass India to have the entire region, flowing from South Asia to West Asia and the African region, in its grip of neocolonial domination, which would lead to India's containment in the region.

Scenario 2: China fails to bring South Asian countries to work against India

Neighbours in South Asia are not unanimously formed to work against India. Neighbours have nothing to do with others in the region. There is no grand coalition in South Asia, hence they cannot go with China against India. It is not clear whether China would gain by expanding its presence in South Asia and contain India. South Asian countries are not bandwagoning with India. Neighbours in South Asia have apprehensions over India's dominance in the region. However, they never collectively come together to express their concern over India. The degree of relations of them with India as well as with

China is not the same. Most of the countries are post-colonial states and do not move closer to China. China's bilateral relation with South Asian countries varies from country to county. For instance, China has very cordial relations with Pakistan for a long time. After the 1962 war with India, and India and Pakistan war in 1965, the relation between China and Pakistan was formed. China sees Pakistan's geopolitical significance in South Asia. Pakistan was seen by China as a gateway to Middle East for it. Pakistan also sees importance of China not only for economic aid and investment but also to counter India's dominance in the region. China was instrumental in Pakistan's nuclear programme. However, China could not rely on other countries in South Asia like Pakistan to work against India. In future, the South Asian countries would try to maintain cordial relations with both countries (India and China) otherwise their national interests would be threatened.

However, on the other hand, similar to scenario 1, the causal explanation of China–Pakistan "all-weather" friendship can be extended to explain that China's increasing foothold over the Indian Ocean region is a cause of India's persistent dilemma that in the future with expansion of BRI and China's increasing political influence in South Asian region (as is evident in Nepal's kowtowing to China on boundary disputes with India, Maldives under the previous administration of Abdulla Yaameen, inching closer to China economically and Sri Lanka's forced handover of strategic assets) China will come to replace India in its own neighbourhood as the leading/dominant power.

Scenario 3: South Asian countries depend on India on traditional security

The region is affected by many non-traditional security threats, which have transnational dimensions, and no individual country would be able to tackle them alone. Now it becomes a challenge for every country to address threats; hence, cooperation among the countries in the region is required. India has more advantage in tackling (non-)traditional security challenges in South Asia, particularly in the domain of human security. The neighbours will seek help from India; otherwise, it would be difficult for them to address the challenges. They also recognised that India is growing rapidly in both military and economic terms, unlike other countries in South Asia, which would depend on it for their development. Hence, India has become the dominant country in the region and will continue to remain as such in the years to come. India's regional preponderance is inevitable, and neighbours have to accept the reality. On the other hand, they maintain relation with China for their development. For them, maintaining cordial relations with both India and China will provide them more bargaining power. As long as non-traditional security threats are becoming a main concern for the South Asian countries, they would largely depend on India to address them.

Scenario 4: China depends largely on Pakistan to counter India

India and Pakistan emerged as major countries in South Asia and were more capable than other countries to change the environment in the region. In other words, India and Pakistan became more capable of maintaining bipolarity in the region. However, in recent times, Pakistan seems to have failed to emerge as a strong country to continue to maintain bipolarity in the region. Pakistan could not attain parity with India (which was one of the goals of Pakistan) to compete with the latter. However, Pakistan and China have the convergence of interests with regard to containing India. Since Pakistan seems to be seen as a failed state, China would fail to counter India with the help of Pakistan.

Scenario 5: China as a factor in strained relations between India and Pakistan

Cordial bilateral relations between India and Pakistan will not only benefit these two countries but also enhance regional cooperation. Cordial relations between them will lead to regional stability, progress and peace in South Asia. However, it does not seem that cordial relations between the two countries are possible in the foreseeable future. The main factor could be China's close proximity to Pakistan and the former's strained relation with India. If there was no war between China and India, the former would have not given ultimatum to the latter in India-Pakistan war, 1965; it would have not been played role in enhancing Pakistan's nuclear and military programme, and as a result, Pakistan could have realised its limitations and could have improved relations with India. If China seeks to prevent India from emerging as an economic power, it would largely have to depend on Pakistan to destabilise India.

As a future scenario it could be extended to India's fear that this strategic rivalry might lead to Pakistan handing over lethal nuclear weapons in the hands of terrorist organisations that it provides safe havens on its soil. If the deadly weapons are under the control of the terrorists, it will bring miseries for India's growth and development. Also, the damage can spill over into Pakistan's neighbouring country Afghanistan and further upset the peace-building process there to the detriment of India, which has significant investments in Afghanistan.

Scenario 6: India and China relations

China and India are neighbours, maritime powers and nuclear states, and both are emerging as major economies in the world. Trade between them is growing. There is a convergence of interests between them and shared interests, such as safeguarding free navigation, focus on development and energy security, eradication of poverty and dealing with social unrest; climate change; environmental, demographic and resources constraints; corruption; political unrest; non-state actors' roles; and so on.

They have increased their collaboration with regional groupings such as BRICS, BCIM and trade and investment. India and China are trying to improve relations to enhance their economic development rather than countering each other. However, some of the issues which are irritants between them are border disputes, the Tibet issue, China's relations with Pakistan, India's relations with the United States, expansion of their presence in the Indian Ocean region and competition over access to resources. China understands that India and the United States are likely to be closer than either one will be to China.[12] It realises the importance of India and the United States to its economic development. It is not clear whether China would gain by expanding its presence in South Asia and containing India.[13] Though India and China do not trust each other, they have to work together for their development. Trade has become one of the motivations for both countries to depend on each other. If these two countries improve their relations, China may have less concern for India's neighbours. Hence, India's neighbours (including Pakistan) would have to improve their relations with New Delhi. Even if this scenario is not possible, India will be recognised as an important player by its neighbours.

India and China realise the importance of each other for their economic development. The Wuhan meeting (Modi–Xi) was held in May 2018 to address that ever-growing divide between China and India over a range of issues (e.g. the boundary dispute, the Belt and Road Initiative, the Nuclear Suppliers Group membership and China's growing naval presence in the Indian Ocean region). However, in recent times (May–June 2020) Chinese troops tried to enter into Indian territory, claiming right over Galwan valley, which is part of India.

India and China should search for areas of cooperation by keeping aside their differences. If the two countries have cordial relations, the following advantages would be available to both:

1. India's involvement in Tibet will not cease, granting China full suzerainty over Tibet.
2. India's alliance with the United States, Japan and other littoral countries in the Indian Ocean would be limited.
3. China would support India to be part of the Nuclear Suppliers Group.
4. China will minimise its relations with Pakistan, and in return, Pakistan will minimise its adversarial activities against India.
5. The majority of their (India and China) trade, which sails through the Indian Ocean, would be secured.
6. Both can peacefully rise as major economies.[14]

The growth of the world economy in the next decade, it is expected, will be powered by Asia. China, Japan and India are important actors in Asia. It is a challenge for the major countries of Asia to collectively work to make Asia an important continent and address their differences among themselves, because the continent lacks strong regional institutions to resolve their problems. Asia's future will be determined by the relations between these two countries and other major countries in Asia, including Japan. Hence, both countries, as responsible actors in the global arena, would opt more for cooperation than confrontation. They can address various issues through cooperation, and they can create a better future for Asia.

Scenario 7: competition between India and China lead to contain each other

India and China have played a significant role in the maritime domain. In 2012, the two countries undertook joint operations against piracy and for sharing technological knowledge on seabed research, which involved coast guards, navies and air forces of both countries. In April 2014, another significant development was the participation of the INS Shivalik in the first maritime exercise organised by China, at Qingdao along with the navies of six other countries. The dialogue on maritime cooperation between India and China was held on 4 February 2016.[15] India and China in April 2005 signed an agreement on Strategic Cooperation and Partnership for Peace and Prosperity. An agreement was made on 4 September 2012 between India and China to boost defence ties during the visit of Chinese Defence Minister Gen. Lian Guangle to India and his meeting with his Indian counterpart A.K. Antony. Both sides agreed to strengthen border security cooperation between the troops in order to maintain peace in the border area. In 2013, both signed a Border Defence Cooperation Agreement (BDCA) for a positive tone to future talks between New Delhi and Beijing. The visits of China's President Xhi Jinping to India in 2014 and Indian Prime Minister Narender Modi's visit to China in May 2015 demonstrated that both sides are willing to improve their relations. Both agreed to establish regular meeting mechanisms between the headquarters of the two armies and also to enhance cooperation in non-traditional security threats.

Both India and China compete with each other in the maritime domain. China has increased its presence in different parts of the Indian Ocean. For instance, China has involved in the BRI project. India refused to join the project because its merchandise and manufactured exports are minuscule. India joined the Quad because BRI is clashing with the free and open passage of oceans.

China's BRI, a multibillion-dollar venture, is connecting 80 countries in Asia, Europe and Africa. BRI covers half of the world's population and a quarter of global GDP, connecting infrastructure corridor over land and sea route corridors. India refused to join the BRI because China had an agreement with Pakistan to take up the project called CPEC, involving the disputed PoK area, impinging on Indian sovereignty; there is corruption and local labour is not being hired in the project. China is trying to create unipolar order through the initiative of BRI. Beijing's economic expansion is strengthening authoritarianism and establishing hegemony.

China plans to build ports, roads and railways in underdeveloped Eurasia and Africa mainly out of political motivation rather than real demand for infrastructure. BRI is to extend Chinese influence and establish itself as a world-leading economy and spread its power. Through BRI, China creates new markets and gets economic benefits by building infrastructure, roads, railways, waterways and communication networks in countries through the BRI project.

Chinese plan to invest in different countries in the name of connectivity may lead to debt trap than development for a recipient country. For instance, in case of Sri Lanka, a state-run Chinese company obtained 99-year lease on the port and 15,000 acres of land to build an industrial zone. There are doubts raised over Chinese investment in Pakistan through CPEC project.

To counter Chinese initiatives, India and Japan are involved in Asia–Africa Growth Corridor (AAGC). Unlike the BRI, AAGC will be a sea corridor linking Africa with India and other countries of Southeast Asia and Oceania, more consultative and private sector funded rather than government funded (unlike BRI), it is claimed. BRI is a debt-based infrastructure project rather than a free foreign aid initiative or simply a network of trade activities. This is designed to maintain a balance with both the power structures led by the United States and China. AAGC that is being envisioned by India and Japan is based more on the consultative nature of cooperation focusing on infrastructure building, enhancing connectivity and aiming to promote the universal character of growth based on people-to-people contacts. Cordial relations between China and India would have influenced Beijing to make BRI more viable as a consultative mechanism. India's proximity with major countries such as the United States, Japan, Australia etc. undermines its initiatives such as BRI. China would understand how to cultivate advantages being closer to India.

The competition between India and China to enhance their presence in the Indian Ocean is seen as rivalries. Robert Kaplan argued that "As the competition between China and India suggests, the Indian Ocean is where global struggles will play out in the twenty-first century."[16] Further, Margolis observes that in the future, "geopolitical tensions between the two uneasy neighbours and rivals easily could intensify as they vie for hegemony over South and Central Asia, Indonesia and even the South China Sea, political influence, oil, resources and markets."[17]

Conclusion

While the author has attempted to construct different scenarios, it must be understood that no single scenario can be said to be the most probable one. A combination of factors, political and economic primarily, would dictate how much any of these scenarios will play out. China's strategic and geopolitical calculations in South Asia have not taken concrete form. China has to realise that without cooperation with India, it would be difficult to enhance its presence in South Asia. China is trying to assert its supremacy in South Asia by ignoring India with a perceptible disregard to the economic and military potential that India has already achieved as a large country in the region. The asymmetric relation between China and South Asian countries do not forecast a potential expansion of Chinese interests in the region, unless a trust-based cooperative framework is established between India and China. Such a framework would also serve as a basis from which smaller nations in South Asia can leap forward to join the global bandwagon of growth. China and South Asia together not only represent half of the global population but also have the potential to shape the future of Asia in terms of maintaining stability, prosperity and peace in the global order.

Notes

1 Oliver Stuenkel, "2040: US Military Supremacy vs Chinese Economic Leadership", 18 January 2013, https://www.oliverstuenkel.com/2013/01/18/2040-us-military-supremacy-in-a-world-economy-led-by-china/#:~:text=In%202040%2C%20for%20example%2C%20China%27s%20economy%20could%20be,States%20position%20as%20the%20world%27s%20second%20largest%20economy, accessed 3 July 2020.
2 Mahmudul Huque, *The Role of the USA in the India-Pakistan Conflict 1947—71*, Dhaka: International Books, 1968, p. 148.
3 Yaacov Vertzberger, *Entente: Sino-Pakistani Relations 1960–1980*, The Washington Papers, New York: Praeger Publications, 1983, p. 47.
4 *Keesing's Record World Events*, New Jersey: Keesing's Record of World Events, vol. 38, no. 3, 1992, p. 3884.
5 *Facts on File*, vol. 23, no. 1166, 28 February–6 March 1963, p. 78.
6 *Ibid*.
7 Meenu Roy, *Thousand Days of Indo-US Diplomacy*, New Delhi: Deep & Deep Publications, 1993, p. 83.
8 A. Subramanyam Raju, *Democracies at Loggerheads: Security Aspects of US-India Relations*, New Delhi: South Asian Publishers, 2001, p. 55.
9 For details, see Neville Maxwell, *India's China War*, Bombay: Jaico Publishing House, 1970, p. 358.
10 *Ibid*, p. 373.
11 See Surya P. Sharma, *The Chinese Recourse to Force against India: A Case Study in Peaceful Coexistence*, New Delhi: External Publicity Division, Government of India, 1966, p. 30.
12 Aaron L. Friedberg, "The Geopolitics of Asia in 2030: An American Perspective", in Ajey Lele and Namrata Goswami (eds), *Imagining Asia in 2030: Trends, Scenario and Alternatives*, New Delhi: Academic Foundation, 2011, p. 472.
13 *Ibid*, p. 475.
14 See Adluri Subramanyam Raju, "Bilateralism in South Asia: Future Scenario", in Adluri Subramanyam Raju (ed.), *New Futures for South Asia: Commerce and Connectivity*, London: Routledge, 2020, p. 59.
15 Anasua Basu Ray Chaudhury, Pratnashree Basu, Sreeparna Banerjee, and Sohini Bose, *India's Maritime Connectivity: Importance of the Bay of Bengal*, Kolkata: ORF, 2018, p. 101.
16 Robert D. Kaplan, "Center Stage for the 21st Century: Power Plays in the Indian Ocean", *Foreign Affairs*, March–April 2009, p. 2.
17 Eric S. Margolis, "India Rules the Waves", *Proceedings of the United States Naval Institute*, vol. 131, no. 3, 2005, p. 67, cited in Lindsay Hughes, "Examining the Sino-Indian Maritime Competition: Part 4 – India's Maritime Strategy", *Strategic Analysis Paper*, 30 January 2014, Australia: Future Directions International Pvt Ltd., Dalkeith, WA, p. 6.

PART II
South Asia and China
Connectivity

3
BRI, NEO-TRIBUTE SYSTEM AND INTERNATIONAL FINANCIAL ASSISTANCE

Perspectives for South Asia

R. Srinivasan

Introduction

The Belt and Road Initiative (BRI) or the One Belt One Road (OBOR) was announced to the world by President Xi Jinping of China during his visits to Kazakhstan and Indonesia in 2013. The BRI comprises a trans-continental passage that links China with Southeast Asia, South Asia, Central Asia, Russia and Europe by land. It includes a sea route connecting China's coastal regions via Southeast and South Asia, the South Pacific, the Middle East and Eastern Africa, all the way to Europe. It is by any standards in political vision or economic aspiration in the history of mankind, the grandest that has been conceived, covering 70 countries, involving nearly 65% of the world's population and a combined GDP of 40% of the world. The programme is expected to involve US$1 trillion in investments primarily into developing infrastructure across its geographic reach to facilitate, amongst its other aims, unimpeded trade.

Chinese efforts to bring in more and more partners to the BRI have drawn as many benevolent endorsements as there are detrimental ones. Though the world appears to be too stupefied by the astronomical growth that China has attained in its economy (and in military potential), detractors to China point out the abysmal human rights records that apparently China holds and its bullying tactics with the littorals of South China Sea. There is also considerable apprehension over Chinese intentions with the Korean peninsula, their build-up against Taiwan and the trade war that China has apparently chosen to levy on United States.

Notwithstanding these distractive developments concerning China, world attention is constantly focused on the BRI. Perhaps the scale to which China has built objectives for the BRI and the way it has gone about securing its interests in Indian Ocean Region (IOR) as well as in Central Asia demand such attention.

Be it the Chinese involvement in Central Asia or in IOR, South Asia remains most affected by developments that aid or detract the BRI, as this region sits at the junction that connects the Middle East to China. It also connects the ambitious Maritime Silk Route to its destinations in the Middle East and Africa. We may hypothesise, therefore, that South Asian cooperation is critical to China for achieving its BRI objectives.

President Xi Jinping announced a new Silk Road Economic Belt during his speech at Nazarbayev University in Astana, Kazakhstan, on 7 September 2013. He was hinting at the expansion of Chinese trade and economic networks across Central Asia, which, together with the CPEC economic corridor and the new Maritime Silk Road, will go on to become the bulwark of the BRI. Chinese interest in Central Asia is at least a millennium old, dating back to Chenghis Khan and the consolidation of China under Kublai Khan. The old Silk Road connected China across the deserts of Taklamakan, mountains of Northern Afghanistan and the plains of West Asia with Europe in the first millennia. Wealth from Europe poured into China along with newer knowledge and technologies. The 7000 km long artery was the harbinger of prosperity. The new Silk Road that Xi was referring to is more important from the point of view of Chinese prosperity; it will satisfy growing Chinese needs for energy, mineral resources and in a sense access to the erstwhile industrial and scientific assets that the Central Asian countries inherited from Soviet era.

South Asia is the emerging region in the world. Home to nearly a fifth of the world's population and blessed as it is with natural and manpower resources, South Asia at present is tied down only by two factors: the rivalry between Pakistan and India, and a mineral-rich Afghanistan that is mired in internal turmoil. The expanding footprints of Islamic State (IS) together with a fundamentalist Taliban are causes for major concern not only for South Asian security but also to China since its restive Xinjian region borders with Afghanistan wherefrom Islamic terror could enter into its Uigur heartlands. Striding the Taklamakan, these security challenges have the potential to upset the objectives of the BRI.

While China goes about creating its footprints across Central Asia and Africa, South Asia remains critical to the achievement of the objectives of the BRI. Apart from its geography, South Asia also offers immense markets to China, and a carefully guided scheme of cooperation will take the BRI to the very doors of Europe across West Asia, which appears to be the motive behind the initiative. Establishing strong footholds across South Asia, China aspires to become the pivot around which the world economic and political orders will revolve.

This chapter considers South Asia as central to the success of the BRI. Contemporary geopolitics may as well show certain cleavages through which China may be appearing to make purposeful strides towards blending this region into the BRI. However, it is believed that an offbeat look into certain historical and contemporaneous developments is necessary to sharpen South Asian perceptions of the Chinese and the BRI. This chapter believes that such perceptions may equip South Asian nations to understand their part in the BRI and evolve their responses that could be in their best interests.

Perceptions on Chinese history

China is one of the four oldest civilisations in the world, along with Indian, Babylonian and Egyptian civilisations. Though the Xia dynasty is credited to be the first dynasty to rule China (2100–1600 BC), Western and Eastern Han (206 BCE–220 CE) unified China and expanded its reach into Korea and Vietnam. In the next 400 years, China's fortune rose and plummeted. Chinese historians refer to a portion of this period (220–589 CE) as a "Period of Disunity" or "Six Dynasty Period." Between 581 and 618 CE, the Sui dynasty unified China and their successors, the Tangs (618–906 CE), expanded Chinese territory in all directions till the Arabs defeated Tangs at Talas in 751. Between 906 and 1368 CE, China was ruled by the Song and Yuan dynasties. The Yuan was an off-shoot of Mongols, the prominent and founding emperor being Kublai Khan. Under the Song and Yuan, China dominated the Silk Road trade. It was an era that marked the monetisation of the economy, growth in commerce and maritime trade, urban expansion and technological innovations, examination system for bureaucratic recruitment and expansion of the empire into the heartlands of Russia and the Middle East. The Mings and Manchus, who followed (1368–1912), oversaw many reforms in agriculture, economy as well as substantial increase in territories of the empire. However, in their later periods, the authoritarian Manchus found it difficult to cope with the cultural and military onslaught of Western powers. A weak central government led to the collapse of the dynasty system, and the republic rose. The Mao-led revolution in 1949 brought in a substantially different form of communist philosophy as the basis of government, earning a new epithet "Maoism."

It is evident from this brief historical narrative that the civilisation of China evolved and modified itself over four millennia. We may paraphrase the evolution of China perhaps in Arnold Toynbee's thoughts: "All human achievement involved challenge and response."[1] In doing so, China also evolved a world view that suited its persona. Every civilisation, Lucien Goldmann in his "The Hidden God" explains, draws its essential insights from the "view of the world" it adopts. The "view of the world" that China developed was based on the lessons that it drew from its interactions with the world through military, political and trade contacts that it had developed, sustained or modified through these four millennia. Two important elements in Chinese thought on the world order merit specific visitation – the Tribute System and, specifically with reference to South Asia, the Five Fingers Policy.

Tribute System

An important element of the "view of the world" that China developed pertains to its view on the states that lay at its borders. Scholars like Fairbanks,[2] Cohen[3] and Zhang believe that it was essentially a Sino-centric view of world order in which the Chinese regulated their trade and diplomatic relations with the countries lying at their borders through what has come to be termed as the "Tribute System." Yongjin Zhang in his introduction to the edited volume "The Tribute System" state:

> There is also broad agreement that a Tribute System of a sort existed and operated to regulate China's trade and diplomacy with its neighbours at least as far back as the Han dynasty (206 BCE–220 CE). There is little dispute that the demise of the Tribute System was brought out by the introduction of the treaty system in China's international relations after the Opium War in 1840, with the conclusion of the Treaty of Nanjing in 1842. It is a matter of intense debate how stable and uniform the Tribute System was throughout China's tumultuous dynastic histories and whether its existence was highly precarious, with occasional breakdowns and constant reconfigurations. There are clear contradictions in the enduring Chinese discourse and varied practices of the Tribute System. The precise meaning of the Tribute System is equally hotly contested. It is sometimes said to have principally served the instrumental purpose of managing China's trade with its neighbors and of instigating frontier pacification. It is also claimed to have been constitutive of a Sino-centric Chinese world order in historical East Asia. It is not clear, however, whether those participating in the Chinese world order actually accept the civilizational assumptions embedded in the Tribute System and the Sino-centric conception of superiority and inferiority in their relationship. The centrality and usefulness of the Tribute System model as an overarching analytical and explanatory framework in understanding traditional China's foreign relations have therefore been a subject of controversy.[4]

Though, as Zhang points out, there are considerable debates as to the centrality of the Tribute System to Chinese foreign relations, the concept behind the system provides an important tool to understand Chinese foreign relations today. This aspect will be visited subsequently in this chapter.

Five Fingers Policy

China's legendary revolutionary leader Mao Zedong, standing in front of Beijing's Tiananmen Square in the 1950s, talked about Tibet and the Himalayas:

> Xizang (Tibet) is China's right hand's palm, which is detached from its five fingers – of Ladakh, Nepal, Sikkim, Bhutan and Arunachal (formerly NEFA). As all of these five are either occupied by, or under the influence of India, it is China's responsibility to 'liberate' the five to be rejoined with Xizang (Tibet).[5]

Mao's description of the five fingers was not based on his vision for China's future; it was based on the historical perceptions that China developed about itself and in ample measure supported by the Tribute System. Historically speaking, it was not until the Mongols expanded their footprints across the Tibetan plateau westwards at the beginning of the thirteenth century that Tibet came to be ruled by a diarchal system imposed by Mongol-Yuan. Ever since then, the Yuan control lasted only till the mid-thirteenth century. Tibet became "independent" of Chinese control for about four centuries, to be ruled by native families and Dalai Lama lineage. From the early eighteenth century, Tibet again came under Chinese rule under the Qing-Manchu empires. Qing stationed troops in Lhasa and in many other important towns of Tibet. The defeat of the 1791 expedition into Nepal actually helped China consolidate its control over Tibet.[6,7] The "palm" that Mao referred to was in Chinese direct control for a little under 400 years. However, commencing from the rule of Genghis Khan, Tibet had played a vital role in the trade with the West over the Silk Road.

China's relations with the other four fingers also present interesting perspectives. Ladakh, which was part of Baltistan, remained independent under its chieftains when direct Tibetan control waned in the mid-ninth century. The Defeat of the Chinese at Talas in 751 (Tibetan troops were with the Chinese in this campaign) apparently had the effect of freeing Tibetan control over Ladakh. The loosening of Tibetan control exposed Ladakh to repetitive invasion and plunder by the Muslim armies from the west for nearly 700 years. In the sixteenth century, the Namgyal dynasty established itself as the rulers of Ladakh. However, they were defeated by the Mughals and later by General Zorawar Singh, bringing Ladakh into the Dogra kingdom. Chinese interest through all these years in Ladakh primarily remained one of trade since Ladakh offered an easier route across the Karakoram to access Kashmir and further the trade routes in Baltistan and Afghanistan.[8]

Nepal, on the other hand, remained a largely independent kingdom that served as the door to Tibet in the north and to the Buddhist sites of the Gangetic plains in the south. Its relations with Tibet span millennia. Nepal had two wars with the Chinese Empire over what apparently were economic reasons. The stoppage of Nepalese coins by Tibet in its trade with Nepal led to the Nepal–Tibet war in 1789. The resounding victory of the Nepalese army over Tibet resulted in the Qing Empire of China coming to the aid of Tibet. The 1789–1791 Sino-Nepalese war resulted in the defeat of Nepal and the Treaty of Betrawati. Nepal, under the terms of this treaty, was to pay a tribute to the Qing Empire every five years.[9] The second Sino-Nepalese war of 1846 over Tibet, however, resulted in a stalemate treaty of Thapathali. Indirectly, Nepalese intervention in Tibet led to the consolidation of Qing control over Tibet. Under the treaty both Nepal and Tibet agreed to acknowledge the Chinese Emperor with respect.

In the case Bhutan, cultural and trade connections with Tibet are a matter of ancient history. While Bhutan maintained strong ties with Tibet, there has been no historical evidence of the shadow of Chinese suzerainty over Bhutan, though one may surmise that with Tibet under Chinese rule during the Yuan and Qing periods, Bhutan had direct contacts with the Chinese Empire. During the periods of Chinese control over Tibet, particularly during the Qing period, disputes over border demarcations between China (Tibet) and Bhutan arose. They pertained specifically to Chumbi Valley and the northern Haa district of Bhutan. In February 1910, the Manchu rulers claimed even suzerainty over Bhutan.[10] The Manchu rule ended in 1912 with the onset of the Chinese Republic and the Mao-led revolution in 1949. In these later periods, China remained silent on its claim over Bhutan. However, in 1993, China offered to renounce its claim over 495 km^2 of disputed land in the Pasamlung and Jakarlung valleys in exchange for the Doklam plateau, a smaller track of disputed land measuring a total of 269 km^2 in the northwest part of Haa district in Bhutan.[11] It is also pertinent to mention that in the eighteenth and nineteenth centuries, there were two military interventions by the British: first in support of the King of Cooch Behar in 1774, and later during the Duar wars of 1864–1865. The Duar wars ended Bhutanese territorial interests in the Siliguri corridor. From then on, Bhutan remained on good terms with British India. Bhutan's firm ties with India after British rule perhaps remain a matter of concern to Beijing.

Sikkim, the fourth finger, had long been an independent kingdom with trade and economic ties with ancient neighbours India and Tibet. When the first Anglo-Nepalese war ended in 1786, Nepalese control over what today is the Darjeeling district was ceded back to the Raja of Sikkim. In the years that followed, Darjeeling was gifted to the British in 1841 through tactical manoeuvres of the Governor General.[12] This created a unique situation by which Sikkim lost its direct access to Bengal provinces and ports, thus becoming entirely dependent on British India for access to the world. Though Nepal and Bhutan resented Sikkimese concession, they were not in a position to leverage it otherwise. The Chinese Empire remained merely a witness to the British consolidation in the Himalayas. When India attained freedom, Sikkim remained an Indian protectorate, eventually acceding to India in 1975. Chinese formally recognised Sikkim's accession to India in the same year.

The history of NEFA dates back many millennia due to its obvious geographical location. The Ahoms ruled Assam for over six centuries before the Burmese invaded Assam in 1817, falling under Burmese rule till 1826. Thus, belligerent Burmese came into contact with British India, bringing a hesitant British to invade Asom and eventually annex Burma. However, vary of the growing Chinese strength evidenced by their victories in Turkestan against the Russians (1863) and their trade interests in Burmese territory, Britain agreed in 1886 to pay customary tributes to the Dowager Empress every ten years. The British annexation of Asom, however, remained undisputed. NEFA, or Arunachal Pradesh, was carved out of the northern reaches of Assam by Nehru in 1948 under the guidance of Verrier Elwin.

The brief historical narrative reveals two points in the discussion over the Five Fingers Policy. One, that Chinese historical claim to sovereign control over the fingers is not supported by history; two, the claims actually emanate from Chinese control over Tibet in Yuan and Qing-Manchu periods cumulatively for about 400 years. Both these aspects need to be borne in mind through the ensuing discussion on the BRI.

The four phases of the BRI

China has gone about its BRI in calibrated phases. The seeds for the present BRI actually were sown in the early 1950s when China gained confidence of Pakistan and built the Karakoram highway across the 20,000 km^2 of northern Ladakh, which was under Pakistani occupation after the skirmishes of Pakistan and India over Kashmir in 1948. China began constructing the Karakoram highway in 1959.[13] China's eyes were set on gaining access to the Arabian sea through the port of Gwadar in Pakistan. In the years after India–China war of 1962, China went about building rail-road networks across TAR region connecting it to Yunnan province and mainland China. Rail lines were also extended from Kunming in Yunnan to Guangzou, a major Chinese port (incidentally, from where the old Silk Road began), 1285 km away. The rail-sea connectivity from Guangzou to Gwadar is expected to cut the cost of transportation by 50%.[14] Chinese consolidation over TAR in the process remains a thorny issue in international politics, specifically influencing its relations with India over the Dalai Lama issue and the functioning of the Tibetan government-in-exile from Dharamsala.

In the second phase, China launched the Shangai Five group in 1996 along with Russia, Kazakhstan, Kyrgyzstan and Tajikistan as its members. The objectives of the group included economic, military and diplomatic relations that were generally perceived to be a Central Asian effort to counter US influence across Central Asia. Barely a month after Brookings report on the subject,[15] China renamed the group Shangai Cooperation Organization (SCO) in 2001, an initiative that brought all five of the Central Asian countries under one umbrella, including Uzbekistan. Today, SCO has eight members (China, Russia, India, Pakistan, Kazakhstan, Uzbekistan, Kyrgyzstan and Tajikistan), four Observer states (Afghanistan, Iran, Belarus and Mongolia), six dialogue partners (Armenia, Azerbaijan, Cambodia, Nepal, Sri Lanka and Turkey) and four guest attendees (CIS, UN, ASEAN and Turkmenistan). SCO is perceived to be the most influential alliance today in terms of economic cooperation and military potential.[16]

The third phase of the BRI also commenced in the early 1950s when China recognised the Palestinian claim for statehood. Unfortunately, the Arab nations looked at China with suspicion and except the Egyptian initiative to recognise PRC in 1956, no progress was made by China in the Middle East. Even though Israel had recognised the PRC in 1950 earlier, support to Palestine by China impeded any meaningful association with Israel almost till 1972.[17] Even though China has taken major strides to increase its footprints in the Middle East, continuous US engagement in the area along with

Russian influence among West Asian states presents a scenario that calls for a pragmatic approach from the Chinese. Rightfully, China has identified Afghanistan as the entry point into the Middle East since Central and Middle East Asian destinies have been intertwined for millennia. Among the Middle Eastern countries, Iran is vital to Chinese interests owing to its energy needs. China imports US$1.5 billion worth of oil every month from Iran. In fact, when President Trump imposed sanctions on Iran, India and China managed to get waivers for the oil till March 2019. It is expected that if India reduces or stops buying Iranian oil due to the threat of US sanctions, Iran may consider handing the Chabahar port to Chinese,[18] wrenching a huge strategic advantage that India now enjoys in the Arabian sea.

The fourth phase of the BRI has the maritime dimensions attached to it. Millennia before Guanzou in China was connected to Venice through the ports in the Indian, Arab and African coasts. Commencing in Nara (Osaka) in Japan, the ancient maritime route connected Guangzou, Poduka (Madras), Muziris (Kodungallur, an hour's drive from modern Cochin), Muscat, Jeddah and Zanzibar (on the Eritrean coast of Africa) to Alexandria. Chinese trade vessels have coursed these waters from the first century AD, if not before. Muziris and later its rival port Calicut were visited by Chinese vessels regularly in the first millennium on their way to the Middle East and African ports.[19] Famous Ming Admiral Zheng He is reported to have visited Calicut seven times with his fleet and it is said that he died at Calicut in 1433 AD during his seventh voyage. From the Tang dynasty of the ninth century to the Mings in the sixteenth-century brisk trade and embassies were exchanged by Chinese fleets with the rulers of Calicut and Muziris. Considering the Indian reservations about joining the BRI bandwagon, China embarked upon wooing Sri Lanka into handing the Hambantota port for development.[20]

On 23 March 2019, China signed a MoU (however non-binding it was made to sound) with Italy by which Italy agreed to join the BRI.[21] The new Silk Road that China has been meticulously canvassing for from 2013, gathering about 70 nations across Central and South Asia and Africa in its fold, formally reached Rome, once again after a thousand years (historically speaking). With this, figuratively speaking, the fourth phase of the BRI reached its historical destination.

Silk Road, Neo-Tribute System and BRI

Scholars across the spectrum have been studying the debt-trap diplomacy that China has allegedly used to extend the reach of its BRI. With over US$3 trillion in its FOREX reserve,[22] its pocket is apparently deep and its terms of offer of financial assistance are appealing to cash-starved nations. Analysts like Philips[23] even cited the US Treasury Department labelling China as a "rogue creditor practicing opportunistic lending." It is more important therefore to understand the government control over business houses in China that gives rise to the concern about "opportunistic lending."

In 1978, Deng Xiaoping led China into opening its markets in a calibrated manner to invite foreign investment. Beginning in 1980,

> the Chinese government established four economic zones – Shenzhen, Zhuhai, Shantou and Xiamen – to experiment with economic development models to attract foreign firms. Market reforms accelerated as a result of Deng's 1992 southern tour speech, and the investment of foreign capital into the country began in earnest. Between 1995 and 1997, the Chinese government began opening up domestic markets with the goal of acquiring WTO membership and also started liberalizing trade by implementing measures such as reducing tariffs. In the latter half of the 1990s, China attracted foreign capital with abundant preferential policies and cheap labour as weapons, thereby establishing itself as the "factory of the world." A plan to develop western China kicked off in 1999, and the opening up of China to foreign markets moved from coastal regions to the country's interior. In 2001, China became a member of the WTO, and with further loosening of foreign capital restrictions in the service industries, China saw a dramatic rise in the amount of direct investment.[24]

The liberalisation programme initiated by Deng also aimed at private ownership of domestic business apart from the predominantly state-owned socialistic model that China follows. From 1999, private ownership has been permitted in China. However, most of the privately owned firms are small and are dependent on financial assistance from banks. Since nearly all the banks in China are state-controlled, even the private businesses come under the purview of government control, however indirectly. When the current President Xi Jinping came to power in 2012, the government control over business, including foreign firms, was strengthened by incorporating Chinese Communist Party representatives into the management of the firms. Richard McGregor observed that

> The party's efforts to place itself inside private companies have been, according to its own figures, very successful. One recent survey by the Central Organisation Department, the party's personnel body, found that 68% of China's private companies had party bodies by 2016, and 70% of foreign enterprises.[25]

Analysts however find that the state control in China over business does not appear to be driven by profits alone. In the words of Ramo,[26]

> the "Beijing Consensus," a development approach driven not by a desire to make bankers happy, but by the more fundamental urge for equitable, high-quality growth – because no other formula can keep China from exploding. ... The goal: growing while holding on to independence.

A combination of the policy of state control over business both at home and abroad, synchronised with the example of "Hambantota Model," presents a unique interpretation to the Tribute System that China has historically followed. Even though scholarly analysis has also argued that the "debt-trap diplomacy" employed by China in the case of Hambantota, Djibouti or Venezuela were spun by the media, bringing into focus the relations between academia, media and policy worlds in creating such meme,[27] such arguments do not help to demystify the transfer of the territory of one country under the virtual control of a business organisation that is totally subject to the political will of its mother country.

Arising from such a conception is the phenomenon that we would term "the Neo-Tribute System." The soft financial power of the state makes it possible for China to increase its sphere of influence in a manner that is distinctly different from the rent-seeking-purely-for-corporate-profit approach of the rest of the corporatised world. In the traditional Tribute System, political control over territories of "vassal" states resulted in revenue for the parent state, so long as sovereign control over the other state prevailed. In the Neo-Tribute System, economic control through its banks and lending mechanisms will raise revenues without the sovereignty of the other state coming seriously into question or motive.

Reviewing international terms of assistance

It is easier to fall prey to the temptation of China baiting on its debt diplomacy. Analysts like Mark Akpaninyie note that it is Crony Diplomacy where "unchecked profit motive is driving Chinese firms to exploit poor nations."[28] However, scholarly opinion on the subject of debt-trap diplomacy is equally divided both in favour of portraying China as using financial assistance to expand its sphere of influence in the Global South in true Bandung spirit as well as casting China in the garb of using financial soft power to aggregate the resources of nations while ignoring the impact of their developmental assistance on the poor of those nations.[29] While a balanced dispassionate view is difficult to arrive at, instead, it must be recognised that nations act in their best national interest rather than purely on charitable international community interest. Chinese terms of lending that appear attractive on two accounts: one, the financial or political stability of the seeker country is not given the type of weightage that IMF, ADB or World Bank will put to scrutiny; two, seeking assistance from China comes with other packages like techno giants/skilled labour from China, which other international lending agencies cannot/or do not usually offer. Three, unlike other international lending agencies, China does not seem to worry about defaults in payments. Hambantota and Djibouti serve as important examples, for in the case of other international lending agencies such "bail out" method has not been adopted nor considered tenable in the international legal order.

As discussed earlier, some scholars do view the functioning of multinational corporations (MNC) as different from the policies of the state. However, that

MNCs abide by three legal frameworks – domestic (of the country of origin), bilateral (that of the country of business interest) and international (of WTO, GATT and other such frameworks) – is a given and valid fact. Extending from this premise, scholarly debate also looks into certain pertinent questions, as by Kim and Milner:

> Do MNCs have outsized influence over politics? And relative to whom? Domestic firms, the public and the median voter, or other interest groups? Our data cannot directly answer this critical question. We can say that they have greater means and seem to use them to exert more influence than other firms, even big domestic ones. But are they more able to convert these means into success politically? Again our data cannot give a direct answer. But the direction of US foreign economic policy in the past decades suggests they have been very powerful. The lowering of trade barriers via the GATT/WTO and various preferential trade agreements, the opening of capital markets and signing of bilateral investment treaties and economic agreements with investment protections, and the harmonization of regulations in many areas in preferential trade agreements are all policies that the US government has pursued actively and ones that MNCs have championed.[30]

A study such as above lends credit to our argument that in a country like China where all businesses and banks are directly or substantially controlled by the Communist Party, it is but inevitable that these would be used to extend the government's interest through all available mechanisms. Therefore, it is perhaps time for international lending agencies to take a call on their lending terms and see whether the "ailing" and needing nations could be extended assistance under more affordable terms to help realise their developmental goals. While doing so, it is also necessary to avoid playing into the hands of geopolitical compulsions that may again push nations to seek assistance from other softer privy purses. The agenda is not to counter China. It is to balance an approach that will help nations to work together to achieve goals that create economic opportunities and prosperity in their own lands.

It is also important that international lending agencies must package their assistance with greater emphasis on transparency and accountability since such liberalised assistance may inadvertently give rise to rent-seeking political interests in those countries, defeating thereby the purpose of liberalisation of the terms of assistance. On their part, the political leaders in those countries should avoid joining the BRI bandwagon for immediate political or even personal gains. They must weigh their long-term national interests before considering assistance through the BRI, in preference to other international agencies, if they choose to.

Especially in the post-COVID-19 world, where economically weaker countries would require huge assistance in reconstructing their pandemic-struck economy, the weighing of options between the BRI and other agencies should gain prominent debate and purposeful analysis.

China, BRI and implications for South Asia

Since November 2012, when he became the Communist Party leader, he may have had no intention of stepping down. Two weeks after his appointment. Xi led the six other members of the Politburo standing committee to the National Museum in Tiananmen Square to view a grand exhibition called "The Road to Revival." The exhibition recalled China's "century of humiliation" beginning with the Opium War. Afterwards, Xi talked about the China Dream, or "the great revival of the Chinese nation."[31] If an academic opinion is to be given credence, it appears that in the annals of Chinese history, the Qin Emperor is revered for unifying China, and Xi wants to go down in history as the man who finally unified China – and possibly the first ruler of "all under the heaven."[32]

Ferdinand Braudel in his classical work *A History of Civilizations* observed that "No civilization can survive without mobility: all are enriched by trade and the stimulating impact of strangers."[33] If we are to extrapolate Braudel's observations, we find that China has embarked upon a careful strategy to supplement its upward mobility in the international order through trade and economic footprints across Central, South and South East Asia as well as Africa. It has also liberally promoted "the stimulating impact of strangers" to achieve its objectives. Today, we are aware that China has expanded its knowledge and technical abilities across all conceivable spectrums of human life. Riding the crest of its acquired abilities superimposed on its Sino-centric "world view," Chinese hope to bring about a world order that acknowledges the supremacy of China. The BRI apparently is the medium through which China aspires to revive its great past.

Unlike the dynastical past when China controlled the order of the world in its physical boundaries through the Tribute System, in the new world order that is based on economic objectives, China perhaps is attempting to extract "tributes" that come in the form of soft economic assistance. The Hambantota project in Sri Lanka and Gwadar in Pakistan may as well deserve in-depth understanding in this regard. Cases of Chinese involvement in infrastructure-building and economic assistance in Africa are wrought with an equal measure of hope and suspicion,[34] even though Chinese scholars have built historical and ethical connections to such activities.[35] It appears that China is exacting a new Tribute System that comes with lending rates that are higher than world donors and hypothecation of assets when the native economy is too weak to repay the economic assistance. While scholarly debates agree and disagree over this point, there appears to be a consistency in acknowledging that China leverages this soft assistance policy to its political and economic advantage. In fact, a researcher at Johns Hopkins University pointed out recently that

China has asked for political returns in exchange for debt forgiveness. Apart from territorial expansion, China has been interested in acquiring ports located in the participant states of the Belt and Road Initiative, including in Sri Lanka, Djibouti and Malaysia. China's territorial interests and port acquisitions have and will continue to elicit responses from competing states.[36]

Conclusion

Michel Foucault, in his own peculiar terminology, calls "dividing oneself off" – that is, in the case of a civilisation, expelling from its frontiers and from its inner life any value that it spurns. "One might," writes Foucault,

> trace the history of the limits, of those obscure actions, necessarily forgotten as soon as they are performed, whereby a civilization casts aside something it regards as alien. Throughout its history, this moat, which it digs around itself, this no man's land by which it preserves its isolation, is just as characteristic as its positive values. For it receives and maintains its values as continuous features of its history, but in the area which we have chosen to discuss it makes its essential choice – the selection [our emphasis] – which gives it its positive nature – the essential substance of which it is made.[37]

China's ancient inheritance and its rise as a leading economic power reflect the truth behind Foucault's theory of a civilisation dividing itself off in the process of shedding the weaknesses that it holds as alien to its persona. President Xi recalling the Century of Shame mentioned earlier, in our opinion, sits well with the conception that China has made some serious reflections into those weaknesses that cumulatively resulted in the sense of shame and therefore, its Neo-Tribute System and aggressive expansion of the BRI are the means through which it is attempting to shed those weaknesses. This hypothesis is essential to analysing and understanding China. While China continues to expand its sphere of influence in Asia and Africa towards achieving its BRI objectives, leaders in South Asia as well as in other lesser-developed parts of Africa have an ominous task. They have to understand the way China perceives its world order and determine what role they would play in the long-term interest of their own nations.

Reviewing international terms of assistance

We would like to add by reiterating that it is important to understand China's BRI initiatives without, we emphasise *without*, being Sino-Phobic. Looking at the phenomena discussed above impartially therefore, we express the necessity to review international terms of assistance from established (conventional, if we may say so) agencies in the following words:[38]

It is easier to fall prey to the temptation of China baiting on its debt-diplomacy. Instead, we must admit a simple fact that nations will act in their best national interest rather than purely in international community interest. China does so by offering terms of lending that appear attractive on three accounts: one, the financial or political stability of the seeker-country is not given the type of weightage that IMF, ADB or World Bank will put to scrutiny. Two, seeking assistance from China comes with other packages like techno giants/skilled labor from China which other international lending agencies cannot offer. Three, unlike other international lending agencies, China does not seem to worry about defaults in payments. We have Hambantota and Djibouti as glaring examples.

Therefore, it is perhaps time for international lending agencies to take a call on their lending terms and see whether the "ailing" and needing nations could be extended assistance under more affordable terms to help realize their developmental goals. While doing so, it is also necessary to avoid playing into the hands of geopolitical compulsions that may again push nations to seek assistance from other softer privy purses. The agenda is not to counter China. It is to balance an approach that will help nations to work together to achieve goals that create economic opportunities and prosperity in their own lands.

China may go ahead and realize its BRI objectives with or without interference from other big players in the arena. That China does so is not necessarily a cause for concern if the community of nations along its way take their calls for cooperation on BRI after due consideration of their long-time national interests. The political leaders in those countries should avoid joining the bandwagon for immediate political or even personal gains.

India remains central to the success of the BRI insofar as South Asia is concerned. Prime Minister Modi, however, while attending the 18th SCO summit at Quingdao on 10 June 2018, made it amply clear that "India welcomes new connectivity projects that are inclusive, sustainable, transparent, and those that respect the sovereignty and territorial integrity of nations."[39] He was evidently referring to the Karakoram highway that China has embarked upon expanding as part of CPEC. The Doklam stand-off earlier was again an indication of Chinese intention to test India's will towards acceding to its ambitions in expanding the BRI.

Amongst South Asian nations, Afghanistan and Bhutan have remained steadfast in their relations with India. Bangladesh in recent times has shown great enthusiasm in becoming a partner through BIMSTEC and BCIM forums. Nepal in recent years has shown a greater tilt towards China perhaps on an ideological basis. However, Nepalese concerns need to be re-evaluated in light of the geographical constraints that it faces in becoming an active partner in the BRI.

The plenary session of the 9th South Asia Summit held at Dhaka in October 2015 attempted to address an important question that comes to our mind: Is political leadership in South Asia ready for implementing the 2030 Agenda? The observation of the session just about sums up our opinion too "Leaders in South Asian countries need to rise above the political dilemmas to collaborate in an inclusive and integrated manner (to implement the 2030 Agenda)."[40]

Post-COVID-19 world, whenever the recovery phase commences, will present multifarious challenges to developed, developing as well as poor nations. Addressing those challenges will entail huge monetary assistance from international agencies. It is a scenario in which underdeveloped countries will be more tempted to incline towards China, even though they may not specifically subscribe to the BRI. With the Neo-Tribute System apparently being packaged across as developmental assistance, it is necessary that developed nations and other international lending agencies redefine their terms of assistance to help underdeveloped members of the international community.

Notes

1 Arnold J. Toynbee, *A Study of History*, vol. 2, London: Oxford University Press, 1964.
2 John King Fairbank (ed.), *The Chinese World Order: Traditional China's Foreign Relations*, Cambridge, MA: Harvard University Press, 1968.
3 Warren I. Cohen, *East Asia at the Center: Four Thousand Years of Engagement with the World*, New York: Columbia University Press, 2000.
4 Yongjin Zhang, *The Tribute System*, London: Oxford University Press, 2013. For more insights, see Yongjin Zhang and Barry Buzan, "The Tributary System as International Society in Theory and Practice", *Chinese Journal of International Politics*, vol. 5, no. 1, 2012, pp. 3–36.
5 Abhijit Bhattacharya, "China's Bhutan Push to Fulfill Mao's Old Dream", *Deccan Chronicle*, Op-Ed, 27 June 2017, see https://www.deccanchronicle.com/opinion/op-ed/270617/chinas-bhutan-push-to-fulfill-maos-old-dream.html, accessed 22 February 2019.
6 Robert Chambers, *Chambers' Encyclopedia*, New York: Pergamon Press, 1967, p. 637.
7 Hugh E. Richardson, *Tibet and Its History*, Boston and London: Shambhala, 1984, pp. 48–49.
8 Shridhar Kaul and H. N. Kaul, *Ladakh Through the Ages, Towards a New Identity*, New Delhi: Indus Publishing, 2004.
9 Sanjay Upadhya, *Nepal and the Geo-Strategic Rivalry between China and India*, New York: Routledge, 2012, p. 42.
10 Manoj Kr. Singh, *Indo-Bhutan Relations and China Interventions*, New Delhi: Anmol Publications, 2014, p. 144.
11 *Ibid*.
12 See http://darjeeling.gov.in/darj-hist.html, accessed 27 February 2019.
13 Mahnaz Z. Ispahani, *Roads and Rivals: The Political Uses of Access in the Borderlands of Asia*, Ithaca, NY: Cornell University Press, June 1989, p. 191.
14 "First Cargo Train under CPEC Leaves China for Karachi", https://en.dailypakistan.com.pk/headline/cpec-china-departs-first-cargo-train-for-karachi/, accessed 21 February 2019.
15 Bates Gill, "Shanghai Five: An Attempt to Counter U.S. Influence in Asia?", *Op-Ed*, 4 May 2001, Brookings, see

https://www.brookings.edu/opinions/shanghai-five-an-attempt-to-counter-u-s-influence-in-asia/, accessed 15 January 2019.
16. Rakesh Krishnan Simha, "SCO's Next Big Challenge: Keeping the Peace in Asia, Russia Beyond", 24 July 2015, https://www.rbth.com/blogs/2015/07/24/scos_next_big_challenge_keeping_the_peace_in_asia_47985.html, accessed 15 January 2019.
17. Xiaodong Zhang, "China's Interests in the Middle East: Present and Future", *Middle East Policy Council*, vol. 6, no. 3, 1999, https://www.mepc.org/journal/chinas-interests-middle-east-present-and-future, accessed 16 January 2019.
18. Brendon Hong, "China: Iran's Lifeline to Overcome Oil Sanctions", *Atlantic Council Blog*, 3 October 2018, https://www.atlanticcouncil.org/blogs/iransource/china-iran-s-lifeline-to-overcome-oil-sanctions, accessed 16 January 2019.
19. C. T. Subairath, "Calicut: A Centri-Petal Force in the Chinese and Arab Trade (1200–1500)", *Proceedings of the Indian History Congress*, vol. 72, Part-II, 2011, pp. 1082–1089.
20. Maria Abi-Habib, "How China Got Sri Lanka to Cough Up a Port", *The New York Times*, 25 June 2018, https://www.nytimes.com/2018/06/25/world/asia/china-sri-lanka-port.html, accessed 14 September 2019.
21. BBC, *BBC News*, 23 March 2019, https://www.bbc.com/news/world-europe-47679760, accessed 4 April 2019.
22. C. J. Neely, *Chinese Foreign Exchange Reserves, Policy Choices and the U.S. Economy*, St Louis, MO: Federal Reserve Bank of St Louis, 2017.
23. M. M. Philips, " G-7 to Warn China over Costly Loans to Poor Countries", *The Wall Street Journal*, 15 September 2006, https://www.wsj.com/articles/SB115826807563263495, accessed 15 May 2020.
24. K. Motohashi, *Comparison of Economic Institutions in China and India. In: Global Business Strategy. Springer Texts in Business and Economics*, 11 February 2015, doi: 10.1007/978-4-431-55468-4_4.
25. R. Mc Gregor, "How the State Runs Business in China", *The Guardian*, 25 July 2019, https://www.theguardian.com/world/2019/jul/25/china-business-xi-jinping-communist-party-state-private-enterprise-huawei, 21 May 2020.
26. J. C. Ramo, "China Has Discovered Its Own Economic Consensus", 15 September 2006, www.fpc.org.uk: https://fpc.org.uk/?s=The+Beijing+Consensus, 24 May 2020.
27. D. Brautigam, "A Critical Look at Chinese 'Debt-Trap Diplomacy: The Rise of a Meme", *Area Development and Policy*, vol. 5, no. 1, 2020, pp. 1–14. doi: 10.1080/23792949.2019.1689828
28. M. Akpaninyie, "China's 'Debt Diplomacy' Is a Misnomer. Call It 'Crony Diplomacy'", *The Diplomat*, 12 March 2019, https://thediplomat.com/2019/03/chinas-debt-diplomacy-is-a-misnomer-call-it-crony-diplomacy/, 25 May 2020.
29. M. Power, G. Mohan, and M. Tan-Mullins, *China's Resources Diplomacy in Africa: Powering Development?* New York: Palgrave Macmillan, 2012.
30. I. S. Kim and H. V. Milner, *Multinational Corporations and Their Influence through Lobbying on Foreign Policy*, Washington, DC: Brookings Institution, 2 December 2019, https://www.brookings.edu/wp-content/uploads/2019/12/Kim_Milner_manuscript.pdf, 22 May 2020.
31. Frank Ching, "With Xi Jinping's Lifetime Presidency, China Could become More Powerful than Ever", *Scroll*, 19 March 2018, https://scroll.in/article/872209/with-xi-jingpings-lifetime-presidency-china-could-become-more-powerful-than-ever, accessed 16 October 2018.
32. *Ibid.*
33. Ferdinand Braudel, translation by Richard Mayne, *A History of Civilizations*, New York: The Penguin Press, 1994, p. 10.
34. Shakila Kamatali, "China's Growing Footprint in Africa", *The New Times*, 11 August 2018, https://www.newtimes.co.rw/lifestyle/chinas-growing-footprint-africa, accessed 16 October 2018.

35 Zhang Quanyi Han Yi, "Understand China's Foreign Aid to Africa from a Historical and Chinese Ethical Perspectives Since 1955", 8 February 2018, PAGEO, https://www.geopolitika.hu/en/2018/02/08/understand-chinas-foreign-aid-to-africa-from-a-historical-and-chinese-ethical-perspectives-since-1955/#_edn1, accessed 14 October 2018.
36 Alvin Camba, "Fact-Checking Critics of Chinese Aid", *East Asia Forum*, 28 November 2017, https://www.eastasiaforum.org/2017/11/28/fact-checking-critics-of-chinese-aid/, accessed 10 October 2018.
37 Braudel, n. 33, p. 31.
38 Srinivasan, Gp Capt (Dr) R, "Post-COVID19: International Lending and Geopolitics", Defence Research and Studies, June 29, 2020, https://dras.in/post-covid19-international-lending-and-geopolitics/, accessed 12 February 2021.
39 Saibal Dasgupta, "India only SCO Member to Oppose China's BRI", *Times of India*, 10 June 2018, http://timesofindia.indiatimes.com/articleshow/64533390.cms?utm_source=contentofinterest&utm_medium=text&utm_campaign=cppst, accessed 10 June 2018.
40 See https://cpd.org.bd/political-leadership-south-asia-not-ready-implementing-2030-agenda/, accessed 14 September 2019.

4
CHINA'S OVERARCHING BELT AND ROAD INITIATIVE VIS-À-VIS INDIA'S PREDICAMENT

Y. Yagama Reddy

Introduction

China's Belt and Road Initiative (BRI), earlier referred to as "One Belt, One Road" (OBOR), has received a great deal of attention since it was first announced in a speech by President Xi Jinping in autumn 2013. The Silk Road Economic Belt (SREB) was one of the two initiatives announced by Xi in a speech at the Nazarbayev University in Kazakhstan, and the other one, the Maritime Silk Road (MSR), during his visit to Indonesia in October 2017. A Vision and Action document titled "Jointly Building Silk Road Economic Belt and 21st-Century Maritime Silk Road" was released by him in March 2015. Xi Jinping's "China dream" to "revitalise the Chinese nation" portrays the BRI as a "new type of great power to supplement the international economic order."[1] The BRI envisaged "a network of regional cooperation and systematic projects of global significance" that will embrace 65 countries. Xi Jinping's description of the BRI as a "community of common destiny" is meant to link the BRI to the Chinese model of socialism to develop the world's poorer regions by bringing them (Chinese neighbours) closer to China geopolitically and bring stability in the region.[2] Prima facie, BRI, which is a heavily Chinese investment project, encompasses multiple international transport and infrastructure corridors on land and at sea. BRI is thus a combination of a land-based Silk Road Economic Belt and a sea-based 21st-Century Maritime Silk Road. As a new manifestation of China's soft power of its "peaceful" and "multilateral" rise, the BRI is one of China's key diplomatic and economic initiatives and a potent symbol of the rise of China-based globalisation. The BRI lies at the heart of China's plan to geopolitically and economically master the region. Chinese authorities used to describe China's BRI strategy as one of the most important foreign policy initiatives in the twenty-first century. China's leaders consider the BRI not merely as their

DOI: 10.4324/9781003146223-4

"historic mission" to bring about China's "national rejuvenation" as the world's most prestigious power, but also a contributing factor to the development of "political civilization." It is designed to cover 55% of world GNP, approximately one-third of global GDP, 70% of the global population (around 4.0 billion) and 75% of known energy reserves.[3] The world has begun to feel surprised over the size, strategic ambition and speed of the BRI project, radiating in all directions from China, and with maritime pivot points all the way to Europe.[4]

BRI: connectivity and cooperation spanning vast geographical area

If the BRI links China to Central and South Asia and onward to Europe, the *New Maritime Silk Road* involves building ports all over the Indo-Pacific region and also links China to the nations of Southeast Asia, the Gulf countries, North Africa and on to Europe. Besides the Asia–Europe land and sea "silk" routes, six economic corridors are envisaged: (1) China–Mongolia–Russia; (2) New Eurasian Land Bridge, a 10,000 km rail link from China to Rotterdam; (3) China-Central Asia-West Asia-Economic Corridor, replicating the ancient Silk Road; (4) China-Indo China Peninsula Economic Corridor; (5) China–Pakistan Economic Corridor (CPEC); (6) Bangladesh–China–India–Myanmar (BCIM) Economic Corridor.[5] China has targeted Southeast Asia as one of the central nodes of its BRI through projects and the South China Sea as economic leverage to support its claims over the disputed territories. Apart from BRI-related construction agreements with six Arab countries, China has obtained affirmations of support for the BRI from four other West Asian countries (Saudi Arabia, Kuwait, the UAE and Oman). Along with China–Pakistan Economic Corridor, China in April 2015 signed 49 agreements to finance a variety of projects with a total expected value of US$46 billion in Pakistan; later in May 2017, it signed a Memorandum of Understanding (MoU) of US$50 billion for the development of the North Indus River Cascade in Pakistan's Gilgit-Baltistan region.[6] Under the garb of a "framework of regional connectivity," CPEC is projected to have a positive impact on Iran, Afghanistan, India, Central Asian Republic and the region. China has also expressed interest in investing in port investments at Gwadar (Pakistan), Hambantota (Sri Lanka) and Chittagong (Bangladesh).[7] Chinese sources have made it clear that the BRI is undeniably a Chinese initiative, but not exclusively a Chinese enterprise. Thus, being the largest infrastructure project ever embarked upon in world history, the BRI is undeniably a staggering infrastructure development plan consisting of hundreds of megaprojects – highways, railways, ports, airports, dams, pipelines, a state-of-the-art power grid and open trade and investment networks – that will encourage connectivity and cooperation spanning a vast geographical area stretching across Asia to Europe and East Africa, involving at least 40 nations. Shivshankar Menon, India's former national security advisor, foresees evident economic advantages for the Chinese economy, but at the same time the proposed connectivity on account of the BRI will also clearly benefit all those exporting countries in Asia seeking better access to markets and supplies.[8]

With no part of Asia or Europe excluded from the initiative envisaging more than 900 different projects under the BRI umbrella, this enterprise requires the active mobilisation of technology, management and human resources on a global basis. China's deputy permanent representative to the UN reported to the meeting of the Second Committee of the UN General Assembly that China has signed more than 190 documents on cooperation with over 160 countries and international organisations and jointly established 82 cooperation parks overseas with participating countries.[9] As per a report of January 2021 by the International Institute of Green Finance (IIGF) of the Central University of Finance and Economics (CUFE), Beijing, 140 countries have joined the BRI by signing a MoU with China (40 in Sub-Saharan Africa, 34 in Europe and Central Asia, including 18 countries of the European Union, 25 in East Asia and Pacific, 17 in the Middle East and North Africa, 18 in Latin America and the Caribbean and six in South East Asia).[10] According to Christoph Nedopil Wang, Director, Green Belt and Road Initiative Center at IIGF, renewable energy investments (solar, wind, hydro) constitute a majority of Chinese overseas energy investments – an increase from 38% in 2019 to 57% in 2020 – despite a total decrease of BRI investments in per cent.[11]

Prospective financial support for the BRI

Depending upon the position of each country in the new emerging connectivity maps, productivity, competition, market opportunities and transport and logistics costs are to be impacted.[12] The BRI is an ambitious effort to improve regional cooperation and connectivity on a transcontinental scale as well as to strengthen infrastructure, trade and investment links between China and some 65 other countries. The "first diplomatic victory" of China was the formal launching in October 2014 of the Asian Infrastructure Investment Bank (AIIB) with a starting capital of US$100 billion in Beijing with an aim to provide financial support to China's Silk Road projects. The expressed interest of 57 countries (including 37 countries from Asia, 20 from outside of Asia and 4 of the G7 countries) in joining AIIB has made the BRI a truly international project. The inability of the Asian Development Bank and World Bank to meet the need of US$8.2 trillion required for infrastructure financing in Asia makes AIIB a viable alternative.[13] China has its efforts increased to mobilise capital through the Silk Route Fund, China Development Bank and the Export-Import Bank, among others. Being the first stakeholder (25–30%) in AIIB, China as of now enjoys de facto veto power. With projects totalling as much as US$900 billion in six land corridors covering more than 60 countries,[14] the BRI projects, according to the report of Renmin University which Xinhua News Agency described as the first think tank report, are expected to be fully realised in about 35 years in 2049.[15] That the BRI is a carefully calculated initiative to increase Chinese influence is well discernible from the observation of Gurmeet Kanwal that "the Chinese leadership hopes OBOR will make a significant contribution towards the achievement of China's goal of becoming the unchallenged ... economic and military power in the Indo-Pacific region by 2049, a century after it won its independence."[16] Chinese outbound investment, according to the statement made by Ning Jizhe, China's Vice Minister of the National Development and Reform Commission in Beijing on 13 May 2017, is forecast to total US$600 billion to US$800 billion over the next five years, with a large share of it earmarked for the markets related to the BRI.[17]

Transnational participation at the BRI summit

In an effort to promote the initiative in the international community, the "Silk Road Summit for International Cooperation" was organised in China from 14 to 16 May 2017, and was attended by over 65 countries (excluding India). In addition, 1500 delegates from 130 countries attended, including more than 30 heads of organisations and heads of states such as Russian President Vladimir Putin, Turkish President Tayyip Erdogan and Indonesian President Joko Widodo, the then Pakistani Prime Minister Nawaz Sharif as well as UN Secretary-General Antonio Guterres, IMF Managing Director Christine Lagarde and World Bank President Jim Yong Kim.[18] Most national leaders and commentators welcomed the proposed logistical connectivity projects. Besides appreciating Xi's initiative as "an example of a creative approach towards fostering integration in energy, infrastructure, transport, industry and humanitarian collaboration," Vladimir Putin also described the BRI as "a unique opportunity to create a common cooperation framework from the Atlantic to the Pacific – for the first time in history."[19] Altogether around 140 nations expressed their consent towards the BRI. China has also reached out to the European Union, the ASEAN and SCO members and West Asian countries. Of much significance was the unfolding of US–China detente, as could be better understood from President Donald Trump's nomination of his special assistant and the point person on Asia in the National Security Council, Matt F. Pottinger, to represent him at the BRI Forum. Deputing a delegation to attend the forum in Beijing, as elaborated by the US Commerce Department on 11 May 2017, was simply Washington's recognition of the importance of China-proposed BRI.[20] Equally shocking for India was the participation of Vietnam's President Tran Dai Quang in the BRI event, with no semblance to India's financial help to Vietnam to buy patrol boats to stand up to China.

India abstained from attending the BRI Forum

The Chinese envoy on 5 May 2017 to India, Luo Zhaohui, in a speech to the United Service Institution (USI) in New Delhi argued that his country had no "intention to get involved in the sovereignty and territorial disputes between

India and Pakistan" and even offered to rename the CPEC – a key component of the BRI – to allay Indian objections.[21] The Chinese communist leadership tried in vain to persuade India to join the BRI bandwagon; yet, India has its serious reservations raised that the CPEC would undermine India's sovereignty. New Delhi views that a change of name matters little since the corridor will involve Chinese investments and projects on Indian territory that is under Pakistani occupation. Having termed India's concerns over sovereignty relating to the CPEC as unwarranted, Beijing had apparently given up and decided to simply ignore Delhi's protestations and proceed with the CPEC projects in a big way in Gilgit-Baltistan. Pushing for the flagship agreement, the Chinese Ambassador maintained, India has put forward the "Act East Policy," "Spice Route," etc., and a number of regional connectivity initiatives, as well as vigorously pushed forward the BIMSTEC. As close neighbours, China and India could be natural partners in connectivity and the OBOR.[22] It is a political and diplomatic snub by China, conveying a frank message to the Modi government to "get lost." India marked its protest by not attending the Belt and Road Forum that China hosted in May 2017. Obviously, the Modi government has trodden along the path of confrontation and rivalry with China which seemed to have portended India's global isolation with an oblique reference to the participation of all of India's neighbours in the BRI.[23] India's opposition would become inimical to India's own economic interests, argued Vinay Kaura, who further added it would no way downgrade China's geostrategic ambition of bringing countries from Central Asia to Europe into its orbit.[24] A year later on 24 April 2018 at the meeting of the Shanghai Cooperation Organisation, all other members of SCO (Russia, Pakistan, Kazakhstan, Kyrgyzstan, Tajikistan and Uzbekistan) reaffirmed their support for the BRI through the joint communiqué issued at the end of the SCO meeting,[25] while India had invidiously chosen not to express support to the BRI and stuck to its opposition to the CPEC.

Mistrust and mockery of the BRI

Ever since its inception in 2013, the BRI has garnered both positive and negative attention. The BRI is a key element of a "new round of opening to the world"[26] which the Western outlets described as "China's Marshall Plan."[27] As expected, the *Global Times* rejected the Western scepticism by maintaining that China's BRI is not an alliance and comes with no political strings attached, in contrast to Marshall Plan, which aimed to control Western European nations and to contain the Soviet Union. The BRI, as per the official Chinese media, intends to present China as a non-threatening and non-revisionist rising power, dissimilar to others in the past. China's BRI, China's Vice Foreign Minister, Zhang Yesui, underlines, is "not directed against any specific country or organisation."[28] While pushing the mantra of "Asia for Asians," Xi Jinping in 2014 has professed in a message that China is willing and ready to lead the region. Chinese projects are designed in such a way that Beijing would end up with effective control over critical infrastructure assets in faraway lands.[29] Further, there arises the need for China to go abroad in order to offset the country's fast-fading trade competitiveness.[30] China's competitive advantage along the MSR is also much weaker; for instance, China and Southeast Asia are bound to compete more intensively, and China will face much greater difficulties along the MSR.[31] The BRI is rather a Chinese neo-imperialist adventure; it looks more like a demonstration of financial "soft power" in the face of US retreat from the international scene. China's capital, technology and management experience, it is feared, will promote the development and prosperity of neighbouring countries, but at the same time, China will encourage its own economic transformation and make itself the centre of the regional economy.[32] Though the participating countries are connected with one another, there is no institutional framework or decision-making mechanism for the BRI.

There has been suspicion among several countries that the main aim of the project is to expand China's influence globally, given its logic on the project is based on geopolitics and on the export of its huge infrastructure-building capacities.[33] The suspicion of other countries over the BRI aims and strategic purposes thus becomes the most serious challenge.[34] For all the Chinese ostensible assertion of BRI's spirit of "peace and cooperation, openness and inclusiveness, mutual learning and mutual benefit," the BRI carries the stigma of raising risks of debt distress, if the World Bank debt sustainability analysis is of any indication.[35] Along with the strain on the resources of the Chinese government, the AIIB and China's domestic banks, the BRI poses substantial risks to the host countries. Understandably, regional powers too are wary of China's rise. It has been implicitly aimed at testing Russia's dominance in the economic and security arenas of Central Asia but also posing challenges to US influence. Russia is equally concerned, with the BRI covering almost the same areas of Russia's traditional sphere of interest. Besides creating stiff competition for European companies on trade, investments and market access in Europe and Asia, the BRI is feared to have the potential to impact European security. In effect, the United States is apprehensive about the BRI as an extension of efforts by the Chinese Communist Party to undermine the security and economic architecture of the international order.[36] The Chinese aid is in no way far from problems; mainly it is the lack of coordination with other donors, the lack of transparency in the aid-granting process and trust deficit that has in a way inhibited unified support for its initiative. The Chinese aid, though appears to be free of political conditionality, expects the recipient countries to be loyal to the "One China" policy.[37] Governments from Washington to Moscow to New Delhi are so uneasy that Beijing is trying to use its "Belt and Road" to develop a China-centred political structure that will erode their influence, and the BRI projects are being cancelled, renegotiated or delayed due to disputes. CPEC and other Chinese investment projects in South Asian countries have met with some resistance, reflecting a rising trend of internal disagreements among China and its BRI partners. Notably, Nepal and Myanmar cancelled plans in November for Chinese companies, and Thailand suspended the high-speed railway. Malaysia's opposition to Chinese investment entailed cancelling several projects and putting the brakes on the 'Forest City' project, East Coast Rail Link, and natural gas pipeline in Sabah is well evident from Mahathir's reaction to the BRI as "a new version of colonialism."[38] Sri Lanka has complaints against the deal as being favourable to China, and Tanzania reopened negotiations with China. Questions are raised in Pakistan about the viability of some of the projects that are part of the US$46 billion investment proposed for the CPEC. Many African and South American countries have come to regret past Chinese investments in extraction industries.[39] China's ongoing investment on the African Continent has been the subject of controversy and suspicion, for some time now, on investing in 293 FDI projects since 2005 to the value of some US$66.4 billion. Local discontent has been there with rising Chinese influence on the continent.[40] At the Bo'ao Forum for Asia in April 2018, Xi ruled out the international suspicions over the BRI as a "Chinese conspiracy." As a part of the damage-controlling mechanism, China has made every effort to better communicate its BRI policies and practices to the world; significantly, the BRI has been transformed into a multilateral initiative through tripartite cooperation with other countries and international development institutions.[41] Of much relevance is that Sri Lanka's debt repayment problems had very little to do with Chinese loans, understandably, the criticism that China is using the BRI to achieve its diplomatic and strategic aims through debt diplomacy is a mere fictitious story.[42]

India's benign and malignant concerns over BRI

India is perplexingly faced with the challenge of managing its relationship with its neighbours and competing to maintain its prominence in the region. In essence, the BRI underscores the growing Sino-Indian competition in the subcontinent and the Indian Ocean region. India sees the initiative not as an opportunity, but as a threat or a form of competition. It took serious exception to the CPEC, which China projected flagship of BRI, and candidly responded that "no country can accept a project that ignores its core concerns on sovereignty and territorial integrity."[43] The four specific corridors constituting India's concerns include CPEC, Bangladesh–China–India–Myanmar Economic Corridor, Trans-Himalayan Economic Corridor and Twenty-First-Century MSR, which are a combination of bilateral infrastructure. China's engagement with India's immediate neighbours through these corridors threatens to alter existing power dynamics in the region. India is concerned with the strategic implications of the Chinese infrastructure projects. Undeniably, CPEC passing through Gilgit-Baltistan of Pak-occupied Kashmir is tantamount to a violation of India's sovereignty, and the presence of PLA troops would be harmful to India's national security interests. India is worried about the strategic implications of China's access to Pakistan's deep-water port of Gwadar, which in consequence would become closer to the landlocked territory of Xinjiang than China's eastern coast.

If at all the mega connectivity project respects sovereignty and territorial integrity, India assured its full support to the initiative, which ensures inclusivity. Given the geopolitical nuances of BRI connectivity projects and India's reservations thereof, there is unlikely any possibility for the two countries to collaborate on the BRI. Arguably, Beijing, which has never accepted Indian primacy in South Asia, is determined to build its own dominance in South Asia and the Indian Ocean, and India cannot afford to lose sight of this dimension as it directly impacts its security interests. BRI-promoting-South Asian regional connectivity essentially undermines both the SAARC system and India's central role in South Asia and makes China the arbitrator certainly between India and Pakistan, and possibly also for other smaller countries in South Asia in their ties with India.[44] It is "Beijing's aggressive anti-India regional diplomacy that has reinforced the feeling that containment of India remains the long-term Chinese objective."[45] It is the mutual mistrust in the Sino-Indian relationship that hampers the positive momentum of the initiatives, of which both are members.

India's counter-initiatives to the BRI

To outweigh China's continued challenge, India is to tread on the path of cooperating in the form of bilateral and minilateral formats with other states as, for instance, Japan and the European Union, including Italy, France and Germany, its South Asian neighbours – Afghanistan and Bangladesh and a few of the Indian Ocean island states.[46] New Delhi in 2014 has come up with a counter-proposal to the MSR, known as Project Mausam to revive (India's) ancient maritime routes and cultural linkages with countries in the region; and since 2015 Modi has been promoting the Security and Growth for All in the Region (SAGAR) concept. Further, India needs to carry out initiatives like BIMSTEC with greater vigour. India is instrumental in buttressing the Indo-Pacific idea to contest the China-centric geo-economic and strategic narrative of the BRI. Of significance is India's closer cooperation in new developmental projects in third states of South Asia in association with the United States on a project of transmission lines in Nepal, and with Japan on constructing a liquid gas pipeline in Sri Lanka. This is India's new cooperation what the then Indian Foreign Secretary Subrahmanyam Jaishankar described that its smaller neighbours seemed to feel safer if there were also "other states in the room" alongside India.[47] Within its extended neighbourhood, India has developed new formats of cooperation with Japan, the United States and Australia, besides Germany and Europe that are directly or indirectly positioned against China. Despite modest success in the efforts in 2017 at reviving quadrilateral initiative (Quad) to oppose China's assertive policies like BRI, AIIB and China's rejection of the Permanent Court of Arbitration's verdict on the territorial conflicts in the South China Sea, India and Japan embarked on Asia-Africa Growth Corridor (AAGC) to create a counter-model, an alternative to the Chinese BRI. In order for India to offset the Chinese increased presence in the Indian Ocean, India has intensified its military cooperation with the island states of Mauritius, the Seychelles, Maldives and Comoros.[48] Of much significance is the International North-South Transport Corridor (INSTC), a multimodal transportation, which was established by Russia, Iran and India on 12 September 2000 for the purpose of promoting transportation cooperation among the member states, including 11 other members.[49] This corridor connects the Indian Ocean and the Persian Gulf to the Caspian Sea via Iran and then is connected to St. Petersburg and North European via Russian Federation. Ever since it was promulgated in 2015, INSTC incidentally offers India access to Afghanistan and three Central Asian republics.[50]

India's initiatives short of expectations

India's China policy turned out to be short-sighted sapped with prejudices which were "hopelessly unsustainable today," as termed by former ambassador M. K. Bhadrakumar. India's boycotting of the BRI event, according to the logical analysis of Bhadrakumar, would in no way solve the J&K issue.[51] It would be prudent to look at the initiative as a culmination of various bilateral initiatives, many of them were projects actually initiated in the early 1990s, much before the BRI itself was formally launched. India's former National Security Advisor Shiv Shankar Menon is also of the opinion that "India could explore the opportunity of the BRI to see if 'portions' could serve Indian interest in improving connectivity and economic integration."[52] India needs to be sensitive to Chinese goals and ambitions in the region, besides being proactive, instead of a reactive policy that would exhaust its limited resources chasing China. Even as connectivity presents India with an opportunity to re-establish its regional primacy, New Delhi is termed as being slow in its approach to connectivity in the region. Given China's wherewithal in implementing its overseas development projects vis-à-vis India's struggle to craft its domestic development plans, India is undeniably seriously handicapped to provide an alternative to China's overtures to the region.[53] Further, resources crunch inhibits its options for pursuing its objectives in economic policy or its strategic ambitions aiming inter alia to establish a multipolar order in Asia. India's resources limitations and its mandate to develop much-needed domestic infrastructure, its ongoing response is so inadequate to provide its South Asian neighbours with a feasible alternative. Chinese investments in India's neighbourhood of South Asia represent a challenge to which India's foreign policy has not been able to find a suitable response. Until and after the Chinese forage into the South Asian region, New Delhi was scarcely threatened by any sort of competition from others, obviously Beijing's influence in the region comes at a cost to India's role and profile as a regional leader.[54] The Chinese Deputy Chief of Mission Liu Jinsong has also driven the point home that CPEC's traverse through PoK is "no fresh news for India" as there was already the Karakoram-Kunlun road built in the 1960s and also drew the attention to the 1963 agreement between China and Pakistan, which referred to the need for China and Pakistan to renegotiate their boundary after the "settlement of the Kashmir dispute between Pakistan and India."[55] As a part of sharpening its response, India needs to clearly account for its resources and capabilities related to connectivity and infrastructure development. Insofar as the other countries like Australia, France, Germany, the United Kingdom and the United States are looking upon India playing a leading role in the region, India needs to identify specific projects, mechanisms and goals for its connectivity initiatives.

Need for *modus operandi* of Initiatives and *modus vivendi* Strategy

Notwithstanding its interest and capacity to contain India, China weighs up its relationship of both cooperation and competition between the two countries in the areas of energy security, economic ties and shaping the regional security framework. The need for India and China to work together in global governance has been repeatedly highlighted by China in recent times. At the Wuhan summit, for instance, Chinese President Xi underscored that "the two largest developing countries and emerging market economies with a population of more than one billion are the backbone of the world's multi-polarisation and economic globalisation."[56] Cooperating with India is the option for China, as it would not become a predominant threat to India; instead, India is the key factor [for] the implementation of the BRI in South Asia. The fact that China is too authoritarian domestically to be democratic internationally limits itself the use of its capacity for military intimidation. China is not the only nation seeking a new role in international affairs; India's membership of BRICS, the SCO and the IORA provide the opportunity for India to be a substantial player in defining and shaping the new world order. Quite analogous to this inference is that BRI infrastructure is meant for everyone to use it, according to Global Strategy Advisor Parag Khanna, who further discards the suspicion of the BRI being advantageous to China alone; the BRI is not an arms race, nor is it an alliance system of traditional geopolitical narrative.[57] Given the new connectivity corridors as, for instance, the India and Myanmar trans-border highway, Ambassador Kishan S. Rana rescinds the attempts at the BRI being painted as a spoiler of India's national interests.[58] Suggesting India and China to ensure that one disagreement does not sour everything and to reassess the errors and miscalculations of both sides, Rana further proposes five ways to get the Sino-Indian relations better: "strategic guidance" to the armed forces to cool things on the border; deeper engagement across a wide spectrum; push on congruence areas in development cooperation; expanded cultural links; and harder effort at resolving the border issue.[59]

Conclusion

India accords strategic engagement with China is a great deal of significance, given the fact that New Delhi has found ways to cooperate with Beijing on matters of mutual interest, such as AIIB, BRICS Development Bank (New Development Bank). India would have justifiably signalled the definition of its national interests; mere opposition to Chinese moves cannot be a strategy, as an adversarial competition and outright strategic rivalry would be a step backward. Without sway over its decision to stay away from the BRI Forum, India needs to engage in the pursuit of achieving strategic reconciliation. India's opposition to China's high-profile OBOR project is in no way a reflection of discord in their relationship. This is fully vindicated by Prime Minister Narendra Modi's statement on 2 June 2017 at the St Petersburg International Economic Forum that "in the last 40 years, not a single bullet has been fired" because India and China have cooperated on trade and investments "despite a simmering border dispute."[60] India's antagonism to the BRI is in no way an option to insulate itself from the consequences, and India needs to adopt such diplomatic niceties as to support countries to stand up to the Chinese onslaught and thereby to project its image as good Samaritan.

Notes

1 François Godement, "'One Belt, One Road': China's Great Leap Outward", *China Analysis*, 10 June 2015, p. 2.
2 Tanner Greer, "One Belt One Road, One Big Mistake", *Foreign Policy*, 6 December 2018, https://foreignpolicy.com/2018/12/06/bri-china-belt-road-initiative-blunder/, accessed 7 December 2018.
3 Li Jinlei, "Report: Silk Road Economic Belt May Be Divided into Three Phases; Initial Completion Predicted in 2049", *Zhongguo Xinwen Wang*, 28 June 2014.
4 T. N. Ninan, "India Doesn't Want to Join China's OBOR, but …", *Rediff.com*, 25 May 2017, https://www.rediff.com/news/column/india-doesnt-want-to-join-chinas-obor-but/20170513.htm?print=true, accessed 20 December 2018.
5 Talmiz Ahmad, "Why India Needs to Take a Fresh Look at China's Belt and Road Initiative", *The Wire*, 2 July 2018, https://thewire.in/diplomacy/india-needs-to-take-a-fresh-look-at-the-belt-and-road-initiative-proposal, accessed 17 December 2018.
6 M. K. Bhadrakumar, "Modi Blew It Big Time on China Policies", *Indian Punchline*, 13 May 2017, http://blogs.rediff.com/mkbhadrakumar/2017/05/13/modi-blew-it-big-time-on-china-policies/, accessed 20 December 2018.
7 Joanna Eva, Qi Lin, and James Tunningley, "China's Belt and Road Initiative: Regional Outlooks for 2018", *Global Risk Insights*, 31 January 2018, https://globalriskinsights.com/2018/01/chinas-belt-and-road-initiative-regional-outlooks-for-2018/, accessed 12 February 2018.
8 Shiv Shankar Menon, "The Unprecedented Promises and Threats of the Belt and Road Initiative", *The Wire*, 24 April 2017, https://thewire.in/external-affairs/the-unprecedented-promises-and-threats-of-the-belt-and-road-initiative, accessed 27 February 2019.
9 "Chinese Envoy Calls for Advancement of Belt and Road Initiative", *The Hans India/Daily Hunt*, 8 October 2019, https://m.dailyhunt.in/news/india/english/thehansindia-epaper-hans/chinese+envoy+calls+for+advancement+of+belt+and+road+initiative-newsid-1, accessed 18 May 2020.
10 Christoph Nedopil Wang, *Countries of the Belt and Road Initiative*, Beijing: International Institute of Green Finance (IIGF) of the Central University of Finance and Economics (CUFE), 2021, https://green-bri.org/countries-of-the-belt-and-road-initiative-bri/, accessed 21 February 2021.

11 Christoph Nedopil Wang, *China Belt and Road Initiative (BRI) Investment Report 2020*, Beijing: International Institute of Green Finance (IIGF) of CUFE, 26 January 2021, https://green-bri.org/china-belt-and-road-initiative-bri-investment-report-2020/, accessed 21 February 2021.
12 Ben Joseph Romain Derudder, Xingjian Liu, and Charles Kunaka, "Connectivity along Overland Corridors of the Belt and Road Initiative", *MTI Discussion Paper* No. 6, Washington, DC: World Bank Group, 2018, http://documents.worldbank.org/curated/en/264651538637972468/Connectivity-Along-Overland-Corridors-of-the-Belt-and-Road-Initiative, accessed 27 December 2018.
13 Agatha Kratz, "China's AIIB: A Triumph in Public Diplomacy", *China Analysis*, 10 June 2015, p. 14.
14 Leiden Asia Centre, "China's Belt and Road Initiative-Regional Responses and Implications", *Asia Current Affairs Forum*, 6 March 2018, http://leidenasiacentre.nl/en/event/acaf-chinas-belt-and-road-initiative-regional-responses-and-implications/, accessed 11 December 2018.
15 Jinlei, n. 3.
16 Gurmeet Kanwal, "China's Belt and Road Initiative: Where Are India's Options", *Rediff.com*, 17 May 2017, https://www.rediff.com/news/column/chinas-belt-and-road-initiative-what-are-indias-options/20170517.htm?print=true, accessed 20 December 20118.
17 Bhadrakumar, n. 6.
18 Vladimir Putin, President of Russia, "Speech at the One Belt, One Road International Forum", *Events-President of Russia*, 14 May 2017, http://en.kremlin.ru/events/president/news/54491, accessed 16 February 2019.
19 *Ibid*.
20 Bhadrakumar, n. 6.
21 Devirupa Mitra, "To Meet Indian Concerns, China Offers to Re-Name China-Pakistan Economic Corridor", *The Wire*, 8 May 2017, https://thewire.in/diplomacy/china-pakistan-india-obor, accessed 17 December 2018.
22 *Ibid*.
23 Bhadrakumar, n. 6.
24 Vinay Kaura, "Understanding India's Response to China's Belt and Road", *Asia Times*, 10 June 2017, http://www.atimes.com/understanding-indias-response-chinas-obor/, accessed 17 December 2019.
25 "India Sticks to Its Own Path, Says No to China's Belt & Road Initiative", *Times of India*, 25 April 2018, https://timesofindia.indiatimes.com/india/india-sticks-to-its-own-path-says-no-to-chinas-belt-road-initiative/articleshowprint/63903471.cms, accessed 17 December 2018.
26 Xi Jinping, "Accelerating the Implementation of a Free-Trade Zone Strategy, Accelerating the Construction of a New Economic Model Based on Openness", *Xinhua*, 6 December 2014, http://news.xinhuanet.com/politics/2014-12/06/c_1113546075.htm, accessed 13 November 2017.
27 David Cohen, "China's 'Second Opening': Grand Ambitions but a Long Road Ahead", *China Analysis*, June 2015, p .4.
28 Antoine Bondaz, "Rebalancing China's Geopolitics, 'One Belt, One Road': China's Great Leap Outward", *China Analysis*, June 2015, p. 6.
29 Opinion, "The Many Problems with China Belt and Road Initiative", *Livemint*, 5 August 2018, https://www.livemint.com/Opinion/Aqj4qxXvt3x7yCDkkyL58M/The-many-problems-with-China-Belt-and-Road-Initiative.html, accessed 17 December 2018.
30 Agatha Kratz, "One Belt, One Road: What's in It for China's Economic Players?" *China Analysis*, June 2015, p. 9.
31 *Ibid*., p. 10.
32 Cohen, n. 27, p. 5.
33 Godement, n. 1, p. 2.

34 Raffaello Pantucci and Qingzhen Chen, "The Geopolitical Roadblocks", *China Analysis*, June 2015, p. 12.
35 Luca Bandiera and Vasileios Tsiropoulos, "A Framework to Assess Debt Sustainability and Fiscal Risks under the Belt and Road Initiative", Policy Research Working Paper 8891, Washington, DC: World Bank Group, June 2019, http://www.worldbank.org/prwp, accessed 12 December 2019.
36 Tanner Greer, "One Belt, One Road, One Big Mistake", *Foreign Policy*, 6 December 2018, https://foreignpolicy.com/2018/12/06/bri-china-belt-road-initiative-bl under/, accessed 7 December 2018.
37 Marlene Laruelle (ed.), *China's Belt and Road Initiative and Its Impact in Central Asia*, Washington, DC: The George Washington University, 2018, p. 171.
38 Andy Mukherjee, "Malaysia Doesn't Have the Appetite for China's One Belt One Road Initiative Anymore", *The Print*, 29 August 2019, https://theprint.in/opinion/malaysia-doesnt-have-the-appetite-for-chinas-one-belt-one-road-initiative-anymore/107494/, accessed 17 December 2018.
39 T. N. Ninan, "India Doesn't Want to Join China's OBOR, but …", *Rediff.com*, 25 May 2017, https://www.rediff.com/news/column/india-doesnt-want-to-join-chinas-obor-but/ 20170513.htm?print=true, accessed 20 December 2018.
40 Eva, Lin and Tunningley, n. 7.
41 Ye Yu, "China's Response to Belt and Road Backlash," *East Asia Forum*, 15 December 2018, http://www.eastasiaforum.org/2018/12/15/chinas-response-to-belt-and-road-backlash/, accessed 24 February 2019.
42 Dushni Weerakoon and Sisira Jayasuriya, "Sri Lanka's Debt Problem Isn't Made in China", *East Asia Forum*, 28 February 2019, https://www.eastasiaforum.org/2019/02/28/sri-lankas-debt-problem-isnt-made-in-china/, accessed 28 February 2019.
43 Ministry of External Affairs, "Official Spokesperson's Response to a Query on Participation of India in OBOR/BRI Forum", New Delhi: Government of India, 13 May 2017, https://mea.gov.in/media-briefings.htm?dtl/28463/Official+Spokespersons+response+to+a+query+on+participation+of+India+in+OBORBRI+Forum, accessed 14 June 2017.
44 Jabin T. Jacob, "What Does India Think of China's 'Belt and Road' Initiative?", *Institute of Chinese Studies*, Occasional Paper no. 19, December 2017.
45 Kaura, n. 24.
46 Christian Wagner and Siddharth Tripathi, "India's Response to Chinese Belt and Road Initiative", *Daily Mirror*, 15 February 2018, http://www.dailymirror.lk/article/India-s-response-to-Chinese-Belt-and-Road-Initiative-145857.html, accessed 17 December 2018.
47 *Ibid*.
48 *Ibid*.
49 The 11 new members of INSTC include Republic of Azerbaijan, Republic of Armenia, Republic of Kazakhstan, Kyrgyz Republic, Republic of Tajikistan, Republic of Turkey, Republic of Ukraine, Republic of Belarus, Oman, Syria and Bulgaria (Observer), besides the founder members of Russia, Iran and India. See http://instcorridor.com
50 Wagner and Tripathi, n. 46.
51 Bhadrakumar, n. 6.
52 Shiv Shankar Menon, "The Unprecedented Promises – and Threats – of the Belt and Road Initiative", *The Wire*, 24 April 2017, https://thewire.in/external-affairs/the-unprecedented-promises-and-threats-of-the-belt-and-road-initiative, accessed 27 February 2019.
53 Darshana Baruah, "India's Answer to Chinese Belt & Road Initiative Should Be a New Road Map for South Asia", *The Print*, 2 September 2018, https://theprint.in/opinion/indias-answer-to-chinese-belt-road-initiative-should-be-a-new-road-map-for-south-asia/110025/, accessed 17 December 2018.
54 *Ibid*.

55 "The Boundary Agreement between China and Pakistan, 1963", http://people.unica.it/annamariabaldussi/files/2015/04/China-Pakistan-1963.pdf, accessed 27 February 2019.
56 Harsh V. Pant, "India's Stature Is Growing in Chinese Eyes", *Rediff.com*, 21 December 2018, https://www.rediff.com/news/column/indias-stature-is-growing-in-chinese-eyes/20181221.htm?print=true, accessed 3 March 2019.
57 Utkarsh Mishra, "Why India and China Won't Go to War", *Rediff.com*, 20 December 2018, https://www.rediff.com/news/interview/why-india-and-china-wont-go-to-war/20181220.htm?print=true, accessed 20 December 2018.
58 Kishen S. Rana, "Why Can't We Have a Better Relationship with China?", *Rediff.com*, 27 May 2017, https://www.rediff.com/news/column/why-cant-we-have-a-better-relationship-with-china/20170527.htm?print=true, accessed 20 December 2018.
59 Kishan S. Rana, "5 Ways to Improve Relations with China", *Rediff.com*, 10 June 2018, https://www.rediff.com/news/column/5-ways-to-improve-relations-with-china/20180610.htm?print=true, accessed 23 December 2018.
60 Press Trust of India, "Not a Single Bullet Fired in 40 Years Despite Border Dispute with China: PM Mod", *Times of India*, 2 June 2017, https://timesofindia.indiatimes.com/india/not-a-single-bullet-fired-in-40-years-despite-border-dispute-with-china-pm-modi/articleshow/58966132.cms, accessed 10 June 2021.

5
BRI
Regional responses and alternatives

Ashminder Singh Bahal

Introduction

During the Renaissance period, China and India controlled almost half the global trade. These two countries today have again become the fastest-growing economies with the centre of gravity of the global economy[1] shifting towards Asia and in Asia from Japan to China and India. China's attempt at significantly improving its *Comprehensive National Power* commenced with four modernisations launched by Deng Xiao Ping and it is in consonance with its belief that historically, it is a great empire (*the Middle Kingdom*); hence deserves to be a global power. The goal of the four modernisations was to strengthen four key sectors: agriculture, industry, technology and defence.[2] It is assessed by various analysts that China's *grand strategy* appears to be to establish a new world order that is dominated by China through significant development of its soft and hard power, including developing a very effective economy, integrated and intelligentised military, aggressive diplomacy and advanced technology. This aggressive rise is creating fears in the minds of its neighbours, especially India.

To sustain aggressive growth, China requires access to natural resources, raw materials and overseas markets. It is appreciated that it intends to achieve this by pursuing soft diplomacy and at the same time make strategic inroads in the Indo-Pacific region. It also appears that any issues that China does not intend to resolve politically are those that it intends to resolve on its terms and conditions, in future, especially with those countries that they perceive may come in direct conflict with their core interests and grand strategy.

One Belt One Road initiative

Xi's One Belt One Road (OBOR) initiative that was commenced in 2013, which is also known as the Belt and Road Initiative (BRI). It is appreciated that whilst promoting globalisation and strong economic linkages to help develop infrastructural facilities for facilitating trade and increasing mutual economic gains, it is also focused on creating a strong Chinese geo-strategic footprint by exploiting the resultant increase in the Chinese influence that would take place as a consequence of enhanced cooperation, especially in South Asia, South East Asia, Central Asian Republics (CAR) and Eurasia. China is wooing Kabul too to extend CPEC to Afghanistan.

The six continental routes and the three Maritime Silk Roads not only provide China access to the warm waters of the Arabian Sea and Bay of Bengal, but they may also get smaller nations into a debt trap that forces them to part with a significant portion of equity of their infrastructural facilities to the Chinese companies, thereby ensuring permanent Chinese presence in a number of countries, including Sri Lanka, Myanmar, Maldives and Pakistan.

The best example of getting into a debt trap is the award of 70% equity of Hambantota Port in Sri Lanka to China for an extended lease of 99 years. Sri Lanka was forced to convert debt to equity when they could not repay the loan for the Hambantota project. Its immediate fallouts were Pakistan and Nepal cancelling their dam projects. China is currently negotiating for 85% stake in Kyauk Pyu port in Myanmar, which is causing significant concern to the local people.

It is also feared that Pakistan too is likely to get into a debt trap and may become an extended influence region of China. A group of US senators have asserted that Pakistan is at risk of debt distress due to the rising current account deficit and external debt obligations caused by CPEC.[3] The US senators further wrote that "In China's String of Pearls strategy for the Indo-Pacific, Gwadar and Hambantota are important footholds that if converted into naval bases will enable the PLA Navy to maintain a permanent presence in the Indian Ocean region."[4]

In Djibouti, China has provided more than $1.4 billion in infrastructure funding, equivalent to 75% of Djibouti's GDP.[5] It would be extremely difficult for Djibouti to service these loans. This debt strategy results in intrusive commercial penetration, which leads to the creation of significant strategic vulnerabilities that help China to increase its geo-strategic footprint and financial leverage, thereby leading to sustained geo-strategic loss to the recipient nations as the Chinese domination increases with increasing financial leverage. Intimate Chinese involvement in South Asia, as well as Pakistan's negative influence, has put effective brakes on the progress of SAARC and other regional alternatives.

It is appreciated that the infrastructure projects created under the BRI are likely to facilitate China to procure as well as transport cheap raw materials from other nations and convert them into finished products such as steel and manufactured goods. Thereafter, sell the cheap Chinese products to the same countries leading to the capture of their markets, thereby significantly increasing their strategic loss. This may result in creating a large trade surplus with a number of nations with whom China trades; taking an example, the trade surplus with India is US$56.77 billion in 2019.[6] This concept clearly follows neo-mercantilism policies that were followed by the colonial and imperial powers to enhance their national wealth in the sixteenth and seventeenth centuries.

China's strategic forays under the BRI by creating Maritime Silk Road as well as the creation of CPEC and China-Myanmar Economic Corridors (CMEC) and investing in the critical infrastructure of South Asian states are shrinking India's geo-strategic space. Their development of bases in Kyakhphu, Gwadar, Hambantota, Colombo and Djibouti are harbingers of larger maritime ambitions in the Indian Ocean region. Their inroads are not just creating concerns of "strategic encirclement" and execution of "string of pearls strategy," but there is a palpable risk of debt-ridden countries compromising their sovereignty and making strategic choices that are in congruence with China's long-term strategy; however, this is against India's geo-strategic interests.

The question then arises is that whilst following a policy of neocolonialism and neo-mercantilism, whether China is willing to accept pluralism and cater to the interests of other nations too? Chinese actions, however, do not behave of a neoliberalist philosophy but give a sense of an evolving imperial power that is significantly enhancing its comprehensive national power to achieve global domination and become the "Middle Kingdom" once again.

The experience gained in the South China Sea and attempts to establish Air Defence Identification Zones (ADIZ) clearly indicate China's ambitions of following classical realism more than pluralism or neoliberalism. To counter the growing Chinese reach and power, there is a need to achieve a strategic balance by countering classical realism with a neo-realist philosophy that borders on carrot and stick strategies. There is, therefore, a need to collate the strengths of concurring nations to create a balance of power to bring about an effective change in China's behaviour and limit Chinese designs to more peaceful rise as well as bring in effective control measures that work towards curtailing their blueprint of global domination.

China though has one major limitation: it faces huge internal adjustments as it tries to rebalance its economy. Its debt to GDP ratio has grown quickly from around 150% of GDP in 2008 to around 317% in the first quarter of 2020,[7] as it expanded credit to keep its economy growing in the face of slower growth. It now takes nine units of credit to generate one unit of GDP. But this investment credit-led recovery has created enormous excess capacity. The BRI has large risks for China and recipient countries as it could create white elephants.

To counter the dumping of cheap goods, India has slapped anti-dumping duty on 90 Chinese items,[8] mostly in steel and some in the pharmaceutical sector. It is also considering restrictions in telecom and power. As tension built at the LAC, the Indian government has banned 118 Chinese apps, including PUBG. These could be seen as retaliatory measures and also signs of trade differences between China and India. It is here that India needs to manage an aggressive China preferably without a military conflict and yet retain its territorial sovereignty; just as Japan and Taiwan maintain theirs with respect to China.

China's investments in Indo-Pacific region

With $15.42 trillion nominal (2020) GDP, China in the last few years has gone past Japan to become the second-largest economy after the United States. The Indian economy was 80% that of China in 1990, but it is now less than 25%.[9] China has also developed close economic, military and strategic ties with India's neighbours. This includes investing in trans-Myanmar oil and gas pipelines; 69 of the Chinese MNCs are involved in developing 90 odd hydropower and oil and gas and mining projects in Myanmar. In January 2020, Myanmar and China signed 33 bilateral agreements, including rail and deep-sea ports linking China to Kyaukpyu.[10] Incidentally, China Power Investment Corporation in an internal report highlighted the disruption of river flow, the disappearance of migratory fish species and flooding of 26,238 hectares of rainforests due to the construction of the Myitsone dam in Myanmar. This report got leaked to the environmentalists and it resulted in stirring large protests. The Myanmar government was then forced to suspend the project.[11] It therefore implies that China is not concerned whether the other countries' environment is affected, till the time its projects progress rapidly. The aim appears to be to exploit Myanmar's rich natural resources whilst getting access to the warm waters of the Bay of Bengal.

An analysis of China's investments in South Asia indicates that they are in the process or have created infrastructure at Sittwe, Chittagong, Hambantota and Gwadar ports with possible agreements for logistics and refuelling facilities there. Similarly, China is investing around US$62 billion in Pakistan to create China-Pakistan Economic Corridor (CPEC). Under CPEC, China envisages key investments in rail and road transportation, energy sector and fibre optics. It is also of concern that the Kashgar highway passes through Pakistan-occupied Kashmir, thereby raising India's sovereignty issues and security concerns.

Phase 1 of the CPEC project is nearly over, with main investments being in the power sector and infrastructure creation. There are serious charges of misappropriation in these projects with Lt Gen Bajwa (Retd.) deeply involved in it. Added to this is the reluctance of China to give concessional loans on the $6 billion rail project upgrading 1872 km line from Peshawar to Karachi, and this is driving a wedge between the two countries as China is concerned with Pakistan's weakening financial position and plans to offer a combination of commercial and concessional loans and not just concessional loans.[12]

It is also analysed that China's infrastructure developments support its geopolitical aspirations. At the same time, the creation of numerous posts in the Indo-Pacific region, especially artificial islands in the South China Sea such as Fiery reef, Mischief reef and Subi reef, imperil free flow of trade, threatens the autonomy of other nations and undermine trans-regional stability. It can also be inferred that China leverages its defence capabilities and economic strategies to compel countries with an aim to create a new order in the Indo-Pacific region. It appears that it will continue to enhance its soft and hard power and work towards the displacement of the United States in the short term from the Indo-Pacific region and transform itself as a global power in the long term.

COVID-19 and China

The breakout of an unprecedented COVID-19 crisis has brought the entire world to its feet. Its consequential effect on the world economy has affected most countries. The free movement of goods, services and people due to globalisation has resulted in rapidly increasing COVID-19's spread. This spread has also been compounded by China's reluctance to warn the other countries in time about the catastrophic impact of Corona at Wuhan, though its effect was clearly evident from December 2019 onwards. Subsequently, it allowed the return of a large number of Chinese and other nationals from China to Europe and to other parts of the world after the Chinese New Year. It was only a matter of time that COVID-19's devastating impact would soon be felt in Europe and other nations too, such as Italy, France, Spain, United Kingdom, Germany, India and the United States.

Whether Wuhan effects were deliberate to create Chinese supremacy in the world order, or it was due to the careless and devious attitude of the Chinese leadership that led to the pandemic in Wuhan, the rapid spread of COVID-19 from February to April 2020 brought in another consequential attention towards biowarfare. Since February 2020, Whilst the world grappled with containing the pandemic, China increasingly exercised its muscle in the South China Sea. It even sank a Vietnamese boat in April 2020.[13] It also held major naval exercises in the South China Sea and undertook fly pasts near Taiwan straits and Senkaku islands. This made the United States send its warships along with an Australian ship in that area. Furthermore, China is creating disturbances in Sikkim (Muguthang), Galwan valley (which resulted in a bloody fight that killed 20 Indian soldiers and unspecified number of Chinese soldiers), Depsang and Pangong Tso lake.

Currently, China has amassed a large number of its troops, armour and artillery as well as fighter aircraft all along the LAC, bringing it close to a war-like situation. It has also obstructed Indian patrolling in Depsang and in some areas of Arunachal Pradesh. Though the disengagement process has started near the Pangong Tso lake, the other areas still need resolution. Furthermore, de-escalation of additional forces that were brought into Tibet has not yet commenced. This clearly highlights China's creeping expansionist policy undertaken over a period of time and the aggressive stance that it takes to resolve outstanding issues in their favour.

Changes in national security concepts: China

Human security till 2020 focused more on poverty, internal dissensions, cross-border terrorism and Maoist movements. However, human security has now got another dimension, a pandemic, which though being invisible, spreads rapidly and affects a large number of people quickly. The way the body count spread in some European countries from April to June 2020 reminded one of the transportation of body bags during World War II. Its economic consequence has had a significant effect on most nations. With less money available, there is less for defence; this has forced the different governments to seriously consider curtailing defence budgets, barring China that increased its defence budget by 6.6%[14] during this period.

It is important to note that China has moved its operational strategy of "Informationalised warfare" to "Intelligentized warfare." "Intelligentization" is the Chinese concept of applying Artificial Intelligence's machine speed and processing power to military planning, operational command and decision support.[15] Intelligentisation has become China's guiding principle for future military modernisation, and it does not intend to merely integrate Artificial Intelligence into its war fighting functions, but it also plans to use it to shape a new cognitive domain; that would lead to a new approach to war fighting.[16] It is appreciated that bio-warfare and the use of directed energy weapons may already have been included in this strategy.

Spoilers to South Asian region's growth

South Asian Association for Regional Cooperation (SAARC), a regional inter-governmental organisation, was founded in Dhaka and its member states include Afghanistan, Bangladesh, Bhutan, India, Nepal, Maldives, Pakistan and Sri Lanka. It comprises 3% of the global area, 22% of the world's population and 3.8% of the global economy. Asian Development Bank (ADB) has estimated that SAARC possessed the potential of increasing exports by US$14 billion/year; however, intra-regional trade is merely 5%. The intra-regional FDI too is low and stands at around 4% of the total foreign investment of the region. Though one of the fastest-growing regions of the world, it houses 46% of the poor and 40% of the illiterate. In addition, physical and digital connectivity in the contiguous states is poor, which also contributes towards lowering intra-regional trade.

SAARC's intra-regional trade and its politico-economic growth is primarily held hostage to Pakistan's meddling in the internal affairs of its member states, including Afghanistan, Bangladesh and India and its aiding and abetting terrorism in the region. Its close links with the Taliban, Haqqani Network, LeT, HuM and JeM have led to the widespread propagation of terror networks. After Pathankot and Uri attack, 19th SAARC Summit was cancelled. After the Pulwama attack, there have been significant international reactions leading to the declaration of Masood Azhar as a global terrorist and the imposition of severe restrictions on Jaish-e-Mohammed's activities. FATF too has indicated that Pakistan should do more to curb terrorism and has continued to keep it on the grey list. At the same time, ISI's furtherance of terror since then has become more covert.

China's intimate involvement with South Asia has complicated the integration within the region and has created significant security and economic concerns. It has also undertaken numerous intrusions along the Line of Actual Control

(LAC) in India. There appear to be deeper reasons for Chinese intrusions especially in tri-junctions, as it seems to follow Kautilya's Mandala theory to intimidate India to abandon its neighbours. India's standing up to China at Doklam for Bhutan surprised them.

China does follow a policy of *"Creeping Expansionism"* as part of a long-term strategy, especially when it claims uninhabited islands, reefs, atolls or less-frequently patrolled areas. This strategy is visible both in the South China Sea and along the LAC. It has created complexities within the *"Nine Dash Line"* by encroaching upon uninhabited islands, reefs, atolls or lightly defended areas. Its decision to enforce Air Defence Identification Zone in the East China Sea has heightened the risks of conflict in the Western Pacific. There is a concern that China posits North Korea card to keep the US security alliance with South Korea and Japan on the horns of dilemma, thereby enhancing instability in the Indo-Pacific region and beyond.

It is appreciated that China's aggressive stance and development of its comprehensive national power forms part of its grand strategy for attaining regional dominance by 2030 and its quest for being a global power by 2049, when it intends to displace the United States in international affairs.

Let us now analyse the various trans-regional and intra-regional alternatives that can limit China to a more peaceful rise.

Trans-regional alternatives

It is appreciated that it is in this century that the Western democracies' strategic and geo-economic interests are aligned with India on one side and China, North Korea and Pakistan's aggressive manipulations on the other side. It is clear that the key potential destabilisers are these three countries, and it is time that India took a decision and went with the democracies. It is also time that a grand strategy is created as how to counter the aggressive attitude of these nations. The first and foremost principle adopted should be to limit trade with these countries as it would ensure that their economic power gets severely degraded. In any case, China has a trade surplus with most countries. Whilst the Western countries and Japan are moving out of China, there is a need for India to attract them by having its own supply chains. India should become self-sufficient in supply chains, which may be slightly more expensive to manufacture, but the goods are produced indigenously. This is where *"Atmanirbhar Bharat"* comes in.

It is in the larger US and Indian interest to craft an enduring partnership in the Indo-Pacific region along with other key nations such as Japan, Australia and some of the key South East Asian Nations to limit the growing Chinese coercive influence in the Indo-Pacific region and the South China Sea. There is also a need to assiduously build on the well-articulated concepts of QUAD and alternative economic corridors such as Asia-Africa Economic Corridor and Indo-Pacific Economic Corridor. An area of deliberation should be to determine how to expand the concept of QUAD to incorporate other strategic partners and make it a mechanism of net security provider in a collaborative framework. This could include a number of ASEAN and Western countries.

Going beyond the ambit of multilateral military exercises, there is a case for the United States to rebalance in the Indian Ocean region and for India to revamp its maritime strategy to achieve a favourable strategic balance vis-à-vis China in the Indo-Pacific. The United States must recognise that enhanced FDI and high-tech injection will boost India's comprehensive national power and transform India as a natural balancer to a perceived hegemonic China and emerge as a strategic vector in the Indian Ocean region and beyond.

There is also a need not only to strengthen Indo-US-Afghanistan Security Dialogue but India should deftly use the aegis of the Shanghai Cooperation Organization (SCO) to garner support from other member countries, including Russia, to combat Jihadi terrorism. In fact, India has the potential of nurturing US–Russia cooperation on the issue of combating Jihadi terrorism to counter Pakistan–China nexus. There is also a need to build strategic trust between the United States, Iran and Russia, in the mid-term to long term, as the three countries together with India and CAR could cooperate to balance the overwhelming Chinese influence. The new Joe Biden's establishment has already given indications of greater India–US cooperation in the coming years.

To counterbalance BRI in Southeast Asia, India has moved from Look East to Act East concept. Under this initiative, ASEAN-India Connectivity Summit (AICS) was commenced to accelerate the existing connectivity prospects, identify issues of concern, evolve suitable policy recommendations and develop strategies to enhance economic, industrial and trade relations. Its focus areas are infrastructure, roadways, shipping, digital, finance, energy and aviation.[17] India has proposed US$1 billion line of credit to the ASEAN for physical and digital connectivity and US$77 million for developing manufacturing hubs in Cambodia, Laos, Myanmar and Vietnam (CLMV). This initiative too needs to be progressed rapidly.

Regional alternatives

Alternatives need to be found in the South Asia region for a more peaceful China rise. Keeping India's geo-political weight in mind, India could play an important role in the Indo-Pacific. It is here that COVID-19 provides an opportunity to exploit India's information technology and pharmaceutical (pharma) capability to provide medical assistance in South Asia. A number of Indian pharma companies are researching on finding a vaccine or working with international agencies to develop a vaccine/cure. There are already two types of vaccines available in India. There is a need to enhance the production capacities of these companies with government support so as to play a major role in getting the subcontinent out of the COVID-19 pandemic situation. Coming to the rescue of our neighbours at this time would create a positive environment for these nations to believe in the Indian leadership role. At this time, India is supplying vaccines to more than 25 countries, including Canada. We must also supply to Pakistan to generate favourable opinion there.

India should decisively enhance its economic cooperation within the SAARC region and especially help those nations that are getting into a debt trap with China. To reduce negative Pakistani influence, the focus needs to be given towards progressing the Bay of Bengal Initiative for Technical and Economic Cooperation (BIMSTEC), even at the cost of India contributing more for the Asian Trilateral Highway and other projects that connect India with Thailand through Myanmar. The funding for the Asian Trilateral Highway, especially the stretch that passes through Myanmar, along with the upgrading of around 73 odd bridges needs to be provided by India. Kaladan Multimodal project too that links India with Myanmar and connects Kolkata to Sittwe Port and then to Mizoram through the river route also needs to be quickly operationalised, though significant progress has been made in the past few years. The cooperation could also be expanded to connect Cambodia, Laos and Vietnam. Multilateral cooperative interactions could pool in South Korea, Indonesia and Philippines, thereby building a grouping of nations favoured towards non-China-centred growth in infrastructure and cooperation.

In addition, Bangladesh, Bhutan, India and Nepal (BBIN) initiative should be progressed rapidly to create infrastructural facilities that provide access to Bhutan and Nepal to the Bay of Bengal as well as enhance clean energy cooperation that leads to large-scale intra-regional trade. Hydroelectric energy has the potential of 30–35 GW, resulting in generating intra-regional trade of US$20 billion. The Motor Vehicles agreement that has been signed between BBIN countries needs to be progressed rapidly by removing the misgivings that different stakeholders in Bhutan have about the agreement. Nepal, after the political crisis at the end of 2020 and China's meddling in the same, is ripe for a more balanced cooperative approach. This is the time to forge enhanced cooperation. COVID-19 vaccines are a nice glue that could bind the South Asian nations together. India must not lose this opportunity.

In this regard, after the current government assumed office for the second term, BIMSTEC countries were invited for the function. This clearly indicates a shift in the focus of India towards the East and which does not get tied down only to the West or Russia. There are talks to extend US$100 million line of credit to Kyrgyzstan for the transfer of defence equipment. Their president is the current chairperson of the Shanghai Cooperation Organization. This could enhance India's relationship in the CAR region.

Thirdly, link Afghanistan and CAR through Chabahar port. It can significantly enhance trade and provide an alternate route to Afghanistan and Central Asia, bypassing Pakistan. The effectiveness of the route has been proven with the dispatch of over one million tons of wheat to Afghanistan through the Iranian port. On the other hand, Chabahar port is likely to benefit from the International North-South Corridor project too. The INSTC is a network involving ship, rail and road routes for transporting goods between India, Iran, Afghanistan, Russia,

Central Asia and Europe. It is in line with the Ashgabat agreement between India, Pakistan, Oman, Iran, Turkmenistan, Uzbekistan and Kazakhstan for creating an international transport and transit corridor between Central Asia and the Persian Gulf. These projects were started with great interest but have slowed down over a period of time due to extraneous circumstances.

Way forward

India must first believe in its economic growth story and take the leadership mantle of progressing the Indo-Pacific region's growth and help the South Asian region to fight COVID-19. It also needs to take lead in developing infrastructure that connects South Asia together. In this endeavour, it must continue to promote its *"Neighbourhood First"* policy that it started so well in 2014 with US$1 billion line of credit to Nepal, US$2 billion to Bangladesh and additional US$1 billion to Afghanistan. It must also take initiative in resolving region's problems. In its quest for developing the region, it must not demand reciprocity, but give more and expect less. Since in Pakistan it is the army that dictates its political functioning, there is a need to engage the Pakistani Army as a key stakeholder in working towards a peaceful environment.

Pakistan may soon become irrelevant if it does not participate in the SAARC growth story. In case it still does not come onboard to counter the negative Pakistani effect, there is a need to follow a three-pronged approach. Firstly, progress BIMSTEC rapidly along with BBIN initiative to create infrastructural facilities in this region to provide access for Bhutan and Nepal to the warm waters of Bay of Bengal as well as in clean energy cooperation, leading to increased intra-regional trade. Secondly, though India has improved its ties with ASEAN in its *"Act East policy,"* it now needs to be expanded from Vietnam and Singapore to other countries of the Southeast Asian nations. Thirdly, link Afghanistan and CAR through Chabahar port bypassing Pakistan.

To augment ties with the CAR region, India has announced its *"Connect Central Asia"* policy in 2012.[18] Chabahar port could play an important role in the transit of goods between Afghanistan, Iran and India with Central Asian Republics in line with these agreements by creating a transport corridor. Chabahar port could also help INSTC to connect the Indian Ocean and the Persian Gulf with the Caspian Sea and also with Russia and Europe. INSTC routes could reduce the transit time from South Asia to Europe from the current 45–50 days to 25–30 days.

Conclusion

India needs to assume the leadership mantle in South Asia, especially during the COVID-19 period to help fight this menace together. This would significantly enhance its geopolitical weight in South Asia. It should also be the key initiator of cooperative mechanisms in the Indo-Pacific region to enhance politico-economic and security cooperation in SAARC, ASEAN, BBIN and BIMSTEC.

India also has to evolve a long-term strategy to appreciably develop the SAARC region by providing infrastructural facilities. In addition, it needs to help the South Asian nations that are getting into a debt trap with China as it is doing with the Rajapaksa Sri-Lankan airport.

If the world's dependence on China is reduced in trade and cheap Chinese goods are not bought, then automatically it would hurt its economy and would limit its aggressive geo-strategic footprint and global dominance strategy. India needs to develop its own supply chains and provide a cheap alternative to China by providing numerous incentives. Pakistan may soon become irrelevant if it does not become part of the South Asia growth story. To realise this vision, India should first develop a great power mentality that does not project hegemony but helps its neighbours when they are in need.

Notes

1 Shobhan Saxena, "Rise, Fall, Rise, Special Report", *Sunday Times of India* (Hyderabad), 22 August 2010, p. 13.
2 "Four Modernisations Era", see http//depts.washington.edu/chinaciv/graph/9cenfour.htm, accessed 8 September 2010.
3 ANI, Pakistan at risk of debt distress due CPEC: US Senators, accessed from the site Pakistan at risk of debt distress due to CPEC: US senators – *The Financial Express* on 15 Feb 2021.
4 Ibid.
5 Ibid.
6 PTI, India, "China Trade Declines over 12 Percent in First Two Months of 2020", https://www.newindianexpress.com/nation/2020/apr/03/india-china-trade-declines-over-12-per-cent-in-first-two-months-of-2020-2125357.html, accessed 30 May 2020.
7 Mish, "China's Debt to GDP Ratio Surges 317%", https://www.thestreet.com/mishtalk/economics/chinas-debt-to-gdp-ratio-hits-317-percent, accessed 30 May 2020.
8 PTI, "Anti-Dumping Duty Imposed on 90 Items", https://economictimes.indiatimes.com/news/economy/foreign-trade/anti-dumping-duty-imposed-on-90-chinese-items/articleshow/74006602.cms?from =mdr, accessed 30 May 2020.
9 "Dealing with No.2, China's Rise Demands a Sophisticated Approach from India", *The Times of India* (Hyderabad), 2 August 2010, p. 10.
10 John Reed, "China and Myanmar Sign Off on Belt and Road Projects", see https://www.ft.com/content/a5265114-39d1-11ea-a01a-bae547046735, accessed 30 May 2020.
11 Megha Gupta, "Environmental Effects of Chinese Projects in Myanmar", https://www.orfonline.org/expert-speak/environmental-effects-chinese-projects-myanmar-64588/, accessed 30 May 2020.
12 *Times of India*, 25 January 2021, Why China-Pakistan ties are unravelling over CPEC, accessed from the site CPEC Economic Corridor: Why China-Pakistan ties are unraveling over CPEC | World News – *Times of India* (indiatimes.com) on 15 Feb 2021.
13 "Philippines Backs Vietnam after China Sinks Fishing Boat", *Aljazeera*, https://www. aljazeera.com/news/2020/04/philippines-backs-vietnam-china-sinks-fishing-boat-200409022328432.html, accessed 30 May 2020.
14 Mike Yeo, "China Announces $178.2 billion Military Budget", https://www.defensenews.com/global/asia-pacific/2020/05/22/china-announces-1782-billion-military-budget/ , accessed 30 May 2020.

15 "Accelerate the Development of Military Intelligentization", https://www.wired.com/beyond-the-beyond/2020/01/accelerate-development-military-intelligentization-, accessed 6 April 2020.
16 Ibid.
17 Ministry of External Affairs, "ASEAN-India Connectivity Summit", New Delhi, 11–12 December 2017, 9 December 2017, http://mea.gov.in/press-releases.htm?dtl/29166/ASEANIndia_Connectivity_Summit_ New_Delhi_December_1112_2017, accessed 10 December 2017.
18 Meena Singh Roy, "International North South Corridor: Re-Energizing India's Gateway to Eurasia", 18 August 2015, https://idsa.in/issuebrief/InternationalNorthSouthTransportCorridor_msroy_180815, accessed 8 December 2017.

6
BRI AND BBIN
Asian economic growth engines

Ujjwal Upadhyay

Introduction

Driven by the importance of connectivity to overcome the economic insufficiency and constrains to the available market linkages, the BRI and BBIN can both be the effective tools to propel emerging economies to lead the world's financial systems consisting of investments, industries, markets and financial institutions comprising of both small and large. the BRI and BBIN as means of connectivity not only connect both big and small nations across South Asia and Eurasia with each other but also let investment and market flow to each other to maintain cross-boundary financial liquidity to consolidate both corporate capitals and also ensure socio-economic development of poor community and people through redistribution of wealth among small entrepreneurs, farmers, businessmen and labour forces who in particular get jobs in larger connectivity-based infrastructure development programmes and jobs along with markets created by these projects. Add to this, upon completion of these projects, bigger markets create more opportunities comprising of both jobs and enterprise to the poor people lying in the lower rung of the society.

Without further delay, these ideas need to be implemented where both issues and concerns of all stakeholders comprising of neighbouring nations will be addressed and benefits are enhanced and facilitated accordingly. China has already dispatched a cargo train on 22 May 2020 carrying goods like clothes, electronic devices, shoes and other fabric products, which is expected to reach Kathmandu within 7 days. The train in the northern boundary of Nepal bringing and posing both opportunities and threats, respectively, to India as cheaper Chinese goods will just be few kilometres away from Indo-Nepal border, India should think of reasonable trade-offs to this rather than opposing this idea, so that they too can serve both as big market and exporter of goods to the nearby railway customs of China in Nepal. Using Nepal's road can help India to find the shortest route to reach China's market, making trade more cost-effective. Endorsing China's BRI initiative will certainly help India to get connected to Eurasia through land as the future lies in land-based transport as no other fuels except mineral oil and natural gas can navigate larger ships, which are running out of stock, and the future lies in renewable energy and electricity and thereby run land-based transport means like trains and freights. China's initiative of trusting land-based transportation in the name of the BRI is not only a substitute of Malacca Strait's insecurity but also the alternative energy-run transportation means.

Simultaneously, BBIN, apart from many actions, can be another initiative which can greatly benefit Bhutan, Bangladesh, Nepal and India, where small ships through rivers as inland navigation can be materialised, ensuring better connectivity within these four countries through implementing both the intra and international transfer of goods and services. Construction of high dams, on larger rivers, at strategic points and further capitalisation of such initiatives like hydroelectricity can be another tactic to overcome many issues like security and defence constraints. This mainly becomes important in the case of Northeast of India, where through Brahmaputra River upon customisation of Farakka barrage larger ships can reach up to Arunachal, ensuring better inland naval connectivity to overcome India's Chicken's neck insecurity.

This chapter mainly highlights on how the ideas of the BRI and BBIN can be best capitalized, where both China and India can go further ensuring mutual benefits to each other along with other nations located around them despite the tensions brewed between these two nations during COVID-19-induced blame game that went globally to isolate and humiliate China, and India too was dragged to the team motivated to isolate dragons from the global forums led by the economically powerful nations. Add to this, few tensions in the border area and most importantly, Nepal's stand on the border issue of Kalapani, Lipulekh and Limpiyadhura, where India started constructing roads undermining the legitimate documents derived through various treaties and understanding but unnecessarily dragged China to this issue, blaming them for provoking Nepal (best friend of India in their words) to create dispute with their southern neighbours.

Context

The BRI is an outcome of China's ambition to enhance its international image and establish better goodwill in the region in all the fields – be it a physical product or its image in the global arena. Understanding its own capability of becoming a leading entity to propel the growth engine of the entire Asia, China seems to have taken this lead. The ideas are derived from the Chinese notion and ideology of reviving history and get guided by it. It was the Silk Road route that helped China not only to show its presence in both East Asia and Europe but also to undertake trades and business in a great deal.[1] India nevertheless greatly benefitted from this, and Buddhism is believed to have spread across South East Asia and the Pacific because of this route.[2] Having massive economic ties and the simultaneous heinous trade deficit with China of US$89 billion and US$63 billion respectively, India's challenge has been to enhance its export to China and minimise the deficit which has been inclined towards China in a wake of a bilateral agreement between these two countries to amplify the trade up to US$100 billion.[3] Chinese train's arrival from May 2020 to Sigatse (Autonomous region of Tibet) just a few kilometres away from Nepal's northern border have raised more pressure on India in maintaining the trade balance with China.

Coming to China's BRI strategy, which could be another attempt to show themselves as a much powerful country than its counterpart – India – sharing the enormous land, population and economy in the South Asian region. It is quite obvious to see India getting sceptical to this approach and having some reservations unlike the United States, which has so far been soft to this idea. Many countries, which are not likely to have any kind of confrontation with China, have supported the BRI in hope of getting something against "nothing to lose."

Certainly, Wuhan meet on 27 and 28 April 2017, in the wake of the Doklam Stand-off, was a great relief to both nations, particularly India and its small neighbouring nations, which can also pave the way to good relations between these two nations. After that Nepal has been fortunate and thus took a sigh of relief after it saw understanding between Modi and Xi in May 2017, which agreed to keep all the conflicts and disputes in a cold freeze and move on. For Nepal there was always a threat of paying price in lieu of developing good relations with China, but thanks to Modi and Xi for reaching the consensus. But such a threat seems to get aggravated again as the tension between India and Nepal is rising because of the tone of the outstanding border issues in Kalapani, Lipulekh and Limpiyadhura, which India has been claiming to be in their territory of Pithorgarh district of Uttarakhand state. Things do not stay here. When Nepal formally requested India not to undermine the understandings made through the various treaties and agreements regarding border issue, Indian Army Chief Manoj M Narvane claimed the land being India's territory and also signed the issue raised by Nepal as not genuine and their own but at the behest of someone else. This statement not only raised the mercury amongst politicians of these two countries but people and media too were agitated and started behaving with each other like enemies. Such conflict can never be beneficial to both China and India and their collaborations as they can neither nullify nor exploit Nepal because of many reasons. One reason is that Nepal is a centre of religious faith for both countries; Indian Prime Minister Modi, being a devotee of Mahadev, never misses to visit Pashupatinath Temple whenever he makes a tour to Nepal, and Chinese tourists' main attraction is Lumbini, the birth place of Buddha.

Apart from the progressive thought slightly influenced by the idea of practicing social, cultural, economic, political and regional power hegemony, the BRI has been the need for China mainly because of its connectivity and energy issues it has been facing or likely to face in the future. China imports much of its fossil fuels (almost 60%) from Middle East, Africa and South America through the Indian Ocean and most importantly through the Malacca Strait.

Due to quite fragile and vulnerable relations of China with both Indonesia and Malaysia and also India's Andaman and Nicobar Navy base and US military being in proximity, China wants to overcome this limitation, "or say it wants to break the barrier," and wants to establish better connectivity with the world.

This must have triggered China to build the road to Iran and Gwadar, Baluchistan and materialise the idea of Eurasia along with paving the way for its own need of fulfilling the fuel and energy demand and broadening the horizon for the market that China seeks.

Plus, the future of energy does not lie in fossil fuel or oil anymore. Renewable energy is the future of the world as countries like Japan and Germany have decided to shut down nuclear power plants and introduce renewable energy technologies.

Many countries have agreed upon to make their nations petroleum vehicle-free. Thus, the future of transport and connectivity does not lie in maritime but through road connectivity as renewable energy cannot run large ships on sea but much larger trains on land as future lies on electricity mainly derived from solar, wind and biogas.

China wants to get connected to the world through road before the world runs out of oils, or say it becomes too expensive.

Belt and Road Initiative – a brief introduction

Previously known as One Belt One Road (OBOR), China's ambitious Belt and Road Initiative (BRI) has created quite an uproar throughout the world since it was first announced by the Chinese President Xi Jing Ping in 2013 and after almost half a decade China's multibillion BRI project has been viewed as Chinese Marshall Plan for Global Dominance. China has already secured its quest for becoming the next big super power and constantly influencing the South Asian geopolitics.

The term derives from the overland "Silk Road Economic Belt" and the "21st-Century Maritime Silk Road," concepts introduced by PRC President Xi Jinping in 2013. These are the two major axes along which China proposes to economically link Europe to China through countries across Eurasia and the Indian Ocean.

This inventiveness is mainly about building infrastructures of development throughout Asia, Africa and Europe that mainly includes connectivity via transportation and hence building roads, railways, sea ports, airports, pipelines and power plants. The BRI is also orientated towards other economic modes of development such as the creation of Special Economic Zones. The larger outline, however, focuses on securing China's ever-growing energy needs.

Although there is no officially recorded or comprehensively stated how many countries have already signed the Memorandum of Understanding (MoU) with

China, but as per Chinese state media "Xinhua," China has signed 123 cooperation documents on the Belt and Road development with 105 countries in Asia, Africa, Europe, Latin America and the South Pacific region and 26 such documents with 29 international organisations.[4]

Weidongliu in her article "Scientific Understanding of the Belt and Road Initiative of China and other Related Research" explains the actual meaning of both the key terms "Belt" and "Road," where belt stands for the revival of old economic Silk Route and "Road" stands for Maritime routes via sea lanes.[5]

Acceptance and global response: the United States

The BRI achieved new heights in March 2019 when Italy became the first G7 nation to pledge support to Beijing and signed the MoU of BRI allured by the global investment plans and optimistic to get rid of Rome's debt-ridden status despite fair warnings from Washington and Brussels. With this, speculations are that Beijing is on the rise and there is no slowing down.

Ironically, the United States, which is China's largest trading partner and is also currently involved in a full-fledged trade war, remained sceptic about the acceptance of the BRI since its inception and adopted the policy of "Wait and Watch," but it seems the United States has now completely taken a hardline stance to avoid the BRI or find an alternative to the BRI, jointly with its allies.

Trump administration's act of banning Huawei, a Chinese multinational technological company, in May 2019 also pinpoints that the United States at least for now does not care about the profits and gains from BRI engagement.

India and BRI

India has maintained its early stance on the BRI and denied China's invitation to be a part of the second Belt and Road Forum held in Beijing in April 2019. India has expressed that China Pakistan Economic Corridor (CPEC), a flagship programme under the BRI, passes through the disputed Jammu and Kashmir, parts of which are illegally encroached by Pakistan. India says this displays China's attitude of ignoring India's sovereignty and national integrity. India has chosen to deny any programmes under the BRI also considering the growing presence of China around the Indian Ocean that could lead to downfall in India's quest of becoming Asia's power house ahead of China. India's apathy towards the BRI can also be explained in terms of much popular but contentious concept of Chinese debt-trap diplomacy.

The term debt-trap, in milieu of China, was in fact introduced by an Indian academician, Brahma Chellany, initially to describe Beijing's sequences of providing loans to countries of South and Southeast Asia.[6]

Indian critiques argue that China under the name of the BRI has been extending huge amounts of loans to some developing countries which are important for it because of their geo-strategic location to build transportation and other modes of infrastructure using Chinese contractors consciously despite clear acknowledgment of the developing nations' poor economic conditions and pushing them under debt trap.

India often cites the Sri Lankan case of Hambantota and how the BRI can go wrong or yield one-sided profit to China. Sri Lanka has lost the Hambantota port as well as 15,000 acres of land for a whopping 99 years, giving China access to tactically important territory which is just a few 100 miles away from China's biggest arch rival in South Asia – India – along with a strong base on the waterway for commercial and military purposes.

The whole India-China saga can be explained by the theory if realism in international relations and prominently with the idea of securing national interest, which India does not envision in the case of the BRI.

Sino-Nepal relations, BRI and rise of Nepal between the titans

In the current scenario, the BRI deliberates the changing dynamics of Sino-Nepal relations and how it is achieving new heights, especially after the rise of the communist-led government in Nepal. The notorious 2015 Nepal blockade that the Nepalese side alleged materialised because its southern neighbour instigated the Madhesi rebels who were dissatisfied with the newly promulgated Nepali Constitution further added to the intimacy of Sino-Nepal relations. We cannot also overlook the recently signed Nepal–China Trade and Transit Treaty and the opportunities for Nepal in terms of developing transport and connectivity – roadways, railways and tourism. The Chinese investments and mega projects that are being executed, or in lieu of being executed in the Nepalese soil, might be a huge boost to the Nepalese economy.

While Nepal views the BRI as the ultimate tool to reach heights in global market and balance its Indian counterpart, Nepal is also vulnerable to deliberately falling under the debt trap that China has already illustrated in some of Nepal's friends under SAARC circle.

When a gigantic country like China decides to tremendously invest in a growing neighbour like Nepal, it is a clear manifestation of Chinese national interest. This chapter tries to explore the Chinese intentions behind these development projects and what could Nepal hit or miss.

It is also imperative to explore how the realm of equation between China, India and Nepal is changing or could possibly change in the awakening of the BRI. Nepal has been known as a yam between two boulders since its inception, the BRI adds new aspects to Nepal–India–China relations. Why is it so important for China to push its BRI objectives in Nepal with regard to its archrival India? Why does it matter to India if Nepal becomes actively involves in the BRI? The Wuhan meet of 2017 might have answered some aspects of these questions but not all.

Connecting BBIN and BRI – possibilities for Nepal

BBIN is a sub-regional initiative under SAARC and/or BIMSTEC, consisting of four nations from the eastern side of the South Asian Quadrangle under SAARC. BBIN is an acronym derived from the name of its four members – Bangladeshi, Bhutan India and Nepal. The BBIN initiative is also referred to as Indian Prime Minister Narendra Modi's strategic approach to proceed without Pakistan in sectors of connectivity, regional integrity and energy security after the attempts to sign SAARC motor vehicle agreement failed in the 18th SAARC Summit, held at Kathmandu in 2014.

BBIN is a much important and much-needed approach, from India's perspectives to overcome its limitation of connectivity to the Northeast. Overcoming the limitation of Chicken's neck could be one of the reasons why India brought BBIN issues into the forefront. BBIN can be more ideal for Nepal for gaining access to global trade and connectivity, including a chance to upgrade its maritime accessibility utilising the Indian and Bangladeshi ports improvising the geo-economic game of Nepal.

India should focus on bringing more opportunities through this initiative, benefitting its neighbours, namely, Bangladesh, Bhutan and Nepal. One major initiative could be letting Nepal access to the sea and practice maritime navigation. In this context, Koshi high dam issue becomes crucial to let Nepal trade through the Koshi River, then Ganga, then to the Bay of Bengal and get connected to the world.

The Trade and Transit Agreement (TTA) signed between Nepal and China has offered Nepal with more selections for third world trade. Beijing, along the signing of the TTA protocol, has agreed on allowing Nepal to use its land and sea ports. The Chinese sea ports permitted for Nepal's use by TTA are Tianjin, Shenzhen, Lianyungang and Zhanjiang. Similarly, the land ports permitted for Nepal's use are Lanzhou, Lhasa and Shigatse.[7] This might benefit Nepal to a certain extent, but practically, the shipping cost, including other charges, comes to be very high; therefore, Nepal should push forward the agenda of Koshi high dam project.

India and China should always agree to keep Nepal away from any kinds of their bilateral tensions. Nepal being one of the global geopolitical flashpoints of many powerful countries should be protected by these two neighbouring giants if they really wish to move forward to propel the engine of global economy and power. Outstanding border issues of Nepal with her two neighbouring countries should be done separately by two nations bilaterally even without involving themselves as a third party. Plus, there must not be any blame-game between India and China during COVID-19 and post-COVID-19 era. Both countries should agree upon supporting each other for the great good of the bigger society and population they have in their countries and surroundings. BRI and BBIN are the great initiatives and also a bigger and very rare opportunity coming on the way to these two nations which should not be missed.

The Koshi high dam project: opportunity for Nepal and India

Upon construction of the Koshi high dam project, Nepal's much awaited dream to be connected to the Bay of Bengal for economic prosperity and third world trade would finally take off. However, because Nepal lacks the ability both financially and technically to complete the project, Indian aid and assistance is foreseeable. With water and irrigation issues on the rise, it is also easy to predict the Indian interest in the construction of the Koshi project.

Through BBIN, Koshi high dam construction can be developed as an inland water transportation system that would enhance the maritime trade and connectivity of BBIN nations, particularly for landlocked nations like Nepal and Bhutan. Additionally, studies have suggested that both transportation cost and travel time are reduced by up to 21 times while shipping the goods instead of using roadways.

Henceforth, developing Koshi high dam as a transboundary inland water route would significantly reduce the logistics costs, making transshipment of goods less costly. The high dam can also flourish the Nepalese reverie of developing and selling hydropower – its biggest asset to India and Bangladesh and advance economic stability.

Nepal in present time has the access to two Indian ports – Haldia port in Kolkata and Vizag port in Vishakhapatnam – for transshipment facility. Nepal could be potentially profited by the Indian government's much ambitious Jal Marg Vikash project that transforms as an economic corridor. The development of Kalughat and Jogighopa terminals under the project will provide connectivity to Nepal and Bhutan.

Although feasibility reports have been conducted for the scrutiny of Koshi high dam Projects, the internal politics in Nepal has obstructed any further progress in the project. Nepal government should work on detailed project report via new feasibility studies with greater emphasis on risk analysis and ways to mitigate it, such as possible floods and landslides.

Linking Brahmaputra to Ganga

Simultaneously, Farakka and Jogighoppa dams in Brahmaputra and its needful customisation in coordination with Bangladesh can greatly benefit India to gain maritime access to Arunachal (up to Dibrugarh). If large ships can reach Arunachal, anything can reach there, including the Indian Navy. This can be a historical achievement for India. In addition, facilitating Nepal to produce more hydropower and selling beyond its borders to Bangladesh and others can be another favour India can do to Nepal to gain more cooperation and support.

The Farakka Barrage discharges more water to Bangladesh and less to India, making navigation difficult in the dry season. Discharging more water to Ganga from the Brahmaputra through the larger canal (Panama Canal) can resolve this issue to make India's navy military presence up to Pasighat and Dibrugarh. This can be a great method of tackling the growing Chinese presence in the Indian Ocean.

Connecting BBIN and BRI: challenges

The Koshi River, a major tributary of the larger Ganges, flows through China, Nepal and India. The Koshi River basin borders the Yarlung Tsangpo basin in the north.

The Yarlung Tsangpo is a major tributary of Brahmaputra – one of the largest and most complex rivers in India. The Brahmaputra originates in Tibet and flows down to India before entering Bangladesh – the point where it meets the Ganges and eventually discharges into the Bay of Bengal.

It is in Yarlung Tsangpo – the world's highest river, that China has planned to construct a hydropower project. The Zhangmu dam, which became operational in 2014 at the Yarlung Tsangpo, is just a few kilometres away from the Bhutan–India border; the dam invited series of controversies and criticisms from the Indian side, alleging China of drying out the rivers and contesting water monopoly.[8]

The construction of the Zhangmu dam and the other three dams have a significant adverse impact on the water share of Brahmaputra to Bangladesh. The future of Bangladesh, which is already suffering from rising sea level, looks dark. This crisis also affects the idea of the Koshi high dam project; therefore, Nepal and Bangladesh should share a unanimous voice along with India, demanding or possibly making a plea to China to continue with the project without disturbing the uniform flow of the Brahmaputra.

China's Malacca dilemma and BBIN – an alternative?

It was as early as in 2003 when the then Chinese President Hu Jin Tao devised and used the term "The Malacca Dilemma" to describe China's overdependence on the Straits of Malacca for meeting its energy demands. Particularly, China needs to secure the petroleum and oil supply.

China imports almost 56% of the total petroleum products required. In February 2018, China exceeded America's record as the world's largest crude oil importer.[9] Most of its energy imports from the Middle East and Central Asia, such as Russia and Kazakhstan.

China's heavy reliance on the Straits of Malacca has not abridged much since 2003 and it is desperately seeking new zones to import energy because the Straits of Malacca is not only prone to piracy but also in close proximity of the Indian Navy at the Andaman Island. The Malacca Strait is also known for growing terrorist presence. This can cause a major hindrance to China and its expanding the BRI.

BBIN serves as a new transit route as an alternative to China that helps achieve its idea of "Asian Panama Canal" linked by the Andaman Sea with the Gulf of Thailand and eventually to Indian Ocean.

Conclusion

The BRI appears to be a far-fetched idea until it is endorsed by its neighbouring country India, because China's thrill to secure its growing energy quest can only be met through co-operation with India. The BRI can materialise only when these two countries share mutually beneficial subsets through their regional initiatives of the BRI and BBIN, respectively. Add to this, India's approach to undermining SAARC and introducing BIMSTEC seems to be another intention to isolate Pakistan and build relations with other neighbours, extending up to Thailand.

The main point of conflict between the BRI and BBIN could be China's growing economic presence in Pakistan and supporting them in many ways. Also, India cannot overlook China's presence in Sri Lanka, particularly after the Hambantota port issue. The BRI and BBIN both must materialise with the spirit of regional development, not in isolation. To take these initiatives far and wide, regional cooperation and development becomes must. Thus, keeping all tensions in mind, including COVID-19-induced and outstanding border issues, both countries should agree to continue their collaborations for mutually beneficial initiatives, which would bring them a rare opportunity of propelling the worlds' growth engine.

Notes

1 A. Bhattacharya, "Conceptualizing the Silk Road Initiative in China's Periphery Policy: Springer Link", *East Asia*, vol. 33, 2016, pp. 309–328.
2 *Ibid*.
3 "China May Have Found a Way to Keep India in the Dark over Trade Deficit", *Economic Times*, 15 April 2019, https://economictimes.indiatimes.com/news/economy/foreign-trade/china-may-have-found-a-way-to-keep-india-in-the-dark-over-trade-deficit/articleshow/68884958.cms?from=mdr, accessed 30 June 2020.
4 "Belt and Road Initiative", https://www.beltroad-initiative.com/belt-and-road/, accessed 6 July 2019.
5 Weidongliu, "Scientific Understanding of the Belt and Road Initiative of China and Other Related Themes", *Progress in Geography*, vol. 34, 2015, pp. 538–544, http://www.progressingeography.com/EN/10.11820/dlkxjz.2015.05.001#1, accessed 6 July 2019.
6 Brahma Chellaney, "China's Debt-Trap Diplomacy", https://www.project-syndicate.org/commentary/china-one-belt-one-road-loans-debt-by-brahma-chellaney-2017-01?barrier=accesspaylog, accessed 20 April 2019.
Through its $1 trillion "one belt, one road" initiative, China is supporting infrastructure projects in strategically located developing countries, often by extending huge loans to their governments. As a result, some of these countries are becoming saddled with debt, leaving them even more firmly under China's thumb.
7 Rajesh Khanal, "China Deal Offers Nepal More Options for Third Country Trade Money", *The Kathmandu Post*, 8 May 2019, http://kathmandupost.ekantipur.com/news/2019-05-08/china-deal-offers-nepal-more-options-for-third-country-trade.html, accessed 7 July 2019.
8 Comment, "Megadams: Battle on the Brahmaputra", *BBC News*, 20 March 2014, https://www.bbc.com/news/world-asia-india-26663820, accessed 7 July 2019.
9 The Maritime Executive, "China Surpasses U.S. as Largest Crude Oil Importer", *The Maritime Executive*, https://www.maritime-executive.com/article/china-surpasses-u-s-as-largest-crude-oil-importer, accessed 7 July 2019.

PART III
South Asian Countries and China

7
INDIA AND CHINA IN SOUTH ASIA
Towards trans-regional politics

Anindya Jyoti Majumdar

Introduction

Rise of a power at a juncture of history is not a unique phenomenon in international relations. History is the witness to the rise and fall of a great many powers. In our time, the new rising power is China, and no wonder, China's rise and its resultant impact on the regions around it or its changing relations with the erstwhile hegemons have become an issue of much interest in the contemporary period. India too has been progressing rapidly over the last three decades and eventually it appears that the "Rising China" story is increasingly being appended with a sub-story of the "Emerging India," and the patterns of relations between the two expanding economies and their future trajectories are fast becoming a matter of vital geopolitical importance.

For some, such trends are nothing but very usual fragments of civilisational history. "[T]he history, tells us that the world is remarkably good at absorbing new arrivals on the global economic scene and benefiting from their presence. China and India, in this respect at least, really are no different."[1] However, China's role and influence in the South Asian region is an important segment of China's growing power and assertiveness. While for the onlookers from a distance, China's increasing influence in the South Asian region would appear as natural and obvious, commensurate with its expanding economic and military reach, India views these trends with much apprehension and consternation, which is also quite natural and obvious, as China penetrates into South Asia, a region that has traditionally been India's playfield.

Independent India and Communist China – two ancient civilisations but young actors in terms of post-colonial organised statehood – followed different tracks for national development within the broad international political canvas marked by Cold War predicaments. The initial attempts at defining operational

DOI: 10.4324/9781003146223-7

codes for bilateral relations, between the two neighbours, were not free from interest-based interruptions and both contributed to the evolution of at best an uneasy friendship in the decades of the last century. Even though the post-Cold War changes have introduced new power equations and strategic partnerships in the world arena, a strand of continuity could be ascertained even in the present century in terms of this uneasy relationship. The two countries have experienced ups and downs in relations, even a war in 1962 that India lost. Though a few conflicts resulted in India's favour in 1967,[2] prudence dictates that India should aim for a degree of mission-specific power equivalence to balance any possible security threat emanating from China while striving for better economic ties.

A number of irritants in bilateral relations exist between India and China, ranging from border disputes, resource sharing, divergent political perceptions and consequent policy-posturing. However, the relations between the two are increasingly becoming pragmatic, which includes working together in some areas, while competing in some other, purely based on a cost-benefit calculus. Both the countries realise that they draw benefits from the existing set up. The Wuhan Spirit (2018) followed by the Chennai Connect (2019) – an outcome of the meetings between the Chinese leader Xi Jinping and the Indian Prime Minister Narendra Modi – recognises that effective management of divergences is the key essentially harping on non-political and functional links that presupposes that cooperation will indeed result in mutual benefit. Neither of these states is essentially a system-challenger. Nevertheless, in 2020, the Line of Actual Control (LAC) between India and China shimmered with tension as both the countries mobilised their armed forces in a stand-off situation charging each other with land grab in the Ladakh region. This resulted in a violent clash leading to casualties on both sides. Only in early 2021 disengagement began after several rounds of talks at the military and political levels.

The rise of China makes South Asia a region of strategic value and a platform for augmenting China's commercial and energy links with regions beyond South Asia towards Africa through the Indian Ocean. China's consequent intrusion in South Asia opens up opportunities for the smaller states to derive not only economic benefits but also political support to balance India's perceived dominance, though the price of such friendship apparently turns out to be very high. The feeling of being encircled by China and the apprehension of being confined to a frosty neighbourhood make India adopt measures to protect and promote its interests by re-balancing China. This re-balancing takes essentially diplomatic, economic, military and non-military forms resulting in security implications.

Rising China and its penetration in South Asia

There has been much interest to understand and interpret China's forays into South Asia by scholars in the field and most agree in general on three aspects:

(i) Though located at the core of South Asia, India, which is economically and militarily the most powerful, could never integrate South Asia into a compact zone on its terms, and its hegemony over the region has been incomplete and inadequate. India, a hesitant hegemon in South Asia, acquired merely a "Big Brother" image that loomed large but did little for India's benefit. Rather, as some may argue, India's attempts to portray the region as part of India's national security and to secure the country's foreign political interests through interventions have proven counterproductive. However, since liberalisation, South Asia is being viewed more as a market that can contribute to India's economic development.[3] To counter India's tentative search for influence and dominance, smaller powers in South Asia might find China's support useful to balance India, especially when, with the advent of globalisation, the traditional concepts of power and dominance were changing. Pakistan, a country that relies heavily on support from China, enjoys an all-weather special friendship with China; its economic and military rehabilitation depends heavily on Chinese investments. For the other smaller countries of the region, "China offers a way of offsetting India's overwhelming presence, as well as being a source of significant investment and aid."[4]

(ii) The economic benefits that China can offer make a huge difference in view of India's limited abilities and resources. India understands that the lure of gain from China's economic assistance surpasses the benefits India can offer. Though the Ministry of External Affairs seeks to focus on these areas offering low-interest assistance, but the Chinese funding packages are huge. For example,

> China is taking a lead in the Bangladesh-China-India-Myanmar (BCIM) corridor by extending a US$31 billion (about Rs. 2.12 lakh crore) funding package for infrastructure development in Bangladesh. ... China's financial investment in Bangladesh now appears to be its second biggest after the US$60 billion China-Pakistan Economic Corridor (CPEC).[5]

(iii) China's cheque book diplomacy is now being dubbed as debt-trap diplomacy because of the high price the recipients have to pay in the long run, and moreover, the countries may actually lack the means to pay back. Nevertheless, the availability of funds and easy access make China a better trade and investment partner when huge investments in infrastructure development are needed. Money works wonders. It is also reported that a Chinese government's proposal of covering salaries of teachers in Nepal who teach Mandarin has prompted many private schools to make it mandatory for students to learn the language.[6] China is making fast inroads in Nepal with aid and investment and it has given port access to Nepal, which being a landlocked country depended heavily on Indian trading routes and ports. In fact, the spat between India and Nepal over the disputed territories of Limpiyadhura, Kalapani and Lipulekh, and Nepal's subsequent attempt to sledgehammer a new map in 2020 are assumed to be encouraged by China. A constitutional approval of the new map incorporating the territories, in physical control of India, makes Nepal inflexible and forecloses or substantially reduces possibility of a breakthrough in negotiations.

(iv) India has religious, linguistic, ethnic and cultural ties that could be used as soft power in South Asia. Unfortunately, the soft power connections fail to work in South Asia as nation-building in the smaller states requires the bogey of an external threat (conveniently emanating from India) for domestic cohesion. Geography favours India in the region in many ways, but in this case, the distance from the region favours China. It is free from such historical baggage and as a view persists, China enjoys a comfortable position in this respect, and it has the image of a "neutral" player in South Asia.[7]

India was synonymous with South Asia in the past, and China's connections with India actually meant its relations beyond contemporary India's borders. On the basis of circulatory connections comprising the movements of people, objects and ideas, Tansen Sen viewed the ancient South Asia–China "circuit of exchanges" as part of a wider world of Afro-Eurasian connections. Different traditions were merged together and different markets were interlinked with long-distance commercial networks. Geographical and technical knowledge was circulated in multiple forms through intermediaries and agencies. Traders, missionaries, pilgrims, scholars, diplomats and tourists have established over centuries a succession of links and ties. However, the nature of present-day relations is marked by "political designation" of the two prime actors leading to greater focus on the bilateral relationship that is necessitated by the requirements of nation-states. Indeed, as Sen argues, the formation of territorialised nation-states in the mid-twentieth century led to contraction of border linkages that had defined and promoted earlier connections. Increasingly, policies focused more on promoting bilateral exchanges under state guidance often with the support of imagined intimate relations recreated at the official levels.[8] The net effect and the oft-repeated general conclusion is that China, by political, economic and soft power yardsticks, is far ahead of India in the competition for expanding or retaining influence in South Asia and India has little ability to stop the Chinese expansion.

Balancing through multiple means

The process, however, is not so smooth, especially if viewed from the other angle. While China's growing presence in South Asia is integral to its global design of economic activities, expanded trade ties, energy supplies and connectivity, a potential clog in the wheel in the region is an emerging India that refuses to be a party to the Chinese Belt and Road Initiative and gives increasingly greater attention to its neighbourhood. In his first swearing-in as the prime minister in 2014, Prime Minister Modi invited all SAARC country leaders and his "Neighbourhood First" policy was aimed at forging stronger links with the neighbours. The general impression has been that "with political authority restored, Modi and his government has moved at breakneck pace to revitalize India's neighbourhood policy, especially at a time when China has made significant inroads in the subcontinent."[9] The policy continues during his second term. Modi began his official foreign visits in 2014 with a trip to Bhutan; in 2019, as his second term began, his first official foreign visit was to Maldives and Sri Lanka. Despite attempts to develop better relations with the neighbours, competition seems to be inherent between India and China, which only sharpens over the years. Moreover, the nature of bilateral relations between India and China as two major neighbouring powers impact upon the countries in South Asia and their independent policy decisions.

The theory of balance in its conventional understanding presupposes a rough equilibrium of power determined on the basis of military terms. Today, on the one hand, soft power involving economic opportunities has come to play an important role in relations among nations and on the other, there is little scope for a state to achieve a decisive military victory over the adversary that involves huge cost but little return. The trend establishes a general global balance of power where no major power of the day can dominate others only by means of military power. Uncertain but potentially effective forms of resistance contribute to balance today. Despite irritants and occasional muscle-flexing, India and China have shown restraint in general as the outcome of a confrontation remains uncertain and potentially disastrous. The case of the stand-off at the LCA proves the point. Tactical manoeuvring continued: as China kept on developing infrastructure in the area, Indian forces moved to occupy strategic hill tops south of the Pangong Tso. Eventually, however, China's aggressive posturing failed to alter substantially the ground realities in the face of firm Indian resistance. Nevertheless, fear of the crisis snowballing into a war of high intensity prevented both the parties from being overtly belligerent.

Since the very conception of security has changed over time, it has been widened and deepened, including various dimensions of human activity, the concept of balance and the conventional understanding of the balance of power must also change and include more than the mere equilibrium of military power. From the traditional idea of balance of military power equivalence, one may shift to the idea of balancing through multiple means. Balancing then may be defined as an attempt to approximate near-equal distribution of influence among the concerned actors based on a combined impact of political, economic, military, cultural, diplomatic and networking elements by mobilising or utilising the resources of the state. It seems to be a suitable grand strategy of the state combining both military and non-military tactics but this too would be dynamic and fragile just like the balance established by military means. "India has been pursuing a mixture of limited hard balancing, soft balancing and diplomatic engagement strategy towards China."[10] This explains why India and China have intensified economic cooperation despite serious security competition.

Reinterpreting structural realism, Charles Glaser came up with the concept of Contingent Realism. His theory did not cause a revolution in mainstream security studies, but he made a few very interesting points to be taken into consideration. For him, self-help does not necessitate competition and the state's choices are conditional. Further, security is much more closely related to mission capabilities than with aggregate resources or power, and military policies can be used to communicate information regarding motives.[11] India–China relations portray the elements outlined by Glaser. One may notice both cooperation and competition, aspirations to build, not traditional balance of power per se but mission-specific abilities, and use of military policies and forces for communication.

Functional cooperation, however, does not automatically lead to better political understanding, rather economic cooperation and geopolitical security considerations might follow two separate trajectories. Some would therefore argue to separate trade and investment relations on the one hand and geopolitical issues on the other. However, the two cannot be separated as economics could be used as a handy tool to foster geo-strategic objectives. One is closely interlinked to another, and deterioration in one area inhibits progress in the other. To a significant extent, geo-strategic apprehensions and possibilities of power play may hinder the prospects of economic connectivity. In the milieu of mutual apprehension and trust deficit, even though the economically viable projects are not abandoned altogether, there can be serious lack of enthusiasm resulting in inaction on part of an unwilling party that slows down the scale, scope and pace of progress of economic ventures. The fate of the BCIM Economic Corridor is a case in point.

It may, therefore, be said that on the one hand economics can be used to create an environment of mutual gains and benefit where political disputes increasingly lose relevance and hence either sought to be shelved or resolved. On the other hand, political differences and strategic goals may remain pre-eminent in relations and thwart meaningful ventures of economic cooperation, especially when the perception of threats is buttressed by the occasional belligerent behaviour of the parties involved. The Indian Foreign Minister S. Jaishankar observes that the bottom line for the relationship (between India and China) is clear. "Peace and tranquility must prevail on the border" (and) "the border and the future of ties cannot be separated."[12] In the contemporary period, often we see a mixture of two trends, and consequently progress in some areas and little headway in others. China and India exemplify this complex situation. Progress in some does not mechanically lead to improvement in all areas.[13] At any given point in time, multiple channels of negotiation and multidimensional avenues of cooperation may run with disproportionate success rates, and security challenges continue to cast a shadow on functional cooperation.

China-India bilateral relations and the world order

When a specific trend becomes predominant in bilateral relations between two global powers, it becomes easy to categorise the relations in terms of partnership or adversarial postures. However, the realities often present a mixture of contradictory trends. Amongst the broad categorisations scholars tend to make, three dominant perspectives can be identified on the evolving India-China relations that are predominantly derived from wide-ranging possibilities.

One perspective harps on the so-called Chindia syndrome. In essence it means that both China and India are rising, developing and expanding which is somewhat worrying for the West. India and China have civilisational links and realise that rivalry could be self-destructive. By extension, it means that despite the irritants in relations, China and India would work together bilaterally and through multilateral organisations (like BRICs) with a potential to provide an alternative to the systems dominated by the West, i.e. both need each other for mutual benefit. As mentioned earlier, both the states are system supporters and not system challengers, and there is a scope of working together against a perceived America-dominated world order, especially when the United States unilaterally decides on measures of self-promotion.

In view of the trade war between China and the United States, China is keen to point out that India too is a victim of the American bullying techniques, so far as imposition of tariffs and discontinuation of the generalised system of preference are concerned, and consequently, China and India must stand up together against the United States, which attempts to promote its interests through extreme pressure tactics. As the Chinese Ambassador to India, Luo Zhaohui, claimed in 2019, "China does not want, and is not willing to fight a trade war but by no means is it afraid to fight one. China remains committed to addressing disputes through negotiations and never yields to any outside pressure. If someone brings the war to our doorstep, China will fight to the end."[14] This bravado was matched by his effort to galvanise support against the so-called bullying techniques of the United States, and Zhaohui highlighted inter-civilisational exchanges between India and China and asserted that

> as ancient Eastern civilizations, both China and India share the philosophy of harmonious relations, inclusiveness, mutual benefits and win-win outcomes and look for deepened mutual political trust, economic and trade cooperation through increased connectivity and people-to-people exchanges between the two countries and joint efforts towards building an Asian century and a new type of international relations.[15]

But the two countries are different. The success of China has inspired many Indians to propagate and emulate the Chinese model of a centralised strong state. However, as the critics point out, "China's dramatic progress has come at significant cost to large sections of its people," and they would point out how right from the days of the "Great Leap Forward" Chinese measures, including One Child Policy, restrictions on rural to urban mobility, a crackdown on the Tiananmen Square movement and actions against the dissidents (like the Uighurs in Xinjiang or in Hong Kong), and the ever-increasing surveillance has created a very powerful state[16] that executes policies regardless of people's choice. It is, of course, widely accepted that a strong authoritarian state can pay less heed to the procedural issues and concentrate on the substance of a policy and execute the policy swiftly, irrespective of the policy being sensible or not. A democratic administration by its very structure often dilutes the focus of the policy because of procedural requirements also causing thereby delay in policy implementation. In democratic governments, the procedure can take over substance, especially if a coalition of parties comes to power. Even a single party enjoying majority takes into account the possible disapproval of a proposed policy from the opposition or the people at large. This is a structural feature that the systems generate making India and China two entities different in nature.

However, irrespective of the nature of actors, fluctuations in relations can lead to shifts in adopted positions: if there is a "Chindia" syndrome, there is a "Chimerica" syndrome as well. Like the China-India relations, the China-America relations in the present time show conflicting tendencies too. As the wider perspective of world politics, induced by the chain of events consequent to the end of the Cold War, takes a new turn, bilateral relations change accordingly and the perceptions and consequent policy measures have an impact upon world politics as a whole. Ironically, each nation's aspirations and endeavours to either mould the existing conditions in its favour or to maintain the status quo if the existing conditions were already favourable carry with it elements of competition and conflict.

Sino-American relations have shown enough maturity in terms of pragmatism and realism during the late Cold War period but at the end of the Cold War; with the end of the threat from the erstwhile Soviet Union, American attention was drawn towards a rising China as the potential challenger to the America-led world order. As the unipolar world showed multi-polar tendencies over time in the 1990s, implications of the China–US convergence/divergence became critical. The possibility of the special G-2 relations (informally labelled by some as "Chimerica") was an issue of speculation in the political circles. As the two most powerful economies and influential states of the contemporary period, G-2 relations focus on working out solutions to the global problems together. However, at the same time, the issue of the freedom of navigation against Chinese assertion over expanding maritime territories, an attempt for re-balancing by the United States, the *Pivot to Asia* policy paving way for informal clubs as Japan, India and Australia become active in the Indo-Pacific geopolitical theatre, trade war, charges of snooping and other economic disputes began to set limits for cooperation and instigate cold conflicts. The US foreign policy, while passing through an unpredictable phase under the Trump Presidency, was at a crossroads. It is generally expected that partnership with the United States might make it easier for India to increase its clout over the Indian Ocean region; however, the possibility of US accommodation of China leading to gradual US withdrawal leaving greater space for Chinese assertion remains. Relations fluctuate over time, and acerbic tones give way to conciliatory overtures based on perceptions of evolving interests. President Trump's anti-China rhetoric might be toned down under the dispensation of Joe Biden though basic points of differences would define the relations as China increasingly came to be viewed as a global security challenge.

The second perspective is of strategic rivalry based on geopolitical narratives. One such narrative is the assumption that China wants a unipolar Asia and a bipolar world. Yet another narrative is that the logic of security and logic of economics do not go hand in hand in the present era. Despite good economic relations, incompatible security interests would compel them to form opposing blocs. Definite trends of impending conflicts, however, are absent though occasional muscle-flexing and intrusions along the disputed border with sudden flare-ups may continue. The Chinese tactics of expanding strategic advantage through claiming territories belonging to others would remain a matter of concern. The Doklam face-off in 2017 began when China sought to build a road through Doklam (a plateau belonging to Bhutan) to Doka La (a junction point of India, Bhutan and China), and India sought to prevent China with the presence of force in the area. Likewise, the stand-off in 2020 began as China intruded into the territory claimed by India, apparently as a response to India's infrastructure development activities at the LAC near the Finger Areas at the Pangong Tso in Ladakh though the intrusion this time carried other messages as well.

The idea of the QUAD in the Indo-Pacific region may acquire greater portents in the coming days. The United States, Japan, Australia, India quadrilateral group advocates a free, open, prosperous and inclusive Indo-Pacific region. Prime Minister Modi pointed out at the Shangri-La dialogue, 2018, that Indo-Pacific is a region "not directed against any country" with "Southeast Asia at its centre" and a space that requires a "common rule-based order."[17] It is for the time being a platform that allows these states to consult and coordinate actions in the Indo-Pacific. If the situation so demands, it can be resurrected fast to form an alliance of democracies against China's provocative ventures.

The Wuhan spirit led to some improvement in the relations harping on non-political functional links. China finally agreed to remove the technical hold so that Masood Azhar could be branded as an international terrorist; the issue has been an irritant in India-China relations. Nevertheless, there is a view that the policies and interests of China are such that it routinely brushes aside Indian concerns. To be overly deferential to Chinese concerns would therefore amount to appeasement. For some, "China's growing presence in South Asia (is) being motivated above all by the search for markets and access to the sea for economic purposes."[18] But India is apprehensive that through capacity funding to South Asian states, China is expanding maritime connectivity in the Indian Ocean region and as it is argued at some quarters that the next conflict with China will be at the Bay of Bengal.[19] China is developing deep sea port projects at Kyaukpyu in Myanmar and at Gwadar in Pakistan, and it has acquired Sri Lanka's Hambantota port on debt swap as Sri Lanka had to grant a 99-year lease over its inability to repay loans. Whether China's intentions are purely commercial or not, the apprehension persists in India that China is building a strategic network of ports – the "string of pearls" – to encircle India.

As T.V. Paul argues, limited contest between India and China in an era of intensified economic globalisation has provided a window of opportunity to small states in South Asia. "The managed limited rivalry between China and India has allowed smaller states to play off one against the other and to gain maximum economic benefits."[20] However, if the contest intensifies, Paul maintains, the small states would have to bandwagon with one or the other and this will drastically affect their bargaining power.

The third perspective aims somewhere in the middle. A new word has been coined, *Frenemy* (half friend – half enemy) to explain the complex relations between the two. Dealing with a *Frenemy* requires innovative strategies. If one deals with the enemy through containment, and deals with a friend through engagement, dealing with the Frenemy requires both these elements being combined into "*congagement.*"[21] This reinforces re-balancing by multiple means. "An increasingly assertive Beijing is in two minds about India," says Joshi,

> At one level it sees itself as above the fray and a great power that seeks to have good relations with all the states of the region. On the other, it sees New Delhi, in alliance with Tokyo and Washington, as a peer competitor that must be checked at every step.[22]

Viewed from another angle, in a greater strategic rivalry with the United States, better relations with India at the moment might prove useful for China in the short run, and if India could be prevented from becoming a part of an anti-China alliance, it would be useful in the long run as well. Mobilisation of forces within the disputed territory in 2020, as Bajpai says, is nothing but a pressure tactic to convey a message to India: "don't join a containment structure or we will show you to be a paper tiger."[23] Such communication however has little worth for an emerging India.

The pandemic times

In 2020, the outbreak of the pandemic COVID-19 that swept the world added a new dimension to the fragile relationship. The usual response should have been focused on collaborative measures and collective efforts by the states in line with the much-touted ideas of human and non-traditional security, but the states did what they knew best and opted for self-help and insularity. There were appeals though, issued by the governments, for global cooperation to lessen the economic impact of the pandemic. There were also virtual conferences among the world leaders, but apart from procuring medicines and protective gears for their citizens, there was hardly a common platform or plan to tackle the pandemic on a global scale.

As the states quarantined themselves and stopped movements across borders, it is argued that the problems associated with China's Belt and Road initiative would be further aggravated as anti-Chinese feelings amplified over its not so transparent handling of the disease that originated in China itself and then spread over the world. However, the Chinese plans for health cooperation in BRI countries – though viewed with suspicion by states – might ensure further Chinese penetration in South Asia. It has been observed that the BRI projects would be delayed due to disruption of supply of Chinese labour and equipment, and changing priorities of a contracting economy coupled with "falling appetite for new loans."[24] However, as South Asia's public health care capacities are limited, the next phase of infrastructure development might include a greater push for hospitals and laboratories, enabling China to implement its version of Health Silk Road – thereby, China would become a global health leader, influence international institutions and secure new markets for its medical equipment, biomedical technology and telemedicine.[25]

After a video summit among SAARC nations, India committed $10 million to the emergency fund and emerged as the first responder to the needs of its neighbours, deploying quick response medical teams and providing essential medical supplies.[26] China too has donated testing kits and medical supplies to the states in South Asia and sanctioned huge loans. However, the smaller neighbours preferred to pursue an "independent" policy and some of these countries also wanted image makeover as partners and not merely perennial recipients of humanitarian assistance.[27] Nevertheless, China ostensibly has greater resources and strategies to use these resources towards its rise as a global leader, and much would depend on the smaller states in South Asia in their ability to retain their "sovereign" hold on their policies. It may also be pointed out that India enjoys some advantage as the major producer of vaccines, and "vaccine diplomacy" keeps India in good stead despite india's own troubles under the severe second wave of the pandemic.

The United States, failing to effectively manage the spread of the pandemic within the country, topping the list of deaths, showed little leadership values and its acerbic relations with China, already vicious over a trade war, further worsened. China on the other hand faced a world distrustful of its intentions and designs as charges of cover up and lack of transparency with regard to the origin and patterns of the pandemic were freely levelled against it. The world faced the challenges of economic hardships, depression and unemployment, and there was little hope that the issues would be sorted out any time soon. Disenchantment grew in China's domestic circles and China was, like many other states, a troubled country fast losing the moral authority to lead.

The stand-off between India and China in May 2020 at the Pangong Lake, Demchok and Galwan valley region is explained on three major counts: (i) a troubled China seeks to divert the attention of the Chinese citizens from domestic discontentment to issues that encourage nationalist feelings favouring the ruling disposition; (ii) from a military tactical perspective, upsetting or scuttling India's plans and efforts for infrastructural developments along the LAC; and (iii) pressurising India to take more subservient positions with regard to its policies going against Chinese interests: be it curtailing the scope of Chinese investments to take over Indian enterprises or supporting an international investigation regarding the origin of the pandemic. However, there is a bigger long-term plan: China can only be the world leader by establishing a unipolar Asia subjugating both India and Japan.

The nature of threat/challenge in South Asia from the Chinese penetration is essentially of three types: (i) loss of India's influence as China surges ahead with its cheque-book diplomacy/debt-trap diplomacy in connectivity/infrastructure projects; and today in the times of pandemic with health care support; (ii) weaning away smaller states and creating a hostile neighbourhood for India; and (iii) encircling and confining India to the region by China and its potential allies.

Before the perceived challenges become actual threats, the measures that India adopts to re-balance China in South Asia can also be mentioned under three broad categories: (i) damage limitations that include increased financial assistance, conscious promotion of mutual interests; implementation of the neighbourhood first policy with greater substance; avoidance of inadvertent disputes and more connectivity within the region; and vaccine support in the times of the pandemic. On 5 May 2017, India launched a South Asia satellite with a mission life of over 12 years for providing communications and disaster support for India and its South Asian neighbours. Pakistan, however, remains an exceptional case in this scheme. (ii) Pragmatic policies based on cost-benefit analysis with China leading to a complex interdependence between the two based on multiple means of balancing. (iii) Reorganisation of regional geography itself where the region loses its "regionality" in two ways: (a) sub-regionalism, trans-regionalism and paradiplomacy become the dominant modes of interaction where regionalism and regional institutions increasingly lose relevance; and (b) the region becomes a component of the macro-region of the Indo-Pacific bringing in the ASEAN, Australia, Japan and the United States into the equation where India's Act East policy objectives converge. "Stronger ties with Southeast Asia are just one component of India's efforts to reorganize the regional geography of Asia," argue scholars. Referring to the benefits that BIMSTEC and BCIM can offer, the scholars observe that the "shifting geopolitics of Asia are offering India new opportunities to strengthen integration with its eastern neighbours and developing its own poor northeastern region."[28] In an exercise in diplomatic symbolism, Prime Minister Modi invited the BIMSTEC leaders to his swearing-in in May 2019 and not the SAARC leaders who were invited in 2014.

Conclusion

A few basic lines of argument can perhaps be summarised at this stage. These on the whole include linkages and contradictions involving emerging international structure vis-à-vis the individual state policies, the context vis-à-vis the content of such policies and the deterministic factors of the world order vis-à-vis the choice or initiatives of the leadership. As India grows in economic and military stature and strategic networking make India a trans-regional nation, India is now in a position to become a hub of connectivity, and a transit corridor fostering development in the region with preferential treatment for the smaller states over time. Despite liberal doses of Sino-mania or Sino-phobia that would be present in any such discussion, whether one rejoices with the Wuhan Spirit that has come to influence the bilateral relations of late, or gets dismayed with the more recent stand-off at the LAC, in ascertaining the trends for the immediate future, basic policy prescriptions would continue to be based on time-tested prescriptions. It may be said that the pandemic will have its impact on the abilities and the attitudes of the individual actors but the basic patterns of international politics would hardly be changed. Under the circumstances, a self-reliant India's pursuit comprises of (i) steady mission-specific military upgradation to thwart and/or reduce chances of conflicts; (ii) intense economic diplomacy towards mutual benefit; and (iii) substantive networking in a web of criss-crossing friends and competitors rather than forming cohesive balancing blocks.

China and India are two ancient civilisations, neighbours, aspirant nations and at present have two strong leaders with a vision to push their countries up in the global hierarchy. As they expand, though one is more powerful compared to the other, they understand that confrontation harms both and cooperation helps. The world has at different turns of history accommodated new arrivals in the major power club, but tension and conflict in the phase of adjustment is not ruled out. In introducing his account of the rise and fall of the great powers, Kennedy observes that major powers still "grapple with the age-old task of relating national means to national ends. The history of the rise and fall of the Great Powers has in no way come to a full stop."[29] States pull down or pull up others irrespective of individual policies, and while all the actors are playing the nascent balancing game corresponding to their abilities, smaller states in South Asia are still enjoying a window of opportunity at the moment. In the meanwhile, as Jaishankar argues, not idealism but enlightened self-interest is at work now[30]; India seeks to reduce possible disadvantages by becoming increasingly trans-regional, reorganising and expanding the region itself and thereby moving beyond the confines of South Asia.

Notes

1 David Smith, *The Dragon and the Elephant: China, India and the New World Order*, London: Profile Books, 2007, p. 238.
2 Probal Dasgupta, *Watershed 1967: India's Forgotten Victory over China*, New Delhi: Juggernaut Books, 2020.
3 Christian Wagner, "The Role of India and China in South Asia", *Strategic Analysis*, vol. 40, no. 4, 2016, p. 317.
4 Manoj Joshi, "Expect Greater Rivalry between India and China in South Asia", 23 February 2018, https://www.orfonline.org/research/expect-greater-rivalry-between-india-and-china-in-south-asia/, accessed 5 July 2019.

5 Saibal Dasgupta, "China Takes Lead in BCIM with Rs. 2L cr Offer to Bangladesh", *The Times of India* (Kolkata), 5 July 2019, p. 16.
6 "Now, Chinese Language Must in Nepal Schools", *The Times of India* (Kolkata), 16 June 2019, p. 17.
7 Wagner, n. 3, p. 318.
8 Tansen Sen, *India, China and the World: A Connected History*, New Delhi: Oxford University Press, 2018.
9 Walter Andersen and Shrey Verma, "Washington's India Pivot: Is It Compatible with Modi's Asian Ambitions?", *India Quarterly*, vol. 71, no. 2, 2015, p. 98.
10 Paul Kennedy, *The Rise and Fall of the Great Powers: Economic Change and Military Conflict from 1500 to 2000*, London: William Collins, 2017, p. 55.
11 Charles L. Glaser, "Realists as Optimists: Cooperation as Self-Help", *International Security*, vol. 19, no. 3, 1994–95, pp. 50–90.
12 S. Jaishankar, *The India Way: Strategies for an Uncertain world*, Noida: Harper Collins, 2020, p. 153.
13 Anindya Jyoti Majumdar, "The Politics of Connectivity: Geostrategic Perception and Misperception Challenges", in Swaran Singh, Anita Sengupta, and Sweta Singh (eds), *Corridors of Engagement*, New Delhi: KW Publishers, 2019, pp. 2–3.
14 Zhaohui, Luo, "China-India: Yes to Civilisation Exchanges, No to Trade Bullying", *The Times of India* (Kolkata), 25 May 2019, p. 10.
15 *Ibid.*
16 Arunabh Ghosh, "Mirage of a Strong State", *The Times of India* (Kolkata), 15 June 2019, p. 14.
17 Gauri Agarwal, "The Pacific Interest of India and China", *South Asia Journal*, Winter 2019, p. 81.
18 David M. Malone, "Soft Power in Indian Foreign Policy", *Economic and Political Weekly*, vol. 46, no. 36, 3 September 2011, p. 35.
19 Jayanta Gupta, "Conflict with China Will Be in Bay of Bengal", *The Times of India* (Kolkata), 16 May 2017, p. 10.
20 T. V. Paul, "When Balance of Power Meets Globalization: China, India and the Small States of South Asia", *Politics*, vol. 39, no. 1, 2019, p. 58.
21 Yeong-Kuang Ger, "From Congagement to Engagement: The Changing American China Policy and Its Impact on Regional Security", *American Journal of Chinese Studies*, vol. 11, no. 2, 2004, pp. 159–80.
22 Joshi, n. 4.
23 Kanti Bajpai, "Chinese Whispers in Ladakh", *The Times of India* (Kolkata), 13 June 2020.
24 Deep Pal and Rahul Bhatia, *The BRI in Post-Coronavirus South Asia*, 26 May 2020, https://carnegieindia.org, accessed 13 June 2020.
25 *Ibid.*
26 Dipanjan Roy Chaudhury, "India Pips China to Extend Medical Supplies to South Asian Neighbours *Economic Times*, 21 March 2020.
27 Atul Aneja, "South Asia Unveils India-China Balancing Act during COVID-19", *The Hindu*, 7 May 2020.
28 Xiangming Cheng, Pallavi Banerjee, Gaurav Toor, and Ned Downie, "China and South Asia: Contention and Cooperation between Great Neighbours", *The European Financial Review*, April-May 2014, pp. 13–14.
29 Kennedy, n. 10, p. xxiii.
30 *Sunday Times of India* (Kolkata), 2 August 2020.

8
INDIA–CHINA TRADE LINKAGES IN THE CONTEXT OF AN EMERGING UNCERTAIN WORLD TRADING ENVIRONMENT

Indra Nath Mukherji

Introduction

As the global economy steers in and moves through 2019 and beyond, several headwinds confront its path. Several reports of international organisations, such as the International Monetary Fund and World Bank, have brought down their past estimates for the growth of the global economy in 2019. Decelerating growth has been projected for most countries/regions of the world.

To make matters worse, protectionist sentiments among advanced countries (once champions of multilateralism), right-wing nationalist transactional diplomacy, US government shut down (longest in recorded history), prospects of uncertain Brexit and trade war between two major powers (the United States and China) has brought about extreme and unprecedented policy uncertainty.

US-China trade war is one of the varied manifestations of imbalances in the global economy. Since both India and China have sizable trade with the United States, in the context of US-China conflict and consequent global trade uncertainty, could we expect some realignment of bilateral trade linkages between India and China to the mutual benefit of both the countries? With a view to addressing this question, in Section 1 the chapter examines the trend in India-China bilateral trade, with a focus on the trade imbalance. Section 2 examines the structural imbalance in bilateral trade of the two countries. Section 3 examines India's trade potential in the Chinese market, consequent to China–US trade conflict. in order of products having the highest potential.

Trends in bilateral trade

China is India's largest trading partner as can be seen in Figure 8.1. Total bilateral trade between the two countries increased from US$68 billion in 2013 to US$84 billion in 2017. However, the direction of trade is heavily skewed in

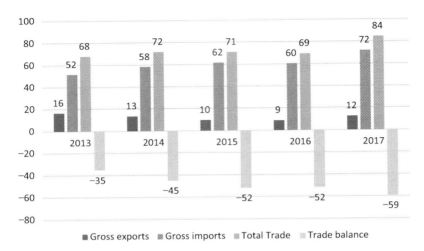

FIGURE 8.1 India China Trade (US $ billion). *Source:* https://www.trademap.org/tradestat/Bilateral, accessed 6 January 2019.

China's favour. India's exports to China fell consistently till 2016, increasing only in 2017. On the other hand, India's imports from China increased consistently during this period. Its import to export ratio, which was 3.25 in 2013, increased to 6.0 in 2017. Consequently, India's trade deficit with China increased from US$35 billion in 2013 to US$59 billion in 2017.

More recent trends in India–China trade, on a monthly basis, has been presented in Figure 8.2. Monthly trade data from June to November 2018 reflects that the problem of trade imbalance remains unaltered when we look at bilateral trade flows in the two countries.

Structure of bilateral trade

In 2010, intermediate goods and raw materials together accounted for as much as 93% of India's total exports to China. The shares of capital goods and consumer goods together accounted for no more than 7%.[1] In 2017, while the shares of intermediate goods and raw materials together accounted for 77%, the shares of capital goods and consumer goods together accounted for only 23%.[2] Thus, over the seven-year period, intermediate goods and raw materials continued to dominate India's exports to China, even though one may notice a modest level of structural transformation with capital goods and consumer goods having increased their shares.

Looking at the structure of India's imports from China, it may be observed that in 2010, intermediate goods and raw materials together accounted for 37% of India's imports from China, while capital goods and consumer goods together accounted for as much as 63%.[3] In 2017, the shares of intermediate goods and raw material together accounted for 77%, while the capital and consumer goods together accounted for

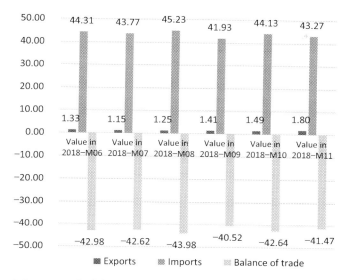

FIGURE 8.2 India's monthly trade with China June–November 2018 (US $ billion).
Source: https://www.trademap.org/tradestat/Bilateral_, accessed 10 January 2019.

23%.[4] It is thus clear that India imported more value-added products from China in 2010. However, in 2017, India imported a greater share of raw materials and intermediate goods and a lower share of capital goods. This is a positive shift indicating that it is importing more intermediate goods and raw materials, the processing of the same will add more value to the domestic economy.

Table 8.1 shows the major product groups in India's average top ten exports to China over the period 2015–2017. It will be observed that the major raw materials exported were cotton, ores, slags and ash. Organic chemicals, copper and articles thereof, mineral fuels, animal, vegetable oils salt, lime and cement were the major intermediate goods being exported to China. Among capital goods, machinery, mechanical appliances and electrical machinery were the major items being exported to China.

It is observed in Table 8.2 that the major capital goods imported by India from China over the period 2015–2017 were electrical machinery, mechanical appliances, articles of iron and steel, optical instruments, floating structures etc. The major intermediate goods imported were organic chemicals, fertilisers, iron and steel, plastics etc.

India's existing export and potential export in the Chinese market

India's export potential in the Chinese market for any product is the minimum of China's import of that product from the world in relation to India's export of

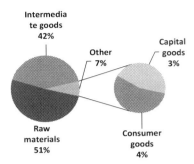

CHART 8.1A   India's exports to China by basic economic categories–2010. *Source:* Estimated from UN comtrade data as obtained from World Bank, World Integrated Trade Solution (WITS) platform, accessed 10 January 2019.

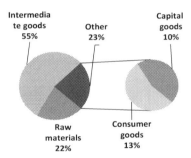

CHART 8.1B   India's exports to China by basic economic categories–2017. *Source:* Estimated from UN comtrade data as obtained from World Bank, World Integrated Trade Solution (WITS) platform, accessed 10 January 2019.

that product to the world, less India's existing exports to China of that product. The top ten potential export products to China (average 2015–2017) is presented in Table 8.3. India's export potential lies in medicaments (pharmaceutical products); medium and light oils and preparations; precious metals such as diamonds worked, gold and gold-plated for non-monetary purposes; frozen boneless meat; parts and accessories of tractors, motor vehicles, aeroplanes, tractors; cotton neither carded or combed; and semi-milled or wholly milled rice.

India–China trade in the context of US-China trade war

The objective of this chapter is to examine the challenges and opportunities that the US–China trade war could have on India–China trade. The two countries in conflict are the largest players in the world economy with India having sizable

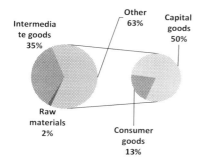

CHART 8.2A India's imports from China by basic economic categories–2010. *Source:* Estimated from UN comtrade data as obtained from World Bank, World Integrated Trade Solution (WITS) platform, accessed 10 January 2019.

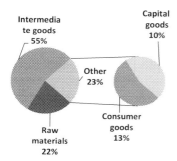

CHART 8.2B India's imports from China by basic economic categories–2017. *Source:* Estimated from UN comtrade data as obtained from World Bank, World Integrated Trade Solution (WITS) platform, accessed 10 January 2019.

trade with both these countries. Hence, it is plausible to assume that the ripple effects of this conflict will be felt across the globe, having bearing on India–China trade as well.

The United States has been the initiator of applying tariffs for all countries since January 2018 on washing machines and solar panels. In March, the United States imposed tariffs on steel (25%) and aluminium (10%), valued at US$2.9 billion. China reacted by imposing tariffs (15–25%) on aluminium, fruit and wine valued at US$2.4 billion in April 2018. The real escalation in the trade war took shape from July 2018. During July–August, the United States–imposed tariffs (25%) on Chinese products valued at US$50 billion in (two tranches of US$36 and 16 billion, respectively), which was equally reciprocated by China. In September, the United States imposed tariffs (10%) on as much as US$200 billion on Chinese products, which was reciprocated by China at the same time, by imposing US$60 billion on US products, with

TABLE 8.1 India's average exports to China of top ten major product groups: 2015–2017 (Average value US$10.33 billion)

Product code (2-HS)	Product description	% of total exports
52	Cotton	14.23
29	Organic chemicals	10.84
74	Copper and articles thereof	10.64
26	Ores, slag and ash	10.06
27	Mineral fuels, mineral oils and products of their distillation; bituminous substances; mineral …	7.45
25	Salt; sulphur; earths and stone; plastering materials, lime and cement	5.61
84	Machinery, mechanical appliances, nuclear reactors, boilers; parts thereof	5.22
85	Electrical machinery and equipment and parts thereof; sound recorders and reproducers, television …	3.54
39	Plastics and articles thereof	3.58
15	Animal or vegetable fats and oils and their cleavage products; prepared edible fats; animal …	3.09
Top ten		74.26

Source: https://www.trademap.org/tradestat/Bilateral, accessed 21 January 2019.

TABLE 8.2 India's average imports from China of top ten major product groups: 2015–2017 (Average value US$646.86 billion)

Product code (2-HS)	Product description	% of total
85	Electrical machinery and equipment and parts thereof; sound recorders and reproducers, television …	34.93
84	Machinery, mechanical appliances, nuclear reactors, boilers; parts thereof	17.62
29	Organic chemicals	9.43
31	Fertilisers	3.25
72	Iron and steel	2.94
39	Plastics and articles thereof	2.94
90	Optical, photographic, cinematographic, measuring, checking, precision, medical or surgical …	2.16
73	Articles of iron or steel	2.01
87	Vehicles other than railway or tramway rolling stock, and parts and accessories thereof	1.85
89	Ships, boats and floating structures	1.85
Top ten		78.99

Source: Estimated from International Trade Centre, https://www.trademap.org/tradestat/Bilateral_, accessed 22 January 2019.

TABLE 8.3 India top ten potential exports to China (US$ million) (Average 2015–2017)

Product code (HS-6)	Product description	India's exports to China	China's imports from world	India's exports to world	India's potential exports to China
1	2	3	4	5	6 = (min col 4,5) – 3
300490	Medicaments consisting of mixed or unmixed products for therapeutic or prophylactic purposes, …	12	10,144	9598	9586
271019	Medium oils and preparations, of petroleum or bituminous minerals, not containing biodiesel, …	122	9446	18775	9323
710239	Diamonds, worked, but not mounted or set (excluding industrial diamonds)	143	6960	21959	6817
710812	Gold, including gold plated with platinum, unwrought, for non-monetary purposes (excluding gold …)	0	61,206	3963	3963
271012	Light oils and preparations, of petroleum or bituminous minerals which > = 90% by volume, including …	532	3855	11740	3322
020230	Frozen, boneless meat of bovine animals	0	2297	3884	2297
870899	Parts and accessories, for tractors, motor vehicles for the transport of ten or more persons, …	28	2246	2443	2218
880330	Parts of aeroplanes or helicopters, n.e.s. (excluding those for gliders)	27	1765	1552	1526
520100	Cotton, neither carded nor combed	250	2105	1622	1372
100630	Semi-milled or wholly milled rice, whether or not polished or glazed	1	1322	5892	1321

Source: Estimated from International Trade Centre, https://www.trademap.org/tradestat/Bilateral, accessed 29 January 2019_

tariffs ranging in four slabs from 5 to 25%. At the time of writing, there is temporary truce between the two countries as official level talks are being held to resolve the issue. The United States has threatened that unless resolved by 1 March 2019, tariffs, currently applied at 10% on goods worth US$200 billion, would be doubled to 20%. Further, the balance US$247 billion US imports from China would also come under tariffs in case China failed to respond to US concerns.[5]

This chapter has restricted its analysis and coverage to include only India's export opportunities for entering the Chinese market, competing with similar imported US products on which China has imposed retaliatory tariffs. This is because China has covered nearly all of its products imported from the United States under its retaliatory tariffs. By contrast, the United States has till to date imposed tariffs on around half of the products it imports from China. This provides an opportunity to analyse India's export possibilities for all major products it exports to in the Chinese market in relation to similar competing US exports to China. The analysis can be done at 6-digit HS classification[6] (HS-2012 format) as this includes all 8-digit level products subsumed under this classification.

Opportunities for India's market access to Chinese market

In the context of China's trade conflict with the United States, China is keen to diversify its source of imports given that it has imposed tariffs on most of US imports. This is also in keeping with China's policy in rebalancing its economy by shifting steadily from its policy of external export-led growth to domestic consumption-driven one. This calls for China to liberalise its imports as well (other than from the United States). China's import liberalisation with India would further help address India's concern of massive and growing trade imbalance with the former country.

This section examines India's additional market access frontier (AMAF)[7] in the Chinese market in respect of all HS-6-digit products exported to that country in 2017. This is compared with the value of China's US imports for the like products in the Chinese market. A minimum of the two values are taken as the maximum potential of India's substitution of US products in the Chinese market. The products are ranked in terms of descending value and the top ten of these are taken up for product-by-product analysis. Table 8.4 presents the details.

Table 8.4 further reveals that among the top ten products identified for access to the Chinese market, some have been earlier granted preferential access to the Chinese market under Asia Pacific Trade Agreement (APTA)[8] concessions offered by China under the third and fourth rounds. This gives India's exporters a further competitive advantage in entering the Chinese market given that while US companies face some 25% Chinese tariffs on these products, Indian exporters get a preferential margin on China's MFN rates for the same products.

India–China trade linkages 119

TABLE 8.4 India's Additional Market Access Frontier (AMAF) with China and possible substitution of US exports in Chinese market (USD Thousand: 2017)

HS-6 (2012 classification)	Product description	India gross exports to China	India gross exports to world	China gross imports from world	China gross imports from the United States	India – Additional market access frontier in Chinese market (4,5)-3	IND – Potential access to Chinese market with import substitution of US products 8 (min col 6,7)	China's preferential margin under APTA (%)
1	2	3	4	5	6	7 min col (4,5)-3	8 (min col 6,7)	
710812	Gold in unwrought forms non-monetary other	0	22,72,508	4,87,40,697	47,44,170	22,72,508	2,72,508	Identified in Table 8.3
870323	Motor cars of a cylinder capacity exceeding 1500 cc but not exceeding 3000 cc	65	14,48,885	3,79,08,637	1,03,17,848	14,48,820	14,48,820	10 % (third round)
841112	Turbo jets, turbo propellers and other gas turbines: (4) a thrust exceeding 25 kN	93,093	15,36,932	27,89,385	17,10,675	14,43,839	14,43,839	100 % (third round)
300490	Medicaments – other	19,025	96,56,150	1,18,85,850	11,26,102	96,37,125	1,26,102	50 % (fourth round)
520100	Cotton, not carded or combed	1,70,811	16,73,471	21,85,602	9,82,687	15,02,660	9,82,687	Identified in 8.3

(Continued)

TABLE 8.4 (Continued)

HS-6 (2012 classification)	Product description	India gross exports to China	India gross exports to world	China gross imports from world	China gross imports from the United States	India – Additional market access frontier in Chinese market (4,5)-3	IND – Potential access to Chinese market with import substitution of US products	China's preferential margin under APTA (%)
1	2	3	4	5	6	7 min col (4,5)-3	8 (min col 6,7)	
848180	Taps cocks valves – other appliances	30,855	7,68,853	34,90,951	5,78,529	7,37,998	5,78,529	35% (fourth round)
392690	Other articles of plastics – other	4,893	5,72,784	32,63,775	4,79,866	5,67,891	4,79,866	35% (fourth round)
720838	Hot-rolled steel sheet of a thickness of 3 mm or more but less than 4.75 mm	0	4,64,330	6,43,361	0	4,64,330	4,64,330	
880330	Other parts of aeroplanes or helicopters	43,279	19,62,342	18,05,278	4,41,607	17,61,999	4,41,607	
847989	Machines and mechanical appliances – other	6,810	3,67,158	86,93,487	7,69,013	3,60,349	3,60,349	50% (third round)

Source: Estimated from UN Comtrade database as accessed from World Bank WITS platform on 25 January 2019.

To provide one illustration, China has offered duty-free entry to both yellow and black soya beans, excluding seed under its third round national list of concessions to all APTA contracting states. On top of this, it has imposed retaliatory tariffs of 25% on soya bean imports from the United States. Assuming that China levies x% MFN duty on soya bean imports from the United States, India will get a landed cost difference of $x + 25$% in case China sources this product from the former country.

At present, India does not export any soya bean oil or flour of soya bean but sends a negligible amount of oilcake obtained from soya bean oil extraction to China. Groundnut exports are subject to a 15% duty in China. India is not competitive in soya bean meal and groundnut exports. The country does not export any soya bean oil or flour of soya bean but sends a negligible amount of oilcake obtained from soya bean oil extraction to China. Groundnut exports are subject to a 15% duty in China. At present, India is not competitive in soya bean meal and groundnut but now given the price advantage, the industry hopes to export US$100 million worth of soya bean meal and around US$50 million worth of groundnut to China.[9]

Some of the imported items from the United States on which China has imposed additional duties of 25% include soya beans, pork, fish, seafood including prawns and shrimp, dairy products, vegetables such as potatoes, tomatoes, onions, shallots, garlic and peas, lentils, nuts including cashews and coconut, fruits including apples, grapes and orange juice and alcohol. India is competitive in exports of such products as it markets them in over 100 countries.[10]

It is notable that China has exempted import tariffs for 28 drugs, including all cancer drugs, from 1 May 2018. The move is expected to boost Indian exports of pharmaceuticals to the neighbouring country as well as help reduce the trade imbalance between China and India in the future. India has time and again asked for greater market access for its goods and services, including IT, pharmaceuticals and agriculture in the Chinese market to reduce the widening trade deficit. Chinese government's decision to remove import duties on key medicines is actually an attempt to bring down its health care cost, which is projected to almost double from US$640 billion in 2015 to US$1.1 trillion by 2020.[11]

This chapter has demonstrated possible cost advantages that India could harness to find entry to the vast Chinese market, as China too seeks to diversify its source of imports. But this does not ensure that even given the unambiguous cost advantage to India in respect of some identified products, such entry would be easy.

The challenges

As has been observed in a background to this study, IMF, in its forecast, reiterates and reinforces its gloom over the global economic outlook for 2019. The further downward revision since October in part reflects carry over from softer momentum in the second half of 2018.¹² In such a gloomy and dismal scenario of such a global economy, the challenges faced by India appear formidable. The US–China trade war is in itself a major factor dampening the growth of the global economy. Just as regional trading arrangements provide the second-best opportunities as against free trade, so also trade wars create the second-best options for trade diversions consequent to the conflict. When two of the largest global economies collide, new alignments are bound to arise in the midst of non-creative destruction and global uncertainty. Harnessing opportunities from new alignments can be very challenging indeed.

To illustrate, a truce or a deal between the United States and China could easily restore the original trading pattern. In the case of soya bean, for instance, China, facing the intensity of the trade war, has agreed to buy more soya bean from the United States as also agreed to reduce tariffs on US automobile imports.

Further, the product being substituted must meet the standard quality requirements of the importing country. It may be recalled that for the past six years the Chinese authorities have banned the import of soya bean meal on the basis of non-compliance with food and safety norms. China imposes non-tariff barriers on a lot of agricultural products such as meals. Barriers such as pending plant inspection and yet to be signed quarantine protocol still exists.¹³ It must be further noted that there are many competing suppliers of soya bean to China, particularly in Latin American countries. Thus, on imposing restrictions on soya bean imports from the United States, China promptly sourced its requirement from Brazil and Argentina. Thus, India needs to be competitive for getting any foothold in the Chinese market.

China uses a complex set of inspection, product testing and quality certification requirements to stifle imports from India. Such restrictions are called non-tariff barriers (NTBs). WTO rules regulate import tariffs but are weak in regulating NTBs. Chinese experts inspect Indian factories. The cost is borne by the Indian side and clearance seldom comes. Only Chinese labs do the product testing, and no appeal is allowed on their decisions. China will not accept Indian basmati rice, while Pakistan's rice is welcome. Indian IT firms cannot take part if the tender size is more than US$100 million.¹⁴

Another challenge arising from the US–China trade war could be the surge in imports for products brought under tariffs in the United States on Chinese products. The products rendered surplus would like to seek entry to its neighbouring countries, including India. Regional trading arrangements such as APTA, in which China is a member along with India and other South Asian countries, could be particularly vulnerable to dumping of Chinese products in the region.

The Directorate General of Trade Remedies (DGTR) (earlier known as Directorate General of Anti-dumping and Allied Duties) was named in May 2018 as an integrated single window agency for providing comprehensive and swift trade defence mechanism in India. DGTR now deals with anti-dumping, CVD and Safeguard measures. Trade remedy measures need to be applied in a judicious, transparent and WTO-compatible manner. These should be reviewed and removed once conditions that prevailed at the time of imposition change for normal.[15]

Post-COVID-19 pandemic, border conflict and bilateral trade

Coronavirus, which originated in China in December 2019 and thereafter spread as a pandemic has severely and adversely affected global, regional and bilateral trade around the world. World trade is expected to fall by 13–32% in 2020 as the COVID-19 pandemic disrupts normal economic activity and life around the world.[16]

India–China trade has likewise been negatively impacted. The trade between China and India fell 12.4% year-on-year to US$12 billion in the first two months amid the coronavirus outbreak, according to the latest data from Chinese customs.[17] The declining trade was largely attributed to the slowdown of the economies of the two countries.

There are now clear indications that the slowdown in bilateral trade will be further exacerbated by the brutal and bloody conflict that occurred on 15 June 2020 around the actual line of control in the Galwan valley of eastern Ladakh between the Indian and Chinese armies, which left 20 Indian and an unspecified number of Chinese soldiers dead.[18]

Generally, trade/investment linkages reflect interdependence and constitute confidence-building measures that stakeholders are keen to preserve. That is why China–Japan or China–Taiwan trade has remained brisk in spite of fundamental differences between the two trading countries/partners. However, since the Galwan valley conflict, the relationship between the two countries has been overtaken by geo-strategic and security concerns, underlying nationalistic dominance/dependence syndrome.

At the time of writing, there seems to be no indication that the stand-off between the armies of both the countries at different conflict points on the line of actual control in eastern Ladakh is likely to be resolved any time soon.

In the meantime, strong nationalistic groups in India are urging the government to ban the import of all Chinese goods, as well as Chinese mobile applications. Further, Chinese participation in highway projects as well as in telecommunications is being opposed on security grounds and on the possibility of theft of data. Enlarging the security parameter to include trade and investments would undoubtedly adversely affect both trade and investment flows between the two countries.[19]

The nature of trade interdependence among trading partners depends not only on the volume of trade but also on its composition. As has been brought out under the second section of this chapter under the structure of bilateral trade, in 2017, the shares of intermediate goods and raw materials together accounted for as much as 77% of India's total imports from China. A close scrutiny of data will reveal that, in fact, India is heavily dependent on China for imports of active pharmaceutical ingredients for its pharmaceutical industry and on auto parts for its automobile industry. Besides, India's major power plants depend largely on the import of Chinese electrical machinery.[20]

Conclusion

This chapter focuses mainly on how the US–China trade war offered both opportunities and challenges for expanding and balancing India–China trade through trade diversion of Indian products to the Chinese market following enhanced Chinese import restrictions on US products as retaliatory tariffs under China–US trade war. The study reveals that significant possibilities exist for India to enter the Chinese market, particularly in products for which China was offering in addition preferential market access to India under APTA.

The study takes note of two strong headwinds that erode substantially the opportunities offered to India by China–US trade conflict. These are COVID-19 pandemic that engulfed the world since early 2020 and the military conflict and stand-off between India and China since May 2020. The scenario likely to unfold in the uncertain gloomy future does not give much hope for stability in future, and a "new normal" in India–China relationship is all that one may expect.

The moot question is "what would be the shape of the new normal?" We are aware that since the past few years China has been trying to re-balance its economy by shifting from an export-led one to one stimulating domestic demand. If that trend continues, it is plausible[21] that China could benefit by sourcing its growing developmental requirements from India. In case this happens, we may expect India's access to the Chinese market increasing over time, with the possibility of India's trade imbalance with China declining. However, in my view, India should not have paranoia about its trade imbalance issue so long it experiences robust entry to the Chinese market. Data for recent months covering the first six months of the financial year 2020–2021 shows that this has started happening, but how long this will be sustained one can only surmise.

Technical Appendix

Additional Market Access Frontier (AMAF) for Product i:

$$\text{AMAF} = \sum \min(SEi, MIi) - ETi \left(i = 1 - n \right) \text{ of product i}$$

where SEi = Supplier's Global Exports of product i; MIi = Market's Global Imports of product i; ETi = Supplier's Existing Exports to partner's Market of product I.

It is the minimum of supplier's world exports and market's world imports less supplier's current

Exports of product i. Summation over products gives the total or sectoral AMAF over all products

Notes

1 India's exports to China by basic economic categories 2010. *Source:* Estimated from UN comtrade data as obtained from World Bank, World Integrated Trade Solution (WITS) platform, accessed 10 January 2019.
2 India's exports to China by basic economic categories 2017. *Source:* Estimated from UN comtrade data as obtained from World Bank, World Integrated Trade Solution (WITS) platform, accessed 10 January 2019
3 India's imports from China by basic economic categories 2010. *Source:* Estimated from UN comtrade data as obtained from World Bank, World Integrated Trade Solution (WITS) platform, accessed 10 January 2019.
4 India's imports from China by basic economic categories 2017. *Source:* Estimated from UN comtrade data as obtained from World Bank, World Integrated Trade Solution (WITS) platform, accessed 10 January 2019.
5 Extracted from China Briefing, "The US-China Trade War: A Timeline", https://www.china-briefing.com/newsm/the-us-china-trade-war-a-timeline/, accessed 26 June 2020.
6 The Harmonized Commodity Description and Coding System (HS) of tariff nomenclature is an internationally standardized system of names and numbers for classifying traded products developed and maintained by the World Customs Organization (WCO) (formerly the Customs Co-operation Council), an independent intergovernmental organization with over 170 member countries based in Brussels, Belgium.
7 The concept is used to give the upper limit of additional market access frontier of supplier country for product under most favourable competitive conditions after netting the existing exports of the supplier country, the supplies being set by the country's world exports and the market demand for the same product by the destination country's world imports. When summed over all such matched products, we derive total AMAF of the supplying country. See technical appendix for definition of additional market access frontier (AMAF). This concept has been used by the author in Indra Nath Mukherji, "Potential for Intraregional Trade in Food Products in South Asia", in N. Kumar and J. George (eds), *Regional Cooperation for Sustainable Food Security in South Asia*, London: Routledge, 2020, pp. 56–84.
8 Initiated by UN-ESCAP in 1975, the Asia Pacific Trade Agreement is a preferential regional trade agreement among countries in Asia and Pacific region. Its current members include Bangladesh, India, China, Sri Lanka, Republic of Korea and Laos.
9 See *The Economic Times*, 12 July 2018, https://economictimes.indiatimes.com/news/economy/foreign-trade/china-us-trade-war-opportunity-for-indian-soya-bean-oilmeal-exports/articleshow/64956147.cms?from=mdr, accessed 26 June 2020.
10 See *The Hindu Business Line*, 13 July 2018, https://www.thehindubusinessline.com/news/world/india-looking-to-take-advantage-of-chinas-retaliatory-tariff-on-usnts_24413713, accessed 27 June 2020.
11 Trade Promotion Council of India, 18 May 2018, https://ibt.tpci.in/blogs/china-removes-import-tariffs-on-pharmaceutical-products-india-china-trade-scenario/, accessed 27 June 2020.
12 International Monetary Fund, *World Economic Outlook Update: A Weakening Global Expansion*, January 2019, https://www.imf.org/en/Publications/WEO/Issues/2019/01/11/weo-update-january-2019 accessed 27 June 2020.
13 See n. 4.
14 For details see https://www.insightsonindia.com/wp-content/uploads/2017/08/India-China-Trade-Gap.pdf, accessed 28 June 2020.
15 Government of India, Directorate of Trade Remedies, http://www.dgtr.gov.in/about-us/about-department#:~:text=About%20the%20Department-,About%20the%20Department,tr0mechanism%20in%20India, accessed 28 June 2020.
16 World Trade Organisation, https://www.wto.org/english/news_e/pres20_e/pr855_e.htm

17 *The Economic Times*, 3 April 2020, https://economictimes.indiatimes.com/news/economy/foreign-trade/india-china-trade-declines-by-12-4-per-cent-in-first-two-months-of-this-year-amid-coronavirus-outbreak/articleshow/74970477.cms?from=mdr
18 Sudha Ramchandran, *The Diplomat*, 5 June 2020, https://thediplomat.com/2020/06/blood-spilled-on-the-china-india-border/accessed, accessed 17 June 2020.
19 For details of perception on Indian boycott of Chinese products, see Basit Arun, *The Wire*, 17 June 2020. Available in https://thewire.in/trade/china-goods-boycott-atmanirbhar-bharat, accessed 5 July 2020.
20 For detailed discussion on these issues, see Amitendu Palit, *The Times of India*, 5 July 2020, https://timesofindia.indiatimes.com/blogs/voices/india-must-work-with-other-countries-to-erode-chinas-economic-influence/ and Roy Horner, *The Indian Express*, 4 July 2020, https://indianexpress.com/article/opinion/columns/india-china-tension-pharmaceutical-industry-covid-19-medicine-6489025/, accessed 5 July 2020.
21 India's trade deficit with China narrowed last calendar year 2020 as exports rose 16.15% to $20.25 billion, led by iron and steel, aluminium and copper, while imports shrunk 10.87% to $66.78 billion. The country's trade deficit with China fell to $45.91 billion from $56.95 billion in 2019. See Kirtika Suneja, "India's Trade Deficit with China Narrows to $45.9 Billion", *The Economic Times*, 24 February 2021, https://economictimes.indiatimes.com//news/economy/foreign-trade/indias-trade-deficit-with-china-narrows-to-45-9-billion-in-2020/articleshow/81178022.cms?utm_source=contentofinterest&utm_medium=text&utm_campaign=cppst, accessed 19 March 2021.

9
CHINA'S REGIONAL ROLE
Should India be worried?

Smruti S Pattanaik

Introduction

China's rise in recent years has often generated a debate on the strategic and economic implications of its rise on the countries within the South Asia region and also beyond. This has assumed significance in the context of the debate on relative decline of the United States and its impact on global power transition. As an emerging power seeking to break the dominance of the United States and US-dominated world order, China's regional strategic presence has generated apprehension among other rising powers in Asia. In the developing countries of Asia, however, there is an expectation that China's rise will ordain prosperity, inject investments and precipitate an economic growth that would help the countries to deliver development to their people. In Asia, Japan is another country that has significantly invested in South Asia and other parts of Asia through generous aid. Interestingly, 59.7% of its Overseas Development Assistance is to the countries in Asia.[1]

In the South Asian region, India is also a rising power and aspire for a global order that is both inclusive and norm based, which is conducive for its economic growth and in the future would facilitate its aspiration to play a larger global role. To achieve this, India wishes for a stable periphery in the neighbourhood. However, India's role as a regional leader lacks the acceptability of its neighbours who feel such regional pre-eminence would constrain their foreign policy. This is because India considers its neighbours as part of its security and has always frowned on external power presence in its neighbourhood considering it as a security threat. India's South Asian neighbours have increasingly engaged China for ostensible economic reasons that are unlikely to be frowned upon by New Delhi. To keep up with this trend of economic engagement that neighbours would be less resistant to, India has stepped up its aid programme which is termed as development partnership as "aid" has a certain imperial connotation. Keeping this in mind, India is also expanding its economic foot print and in the last few years it has invested in connectivity projects both at home and in the neighbourhood. It is simultaneously trying to improve trade infrastructure, i.e. building integrated check posts and negotiating free trade regimes and expanding trade in service. It has adopted multifaceted approach to regional cooperation – bilateral, trilateral, subregional and regional mechanisms to implement various connectivity projects for integrating the region. It is true that China's BRI and its ability to provide an alternative to the smaller countries' dependence on India has successfully blunt India's ability to use the disaffected ethnic and political groups to pressurise the ruling regimes in the neighbourhood for their political accommodation. Interestingly, China's military footprint was prominently visible in South Asia much before its economic diplomacy took root. As the process of democratisation has gained currency in the region with the dismantling of military and other authoritarian regimes, the policy of economic development has become a new code word for China's engagement. Therefore, prosperity and development have overtaken the security narrative. However, at the end, economic presence makes a compelling case for securing assets and also, like India, China will have a stake in political stability by pursuing regime stability as was seen in Nepal in 2020. The difference between India and China is that both seek stability for different reasons. For India, stability would ensure the dimension of domestic conflict in each of the neighbouring countries does not have a spillover effect on India's security and stability. For China, regime stability would ensure a return on its investment and in some countries, especially in Nepal, it would additionally mean to rein in the Tibetan refugees so that they do not pose a threat to Chinese interest.

China's relation with South Asia has often been a point of friction between New Delhi and its South Asian neighbours, especially so after the 1962 India–China war. While during the cold war period India had to contend with other external powers, in the post cold war period China remains the main contender to India's natural pre-eminence in the region. Its close strategic ties with Pakistan, a country it has nurtured as a strategic balancer to India in South Asia, has now prodded India to think of a possibility of a two-front war in the future. However, of late, China's presence in the region also has a salutary influence over India's bilateral relations and has pushed India to gear up its delivery mechanism from the usual sluggishness to act and deliver faster on its promises and wherever possible, to simplify the official mechanism to facilitate trade and transit. To the South Asian neighbours, China's presence has compelled India to act swiftly and its infamous ability to not take decisions and often sit over issues for a long period of time. Most of the neighbours have benefitted by engaging both and have deftly played their rivalry to profit or gain. Bangladesh is one of the countries that has successfully engaged the two countries to a very large extent,[2] unlike other countries of the region with the exception of Bhutan.

India and China are not only competing for influence but are also looking for markets for their exports of the finished product. This compels them to scout for resources to fuel their economy to meet both domestic and external demands. As a result, they are competing in both Asia and Africa building infrastructures and investing in development. China's policy of extracting mineral resources for exporting them to China has often come under criticism. The two countries therefore share a relationship of "congagement" – which is both conflict and engagement. While the two countries have a dispute over their boundaries and fought a war in 1962, they are also engaged in expanding bilateral trade which is going to touch US$100 billion. However, this may change as China's creeping territorial expansion in Ladakh has exposed the limitations of the India-China relationship. This is going to have several implications for India's policy towards the South Asian region. India is apprehensively watching the growing Chinese presence in the region and its likely implications for India's strategy in the neighbourhood. It is slowly acknowledging the Chinese presence as a strategic reality in South Asia. The possibility of China actively playing a role to the detriment of India is now a reality. China's presence in the region has a larger global context. It wants to emerge as a global hegemon and an unchallenging power in Asia and it sees India as a major threat to its desire to emerge as sole hegemon. India's growing close relationship with South Korea and Vietnam and economic partnership with Japan is seen as a major challenge to China and indicate its growing clout. India continues to adopt a hedging policy towards China and is reluctant to enter into any relationship with major powers that would change the dynamics of its bilateral relations with China. Chinese occupation of territory in Ladakh, in spite of their decision to gradually disengage, is going to bring a strategic shift in India's posture. It would now keenly watch Beijing's relations with the countries of the region.

China's ability and willingness to invest without political strings or preconditions and its capacity to efficiently complete projects remain a major attraction for the countries in South Asia which are looking for investments and also perceive China as a strategic ally to cope with an uncertain future. Comparatively, India's decision-making apparatus has been sluggish and at times it has struggled to complete projects and has to contend with the escalation costs which can largely be attributed to the slow implementation of projects. Therefore, India suffers from a delivery deficit even though the majority of its credit line has an interest rate which is less than 1% and a part of its credit line sometimes is converted into a grant. The bureaucratic lethargy and red tapism coupled with shoestring budget only add to the delivery deficit. While China's role in the region has expanded dramatically since the end of the cold war, India is grappling with the much advertised "neighbourhood first" policy. Though India has taken few steps to address the delivery deficit and is engaged in mutually beneficial projects to tailor it to the shoestring budget, in no way it can match China's purse. Many in India's foreign policy establishment argue that New Delhi does not need to match China's investment per dollar; nevertheless, there is a recognition of India's lack of capacity to implement projects in time due to various reasons, including extraneous factors and domestic politics in the host countries where it has invested or propose to invest – for example: the Ramphal power project in Bangladesh, the agreement on Trincomalee Oil Tank or the Eastern Container terminal in Sri Lanka where the government has disregarded the MoU. All these projects that the host government approved have become part of domestic political contestation either over environmental concern as is the case with opposition to Rampal or it is general opposition to Indian investment due to partisan politics in Sri Lanka. This brings in five questions that this chapter seeks to examine. What is the nature of China's role in the region? To what extent China's presence impinges on India's geo-strategic interest? What are the likely consequences of Chinese investment? What is India's approach to the neighbourhood and finally should India be worried about China's regional role?

Nature of China's engagement in the region

As Michael Vlahos pointed out in his article titled "Strategy and the sacred narrative in the context of US's wars," "Narrative is actually the foundation of all strategy, the foundation on which all else – policy, rhetoric, and action – is built."[3] Though this is true given this is the age of social media, narratives are often a method of strategic communication aimed at attracting the attention of the elites and those who have an interest on the issue. Two factors make the narrative portent, which helps its translation into intended objectives. Firstly, the strategic environment that shapes it and, secondly, the perceived threat perception that takes into account the past omissions and commissions and the shift in the global power structure. The strategic environment in the South Asian region is greatly shaped by India's geographical location: India shares border with each of the South Asian countries, and except for Pakistan and Afghanistan, none have a border with another country in the region. To a large extent, this has resulted, naturally so, in numerous bilateral disputes over borders – largely a British colonial legacy, and also India's own strategic vision that has frequently been in conflict with its neighbours. This conflict over India's vision of security which often is contrary to its neighbours' perception has created a strategic mismatch. Added to this narrative is the legacy of partition and centrality of religion that portrayed "Hindus" and "Muslims" are separate and incompatible "nations." This often creates a space for distrust and suspicion and India is labelled as an "enemy" which needs to be contested, contended and balanced. This strategic distrust, though contributed by India's omissions and commissions, is largely shaped by the ruling elites in the neighbourhood who sometimes see India as a challenge to their regime interest, has been at the root of the success of China's economic-strategic foray into South Asia. The main argument of this chapter is, given the carefully constructed narratives spawned by the strategic elite in the neighbourhood and also taking into account the presence of China and its interest to project itself as a counterbalance to India in the region, India needs to calibrate a strategy to further its economic interest and engage in "beneficial bilateralism" wherever possible and draw a redline between the issues that directly impinge on its strategic interest and economics of trade and investment.

The dominant narrative in South Asia is that China is a "benign" neighbour that wants to help the countries and it has no intention to dabble in the domestic politics and treats small and weaker powers as sovereign equal. This, even though not true as the cases in Nepal and Sri Lanka proves,[4] has facilitated acceptability of China's presence and has furthered its interest. Conversely, it has equally helped the South Asian countries to unquestionably engage China without raising suspicion domestically on the nature of the engagement. In most of the countries, China enjoys bipartisan support of the political parties. Though one can analyse to what extent this narrative holds ground, but such a general perception does exist in South Asia and perception matters in contested polity where political factions vie to politically undermine the other.[5] Compared to India, which is not only the dominant power in the region but also shares its border with most of the South Asian countries, the classical "balancing game" can be seen playing out vis-à-vis South Asian countries' relations with China.

China's presence provides a psychological assurance. Beijing's relationship with the militaries in the region is especially important, given that the military in many countries are dominant actors in politics and they are also nationalistic force whose strategic doctrine is modelled on India as an enemy. China's role in the region gets further enhanced due to the pursuant of this doctrine. Unlike China's approach in the 1980s, when there was a rapprochement with India at work and China followed a policy of not undermining India's relations with its neighbours or taking sides in the bilateral disputes that the South Asian countries had with India. To quote an eminent China watcher,

> China's assertion of its right to multidimensional relations with its South Asian neighbours is tempered by a pragmatic realization that if it asserts those rights too vigorously, relations with India will suffer. Throughout the 1980s Beijing understood that, to some degree, it had to choose between thicker relations with the smaller countries of South Asia and better relations with India.[6]

However, this is not the case now. China's economy is five times more than India's, unlike in 1980 when they enjoyed economic parity.

China's relations with South Asia are multidimensional. It not only has close economic relations, but has also emerged as the largest trading partner to many countries of the region. It also has close military ties with the militaries of South Asia. Two of the countries in the region, Pakistan and Bangladesh, are respectively the largest and second largest receiver of weapons from China. It shares extensive strategic relations with the militaries who often portray India as a threat, given the nature of their conflict with India or their fear of India's dominance or to protect their institutional interest. Without a threat perception budgetary support to the militaries, it is feared it would be miniscule. This also enables the military to purchase weapons from the international market and have a say in strategic decision-making. Apart from the perceived strategic requirements, China also wants to expand its market for selling weapons and it has emerged as an important partner for the armies in the region. China always had a strategic interest in the region as proved by its nuclear nexus with Pakistan. However, from the perspectives of India's neighbours, they clearly perceive a balancing role for China even though they appear to have engaged China to develop infrastructure and ports and invest in the energy sector. According to China's defence White Paper released in July 2019,

> Overseas interests are a crucial part of China's national interests. One of the missions of China's armed forces is to effectively protect the security and legitimate rights and interests of overseas Chinese people, organizations and institutions. ... To address deficiencies in overseas operations and support, it builds far seas forces, develops overseas logistical facilities, and enhances capabilities in accomplishing diversified military tasks.[7]

Therefore, the Chinese presence has clear strategic intent and is oriented towards boosting its power projection to achieve the mentioned objectives.

Politics and constructing strategic narratives in the neighbourhood: making space for China

It is significant to understand the prevalent narrative in India's neighbourhood to understand why China has found it convenient and enjoys conducive atmosphere to expand its strategic footprint. It is true that most of the countries in South Asia are dependent on investment to create connectivity network that would boost their economy. Modern infrastructure is an essential part of growing economies. China does have the capacity to fulfil those requirements in cash-strapped countries in India's neighbourhood. However, it is incorrect to assume that it does not have strategic intent as elites in some of India's neighbourhood try to explain. Rather China's presence is sought to balance India. While any investment proposal from India is critically evaluated by the elites in the neighbouring countries in terms of debt, it may create or benefit that may accrue to the country, such scrutiny of China's investment is completely lacking. Or at least, one did not see any opposition to China's developmental activities in the region. For example, India's proposal to invest in Trincomalee oil tanks or its proposal to build a port at Kankesanthurai or develop the Eastern Container Terminal (ECT) of the Colombo port is seen from the point of view of undermining of sovereignty and various motives are attributed to India's keenness to investment.[8] In fact, the MoU on ECT has been held in abeyance as Sri Lanka decided to develop the ECT on its own after politically motivated protest took place.[9]

Some countries have however started to look at Chinese investment critically in terms of the debt burden it may create after Hambantota port was leased out to China for 99 years.[10] Interestingly, Hambantota Port was not seen as a sovereignty issue by those who are protesting against India's investment proposal in Sri Lanka. Even though the issue of leasing Hambantota was an election issue in the presidential election of 2019 in Sri Lanka, President Gotabaya said he would renegotiate the lease deed if he is elected to power. However, after election, he announced that there would be no revision of the treaty, yet this announcement did not receive any criticism in Sri Lanka. The possible reason is China is seen as a balancer to India's regional role. And India has not hesitated to make it clear that it has a stake in domestic stability and inclusive government in the neighbourhood so that the cross-border ethno-cultural linkages and political disaffection should not emerge as a security liability for India. India has been home to the refugees from the neighbourhood given the ethno-cultural linkages between the people of the subcontinent.

Stability is an important consideration for India in its neighbourhood policy. India looks at any conflict in the neighbourhood from the security point of view and examines the extent of its impact on its own security. It has been extremely important to see that this conflict does not have a spillover effect on its own security. In the past, external powers have been keen to intervene in these conflicts to furthering their regional interest. Since independence, this quest for stability and security has made India look at the presence of external powers with suspicion. India's fear of external powers ability to intervene/influence developments in the region which could directly impinge on India's security interests has not just governed India's approach to South Asia but has also shaped the response of India's neighbours. In this equation, China has emerged as a major strategic balancer, especially in the context of the apprehensions that China has about India's close relations with the United States and their rivalry with China. The South Asia political strategic ecosystem has helped China to move in and it is willing to collaborate with India's neighbours to keep New Delhi embroiled in South Asia, which could clip its ambition to play a larger global role. The Sino-India border dispute has only added to the intensification of this rivalry and India's suspicion of Beijing's intent. It is true that China's desire to emerge as a dominant power and its strategic and nuclear nexus with Pakistan is geared towards checkmating India's emergence as a power in Asia which China has to contend with in its path to global dominance. In the post-Cold War period, one observes a new trend where in some cases neighbours have engaged both these countries for political, economic and strategic reasons and have tried not to fall into their bilateral relational dynamics, whereas in other cases China is projected as a countervailing power to checkmate India when a particular regime is threatened. Some examples would suffice this argument: Prime Minister Oli of Nepal seeking China's help to counter India's "blockade" in 2015, Mahinda Rajapaksa's cultivation of China to restrain India's possible diplomatic intervention on behalf of the Tamils or Abdullah Yameen, former President of Maldives move to embrace

China when he faced international criticism over his treatment of opposition and democracy in the Maldives.

The strategic narrative in the neighbourhood has demonstrated that China provides a strategic cushion to India's neighbours in terms of strengthening militaries of these countries. Since India is portrayed as a threat to all the neighbouring countries, baring Bhutan, China becomes a security provider in traditional military terms. Each time a neighbouring country has faced a political challenge, they have reached out to China to make Delhi uneasy and have played the China card as a strategic retaliation to India's policies. These are sovereignty-enhancing strategy because of the asymmetric size of the countries in the neighbourhood vis-à-vis India. Therefore, it is not surprising to see the joint statements that China and the neighbouring countries produce after each high-level visits that contain phrase like "sovereign equality," "non-interference," etc., which one does not find in any other joint statements that China has made with any other countries. For example, the joint statement with Nepal, "The Chinese side reiterated its firm support to Nepal in upholding the country's independence, sovereignty and territorial integrity."[11] Compare this with Prime Minister Narendra Modi's visit to Nepal. The joint statement reads cooperation on the "basis of the principles of equality, mutual trust, respect and mutual benefit."[12] During Xi's visit to Nepal in October 2019, to enhance security, the two countries have signed an agreement on Boundary Management System, which will improve the level of boundary management and cooperation for both sides.

Nepal which shares an open border with India and has a 1950 Treaty of Peace and Friendship that governs its bilateral relationship has often sought China as a balancer. It was not only during the Panchayat regime that the relationship with China flourished as Tibet ceased to exist as an independent country, but such relationship with China continued after Nepal's transition to democracy. It received a boost when communist regimes were elected to power. This is in spite of the fact that India supported the democratic movement in Nepal and the Nepalese politicians shared close relations with their ideological brothers in India and India was instrumental in the mainstreaming of the Maoist and was chief architect of the 12-point programme that saw the end of monarchy in Nepal. Nepal's monarchy, which shares close familial ties with the royal families in India, has never hesitated to develop a close relationship with China, arguing that Nepal wants to maintain equidistance with both countries. After the transition to constitutional monarchy and democracy, India became a factor in Nepal's domestic politics. As the two main parties contested, they tried to leverage their relations with India and China. For example, Nepali Congress (NC) tried to exploit its closeness with Indian leaders, while the Communist Party of Nepal tried to engage China closely to counter NC and India. Depending on the support base, one saw the emergence of contested narratives. Coupled with the issues of nationalism, the question of Madheshis, perceived treatment and reception of Nepali leaders, alleged Indian interference created an environment of mistrust and suspicion. China, which often questions the 1950 Treaty by saying that it undermined Nepal's sovereignty and indirectly encouraged to question this treaty emerged as a strategic balancer.

In the context of Sri Lanka, China is an important strategic partner. It has often been argued that their relations go back to Rice-Rubber pact of 1952. Sri Lanka had always been keen to partner a third power against the perceived threat from India that is historically etched in the mind of Sri Lankans: whether it was signing a defence pact with the British to use Trincomalee and Katunayaka or later allowing the Americans to open a Voice of American transmission network in Trincomalee. Except for UNP government led by Dudley Senanayake, the government of Jayawardane like his predecessor Sirimavo followed a policy of cultivating China and Pakistan to establish his credential and demonstrate that he is following independent foreign policy. Whether it was the decision to allow refuelling of Pakistani aircraft during the 1971 war which one analyst argued was necessary "for the integrity of Pakistan and the preservation of the existing balance of power in South Asia" as "one of the cardinal principles"[13] of Sri Lanka's foreign policy or Sri Lanka's policies in the early 1980s when it was facing Tamil militancy. China saw Sri Lanka's effort to militarily deal with the Tamil insurgency as its effort to preserve its independence, territorial integrity and sovereignty and in November 1985, it sent a 3000-ton guided-missile destroyer and a supply ship for a friendly visit.[14] Coinciding with Sino-Indian rapprochement, it refrained from making any strong statement on 1987 Indo-Lanka Accord. However, China has renewed closer relationship with Sri Lanka, especially since mid-2000 when its strategic presence became more visible. China perceived the close Indo-US ties may create problem for it in the Indian Ocean. Moreover, China was expanding its navy and had an ambition to expand to the Indian Ocean to overcome its Malacca Straits dilemma. It not only provided weapons to the Sri Lankan armed forces but also facilitated Pakistan's supply of weapons when India refused to sign a Defence Agreement with Sri Lanka during the war with the LTTE due to the pressure exerted by Tamil Nadu. As India confined itself to supply of "non-lethal" weapon – which provided critical intelligence that was crucial for Sri Lanka's victory – China emerged as a winner – a true friend – in public perception in Sri Lanka. Both India and Sri Lanka for domestic political reasons did not want to publicly acknowledge the help that India extended. China has close military ties and has become one of the largest exporters of defence weapons to Sri Lanka. It has recently gifted a Frigate to the Sri Lankan navy. The berthing of Chinese nuclear submarine in Colombo Port created an uproar in India and brought to the fore the security threat that Sri Lanka with the help of China can pose to India. India has now developed close ties with Sri Lankan Army, but unlike China, its supply of defence weapons has been confined to radars, two offshore patrol vehicles and its gift of a coast guard patrol vehicle. India has training programme for the Sri Lankan army and it also conducts military exercises – SLINEX, trilateral Dosti series of exercise and Mitrashakti series of exercise, apart from Annual Defence Dialogue. However, India's stand on the ethnic issue would determine the future of India–Sri Lanka relations and the relevance of China in this context.

Maldives's relation with Sri Lanka has deepened only in recent times during Abdullah Yameen's regime. Though India is not seen as a threat traditionally, but during Yameen's rule India was perceived as an adversary. Yameen government perceived India as close ally of his main political opponent, the outgoing President Mohammad Nashid. India was very vocal about the political developments in Maldives. For example, the then External Affairs Minister Sushma Swaraj said, "maintaining public trust required strong adherence to due process and therefore, the space for legitimate political dissent must be safeguarded." During his visits to India, though Yameen emphasised on Maldives' "India first" policy, in reality the government did everything to undermine India's interest – whether it was annulling the GMR contract to build Ibrahim Nasir airport or signing the first FTA with China without consulting the Parliament. In spite of former President Nasheed's twitter appeal to India to intervene in Maldives, India took a cautionary stand. China, which has growing stakes in Maldives, accumulated especially during Abdullah Yameen rule, was quick to issue a statement that cautioned against any interference in Maldives' internal affair. This illustrates how China builds its relations with regime without acknowledging those who contest the regime from below. China has built a bridge that connects Male to the airport, it is building Ibrahim Naseer Airport and a hospital worth US$140 million. According to the Finance Ministry, "data show that these guarantees amount to US$935 million, on top of the US$600 million directly owed to Beijing by the government,"[15] which has created a debt trap for Maldives.

Bangladesh's threat perception has primarily determined its relations with China. China which recognised Bangladesh only in 1975 moved in swiftly taking advantage of the deteriorating Bangladesh-India relations in the post-Mujib period. Bangladesh army, which took over power after Mujib's death, was unhappy with Mujib's decision to sign a 25-year Treaty of Peace and Friendship with India in 1972 since it felt that such a treaty goes against the institutional interest of the army and was aimed at weakening the army. Therefore, China emerged as a balancer to India during the military regime of Zia-ur-Rahman. It helped the Bangladesh Army to emerge as an effective fighting force through supply of weapons. As it stands today, Bangladesh is the second largest receiver of defence weapons from China and in recent years such weapons include frigate, submarine and tanks. China also fits into Bangladesh's narrative that sees India as an adversary having the offensive capability to inflict a defeat on Bangladesh with which it shares more than 4000 km of porous border. Army-to-army cooperation between Bangladesh and China is close which includes training. There is a growing opposition to any close defence cooperation with India. The elites in Dhaka, who never questioned the 2001 Bangladesh-China defence cooperation agreement, are opposed to any idea of close defence collaboration with India.[16] While the detail of Bangladesh's defence agreement with China is not public, the elites speculate about secret agreement with India in spite of MoUs being publicly available. On the issue of military-to-military cooperation, merits of China's huge supply of weapons, including frigates and submarines, rarely raises eyebrows; yet India's extension of US$500 million defence credit line agreement to set up coastal surveillance system has drawn sharp criticism from the detractors of the ruling regime on the ground of the quality of the system, its impact on its security and debts it incurs.[17] This is notwithstanding the fact that India has supplied defence equipment to all other neighbours except for Pakistan. Therefore, it is obvious that India is seen as an adversary which needs to be balanced with China. In this context, India's defence cooperation with Bangladesh remains minimal. In 2017, it has also signed several MoUs for cooperation and training between the militaries of the two countries. It has Sampriti series of anti-terror exercises and coordinated patrol between the navies which commenced in 2018. However, cooperation among the border forces has been strengthened in recent years with the introduction of coordinated border patrol and meeting of District Commissioners/District Magistrates and Police Chiefs serving in the border region of both the countries.

Pakistan is the only country in South Asia whose relations with China has been shaped by its antagonism towards India. Since the signing of 1963 border agreement with China, the relationship has deepened further. China has become an alternative to the United States as far as defence and security of Pakistan is concerned. The deep relationship has fructified in terms of close collaboration in nuclear and missile development. China has helped Pakistan to emerge as a challenge to India in South Asia. The India–Pakistan conflict has allowed China to move India's focus away from its territorial problem it has with China. Its current proposed investment of US$62 billion is likely to make the bond stronger even though many see it as debt trap which will push Pakistan to become a colony of China. However, the Ladakh crisis has brought to fore how China is nibbling away Indian territory slowly, each time contesting the LAC by making slow military advancement through aggressive patrolling and a possibility of two front war cannot be ruled out.

The development narrative: engaging India and China

Over the period of time, India's South Asian neighbours have started to look at both India and China from developmental perspective and have weighed their importance in terms of their support to various developmental projects in their countries. For example, Bangladesh development priorities have determined the contours of its engagement with India and China while being extremely careful to stay away from their strategic rivalry. During the military rule Bangladesh sought to balance India since it clearly saw New Delhi's close relationship with the deposed Mujib regime with suspicion. It forged close military ties with China to counter India while constructing India's image within the "hegemonic" framework. The discourse on power and balance emerged as a strategy of the ruling military regimes and the same approach was adopted by the Bangladesh

Nationalist Party that based its electoral politics on opposing India and befriending China. China's Belt and Road Initiative found supporters in Bangladesh, who saw Beijing's initiative from the economic perspective and dismissed its strategic content. Many in Bangladesh argue in favour of close relationship with China due to its capacity to bring in huge amount of investment. Some analysts often compare the small investment of India and the huge investment proposed by China to point why China is preferred. While Indian investment in each of the sectors is contested, Chinese investment is often seen as beneficial. In spite of this, India has extended US$7.5 billion credit line to Bangladesh which is mostly invested in developing connectivity network that would economically transform the region. It has High-Impact Community Development Projects that are operated under Indian grant-in-aid. Apart from transport connectivity, both the countries are engaged in energy trade and collaborating in subregional cooperation. Therefore, economic cooperation and development partnership has been cornerstone of India-Bangladesh bilateral relations often overshadowing the likely repercussion of China's dominance in defence sector from the security point of view.

Anti-Indianism, which is often synonymous for Nepali nationalism, has emerged as a tool to push back India and raise suspicion on Indian investment. Like other South Asian countries, Chinese investments are encouraged to "teach India" a lesson for its "hegemonic ambition" and its "expansionist" desire and "imperialist motives." China's investment and interference are not seen as transgression of Nepal's sovereignty or exploitation of its resources as is the case with India. Rather, Nepal-China Joint Commission on Economy and Trade has been established to facilitate trade and investment. The economic content of India-Nepal relations is deep. The fact that Nepal has 25 border entry points and has a free border speaks of the voluminous relationship. The economic relationship has been cemented by familial ties, this is only area where China cannot match, yet it is another issue that India has not been able to leverage. In investment, India cannot match China.[18] In 2019, China emerged as the largest investor.[19] It is building an international airport at Pokhra even though cooperation on West Seti Hydropower project has been halted for the time being.

Though China has emerged as a security partner of Sri Lanka, its economy forays have larger strategic implications. It is developing the Colombo Port city project where it has reclaimed land from the sea and is building a modern port city, it has now taken over the Hambantota Port on 99 years lease as a part of debt-equity swap,[20] 15,000 hectare of land to develop it to special economic zone and built the Mattala Airport in Hambantotta, Colombo International Container Terminal as part of Colombo South Harbour expansion project where the Chinese Company has 85% stake, Jaya Container Terminal (JCT) and Port City in Colombo at the cost of US$1.4 billion and roads. Chinese investment in Sri Lanka is to the tune of US$7 billion as per some estimates. Most of these projects are yet to become economically viable to help the Sri Lankan government to pay back the debt. In contrast to China, India's investment has been minimal. Its aid is confined to the reconstruction of houses in the war-ravaged area, rebuilding of Jaffna library and laying of railway tracks. However, its commercial projects and investment are yet to take off as there is a resistance to allow India to have a stake in Trincomalee oil tank, develop Palali airport and Kankesanthurai Port as India is seen as a stakeholder in Island's ethnic conflict. The Island nation will face the dilemma to engage India in developing large projects but when it does, it would balance it with Chinese investment.

Should India be worried?

The question here is what does China's presence means for India and whether India can or should prevent China's presence in the South Asian neighbourhood. Therefore, should India be worried?

Since 2000, China has made its presence through large-scale investment in the neighbourhood. Some of its presence is shaped by the shift in global geo-politics and China's own power calculation. While its presence and close ties with Nepal is borne out of the fact that it perceives its Tibetan region being vulnerable to the threat from the south given the presence of Tibetan refugees in Nepal. With the help of Nepal however, it has addressed the issue of the Tibetan refugees who use Nepal border with China to reach Kathmandu. It also took Nepal's help in curbing anti-China activities by Tibetan refugees. Therefore, China has vital security interest at stake in Nepal. However, many in India argue that the issue of border dispute with India and Prime Minister Oli's decision to ratchet up conflict with India by publishing a new map has been done with the instigation of China or Nepal's ability to challenge India has the support of Beijing. This deterioration of Nepal's relations with India is to the advantage of Beijing. In the context of Bangladesh, it has traditional security ties and China's economic ties are linked to economic development of its periphery and linking it to the nearest seaport. Its presence in Sri Lanka is linked to its Indian Ocean strategy to prevent domination of the Indian Ocean by any power which will affect its maritime trade. It should also be seen from the perspective of shift in global politics. Its presence in Maldives is also part of its larger Indian Ocean strategy. However, its focus on Pakistan is not only geared towards linking its restive Xinxiang region to Gwadar and Middle East but it also has a significant Indian dimension. Given the dynamics of India-China relations, China's presence in the neighbourhood impinges on India primacy in South Asia. It will motivate these countries not to resolve their internal issues, which will have repercussion to India's stability given the cross-border ethnic ties. Moreover, India's neighbours perceive India's growing ties with the United States as being directed against China, which they feel would empower India both in regional and global context.

While India should not be unnecessarily worried about the economic transaction that China has, it will certainly be concerned about a Hambantota type of situation where economic vulnerability of the countries in the region and their inability to profit from Chinese investment can lead to China's takeover of strategic asset. This would lead to robust presence of China in the neighbourhood. China's investment would facilitate its political presence. As a result, India's ability to empathise with marginalised groups and their aspiration for inclusion in governance may not materialise. For example, after 2015, India has tried to distance itself from the issue of marginalisation of Madheshis and its approach to Tamils in Sri Lanka has been to adhere to 1987 accord – which remains part of intense domestic politics that swings between Sinhala majoritarianism and Tamil political aspiration. It is not surprising that Tamils are now interested in internationalising the issue realising Indian constraints. China's presence has constrained India in its approach to some of these issues, however, this in the future may lead to larger internationalisation opening up space for external power intervention which India historically tried to prevent.

Conclusion

It is difficult for India to prevent China's presence in South Asia. Therefore, India needs to look at its bilateral relations with its neighbours on the basis of its own merit and the potential it has for expanding it further. It needs to reinvigorate its ties and take a holistic approach rather than having preference for particular parties and leaders. Over a period of time, India has tried to break this party preference and has tried to establish contact with all the important political actors in the neighbourhood. Role of India in the neighbourhood should be seen from the perspective of India being a stakeholder in stability. Whether it was midwifing the 12-point agreement between the political parties of Nepal in 2006 or the Chittagong Hill Tracts (CHT) Accord in 1997 which saw peace in CHT of Bangladesh or its attempt to bring peace in Sri Lanka in 1987 by signing Indo-Lanka Accord, India would remain crucial to the stability in the neighbourhood as neighbours would be crucial for India. The close socio-economic ties that India shares with its neighbours will help it to overcome mistrust that may crop up from time to time. Rather than being complacent, India needs to work on the delivery deficit where even small projects get delayed for long time. It is not about matching each dollar for dollar invested by China. Rather, it is implementing projects in time. After the establishment of Development Partnership Administration, such delivery deficit to some extent has been bridged.

Should India be worried about the China's presence? Perhaps not. Security has many dimensions. In the context of non-traditional security like terrorism, humanitarian assistance disaster relief and given the geographical proximity, India will remain a significant partner of its South Asian neighbours. It can reach them in the time of natural calamities. In the recent past, both China and India have reached out to South Asia to help them to battle COVID-19 pandemic. India vaccine diplomacy is also a case in point. India supplied COVID-19 vaccine to Bhutan, Bangladesh, Nepal, Sri Lanka, Afghanistan and Myanmar as part of its "neighbourhood first" policy. China's incursion in 2020, however, would deepen India's strategic suspicion of China. While it may have reservation about China's presence, India needs to draw security redline and should take up issues with its neighbour when it directly impinges on its security rather than merely objecting to China's economic and strategic ingress. The more India shows its concern, the greater is the propensity of some of the regimes in the region to engage China as a method of strategic communication. India needs to play the balancing game with China elsewhere than in South Asia.

Notes

1 Ministry of Foreign Affairs, Japan, *White Paper on Development Cooperation 2018*, https://www.mofa.go.jp/files/100004330.pdf, accessed 21 February 2021.
2 Smruti S. Pattanaik, "Engaging the Asian Giants: India, China and Bangladesh's Crucial Balancing Act", *Issues & Studies: A Social Science Quarterly on China, Taiwan, and East Asian Affairs*, vol. 55, no. 2, June 2019.
3 Michael E. Vlahos, "Strategy and the Sacred Narrative", *American Intelligence Journal*, vol. 25, no. 2, Winter 2007/2008, p. 4.
4 In Sri Lanka, during the 2015 election, there were posters pasted behind tri-rickshaws (tuk-tuk) explaining how China's investment has created job in Sri Lanka. Many saw this as a bid to support Rajapakse. In Nepal, the Chinese Ambassador met top Nepali leaders, ostensible to discuss China-Nepal relations and this visit came amidst the political crisis within the NCP. However, after the meeting with the Chinese Ambassador, the two sides patched up and Prime Minister Oli continued as Prime Minister. "Chinese Ambassador Meets Ruling NCP's Top Leaders", *My Republica*, 1 May 2020, https://myrepublica.nagariknetwork.com/news/chinese-ambassador-meets-ruling-ncp-s-top-leaders/
5 For details on China's engagement with Nepal, Sri Lanka and Maldives, see Smruti S. Pattanaik, "India's Policy Response to China's Investment and Aid to Nepal, Sri Lanka and Maldives: Challenges and Prospects", *Strategic Analysis*, vol. 43, no. 3, 2019, pp. 246–52.
6 John W. Garver, "China and South Asia", *The Annals of the American Academy of Political and Social Science*, vol. 519, 1992, p. 73.
7 The State Council, "China's National Defense in the New Era", 24 July 2019, http://english.www.gov.cn/archive/whitepaper/201907/24/content_WS5d3941ddc6d08408f502283d.html.
8 The workers of the Port Authority on 2nd July threatened to go on an indefinite strike if the government allowed a foreign country to develop the Eastern Container Terminal (ECT) and accused that India is preventing Sri Lanka to develop the ECT on its own. PTI, "Sri Lankan Port Workers End Protest over Alleged 'Indian Pressure' after Talks with PM Rajapaksa", *Deccan Herald*, 3 July 2020, www.deccanherald.com/international/sri-lankan-port-workers-end-protest-over-alleged-indian-pressure-after-talks-with-pm-rajapaksa-856570.html

Also see Reuters, "Sri Lanka's Oil Firm Workers Call Off Strike over India Deal", *Financial Times*, 25 April 2017, https://www.financialexpress.com/world-news/sri-lankas-oil-firm-workers-call-off-strike-over-india-deal/640876/
9 Spokesperson of Indian Embassy Colombo said, ""I would like to reiterate the expectation of the Government of India for expeditious implementation of the trilateral Memorandum of Cooperation (MOC) signed in May 2019 among the Governments of India, Japan, and Sri Lanka for the development of ECT with participation from these three countries. The commitment of the Government of Sri Lanka in this regard has been conveyed several times in the recent past, including at the leadership level. Sri Lanka cabinet also took a decision three months ago to implement the project with foreign investors. All sides should continue to abide by the existing understandings and commitment." See *Sunday Times*, "Confusion Reigns as ECT Deal

Sinks and UNHRC Pressure Rises", 07 February 2021, http://www.sundaytimes.lk/210207/columns/confusion-reigns-as-ect-deal-sinks-and-unhrc-pressure-rises-431857.html

10. Tahir Mashhadi, Chairman of the Senate Standing Committee on Planning and Development, said, "Another East India Company is in the offing; national interests are not being protected. We are proud of the friendship between Pakistan and China, but the interests of the state should come first", see Syed Irfan Raza, "CPEC Could Become Another East India Company", *Dawn*, 18 October 2016, https://www.dawn.com/news/1290677

11. "Joint Statement between Nepal and the People's Republic of China", 13 October 2019, https://mofa.gov.np/joint-statement-between-nepal-and-the-peoples-republic-of-china-2/.

12. "India-Nepal Joint Statement during the State Visit of Prime Minister of India to Nepal, 11–12 May 2018", 12 May 2018, https://www.mea.gov.in/bilateral-documents.htm?dtl/29894/IndiaNepal_Joint_Statement_during_the_State_Visit_of_Prime_Minister_of_India_to_Nepal_May_1112_2018.

13. S. U. Kodikara, "Major Trends in Sri Lanka's Non-Alignment Policy after 1956", *Asian Survey*, vol. 13, no. 12, December 1973, p. 1134.

14. Garver, n. 6, p. 74.

15. Simon Mundi and Kathrin Hille, "The Maldives Counts the Cost of Its Debts to China", *Financial Times*, 11 February 2019, https://www.ft.com/content/c8da1c8a-2a19-11e9-88a4-c32129756dd8

16. List of Agreements/MoUs exchanged during the State Visit of Prime Minister of Bangladesh to India, see https://www.mea.gov.in/bilateral-documents.htm?dtl/28360/List_of_AgreementsMoUs_exchanged_during_the_State_Visit_of_PrimeMinister_of_Bangladesh_to_India_April_0710_2017https://mea.gov.in/bilateral-documents.htm?dtl/31911/IndiaBangladesh+Joint+Statement+during+Official+Visit+of+Prime+Minister+of+Bangladesh+to+India.

17. Khawaja Moin Uddin, "Bangladesh's Act of Balancing Asian Giant Foes", 13 October 2019, https://www.aa.com.tr/en/analysis/analysis-bangladesh-s-act-of-balancing-asian-giant-foes/1611893

18. Sanjeev Giri, "Nepal, China Sign Deal on OBOR", *Kathmandu Post*, 12 May 2017, https://kathmandupost.com/national/2017/05/12/nepal-china-sign-framework-deal-on-obor

19. "Over 90 Percent of Total FDI to Nepal Comes from China", *Xinhua*, 7 November 2019, http://www.xinhuanet.com/english/2019-11/07/c_138535703.htm

20. Maria Abi Habib, "How China Got Sri Lanka to Cough Up a Port", *New York Times*, 25 June 2018, https://www.nytimes.com/2018/06/25/world/asia/china-sri-lanka-port.html.

10
INDIAN MEDIA'S PERCEPTION OF CHINA

A montage of national and regional dailies

Rakhahari Chatterji and Anasua Basu Ray Chaudhury

Introduction

The print media in India, both national and regional, despite the strong presence of the electronic media, enjoys enormous reach and has great impact on the minds of its readers, enriching their information, shaping their perceptions and providing them with choices. Hence, among other things, undoubtedly it also has a role and a responsibility in creating proper understanding between neighbouring countries.[1] This is why an exploration of media perception with regard to China may be considered urgent and interesting.

This chapter is an attempt to examine the role of the media in achieving better perception of India's most important neighbour in the north, i.e. China. The objective of this chapter is twofold: firstly, it attempts to explore the perception of China that India's national and regional print media promote among its readers and, secondly, it makes a comparative assessment of media perception at the national and regional levels.

The national newspapers chosen from India are the following: *The Times of India*, *The Hindu*, *The Indian Express*, *The Economic Times* and *The Financial Express*. The first two rank first and second, respectively, in national circulation among English newspapers in India. *The Indian Express* has been selected as it is a nationally reputed paper, and the last two provide the perspective of economic reporting, at a time when trade relations are being prioritised by both countries. In each of these newspapers, the authors have looked at the editorial pieces relating to China – as these articles are indicative of a newspaper's overall perception.

For the regional print media, the selection was restricted to *The Assam Tribune* and *The Arunachal Times*, the two newspapers representing India's north-eastern border regions with China. For all the newspapers, apart from *The Assam Tribune* for which it became necessary to look into hard copies, the web versions were taken. Each day's publication in all these newspapers were examined for finding China-related editorials.

The analysis of editorials is a combination of quantitative and qualitative method. The time frame of the study was three years extending from 2012 to 2014, during which period both India and China witnessed leadership changes and the new leaders in both countries appeared equally determined to strengthen their bilateral ties. While widely publicised visits were taking place between the two countries and their leaders were meeting on the sidelines of other international fora regularly, border skirmishes of longer and shorter durations were also taking place, sometimes even during the high-profile visits. These years also marked two important policy changes: China's declaration of Belt and Road Initiative (BRI) and realignment of India's Look East into Act East policy. Expectedly, the media had enough fodder to grapple with during this period.

Before going into the issue of the print media's perception of China as projected through their editorials, two other issues were explored. It was necessary as well as interesting to know how much attention the print media paid to China-related issues, and, secondly, it was also important to know if Indian media's areas of concern vis-à-vis China could be identified and if it would be possible to classify those areas in terms of editorial themes. The following sections present the findings on these three issues for the national and regional newspapers.

Scoring editorial attention

A glimpse of national media

A total of 167 editorials from five national dailies could be considered China related. Of these, 30 were published in 2012, 41 in 2013, with sharp rise to 96 in 2014. The editorials studied covered a wide spectrum of issues ranging from geo-politics, strategy, India–China border, international institutions, trade and economy, environment and even Chinese domestic issues. To gain a robust understanding of national media's interest in India–China relations during the three years of 2012–2014, an "attention score" was devised. The attention score for each newspaper is computed by taking the number of editorials it has published every 365 days for these three years, multiplied by 100, to get a standardised score. According to this scale, a newspaper scoring 100 would have published at least one editorial piece on China every day of each year and a score of zero would mean it did not carry any editorial at all in the same period.

The Indian Express happens to be most attentive to China-related issues during the period under scrutiny followed by *The Hindu* and *The Times of India*. Amongst the financial newspapers, it was *The Economic Times* which expressed significant interest.

Table 10.1 presents the attention scores of individual newspapers for each year as well as the aggregated scores for the three-year period.

TABLE 10.1 Attention score of national dailies

Newspaper	2012	2013	2014	Aggregated score	Mean score
The Indian Express	1.37	5.48	7.67	14.52	4.84
The Times of India	1.92	1.64	3.01	6.57	2.19
The Hindu	1.09	1.37	6.02	8.48	2.83
The Economic Times	2.19	2.46	6.3	10.95	3.65
The Financial Express	1.64	0.27	3.28	5.19	1.73

Source: Prepared by the researchers working under the ORF project "Understanding public perception."

Table 10.1 shows that apart from marginal decline in attention score of *The Times of India* and *The Financial Express* in 2013, for all the newspapers under study it has moved upward during this time period. It also shows that the degree of attention has varied across the newspapers. The decline in attention of *The Times of India* and *The Financial Express* in 2013 is somewhat unexpected given that in that year there took place a number of more or less serious border incursions allegedly by China as well as the much acclaimed first foreign visit by the new Chinese Premier, Li Keqiang, to India.

Regional media's attention score at a glance

Compared to five national dailies' 167 editorials, the editorial count was 89 for two regional dailies (*The Arunachal Times* 31 and *The Assam Tribune* 58), i.e. on an average, the selected regional dailies have editorialised China more frequently than the national dailies during this time period. Starting with only 11 editorials in 2012, the number of editorials shot up to 38 in 2013 and remained in that neighbourhood with 40 editorials in 2014.

The Arunachal Times had the highest number of China-related editorials published in 2014 and *The Assam Tribune* had the highest number published in 2013. Looking at the attention score of each newspaper, it can be noted that *The Assam Tribune*'s aggregated score and mean score were higher than *The Arunachal Times*. However, the separate scores demonstrated that *The Arunachal Times* consistently increased its attention on China-related issues with highest score in 2014 while *The Assam Tribune*'s interest went up between 2012 and 2013 to register a slight fall in 2014 (see Table 10.2).

Interestingly, as mentioned, the number of editorials per newspaper from the border region of India was significantly more than the corresponding figure of the dailies located in the national capital. As a measure of editorial attention, it amounts to saying that the media near the India–China border show more sensitivity to China than their counterparts in Delhi. It is also apparent that the section of the print media under study, both national and regional, has shown increasing sensitivity to China-related issues over these years.

TABLE 10.2 Attention score of regional dailies

Newspaper	2012	2013	2014	Aggregated score	Mean score
The Arunachal Times	0.54	3.01	4.93	8.48	2.83
The Assam Tribune	2.46	7.39	6.02	15.87	5.29

Source: Prepared by the researchers working under the ORF project "Understanding public perception."

Editorial themes: exploring Indian media's areas of concern

To identify the editorial themes in the selected national and regional newspapers, it was necessary to decipher the substantive thrust of an editorial. While dealing with quantitative representation wherein the study had to convert the textual information into quantities, caution was taken to avoid or reduce subjectivity. A group of researchers coded the textual material separately following which they repeated it jointly with the objective of attaining as much inter-subjectivity as possible. By so doing, six distinct themes could be identified: "China as a Rising Power," "India–China Border," "Domestic" (i.e. domestic issues of China), "Economy," "Ecology" and "Connectivity" in both national and regional dailies. However, in national newspapers, yet another theme, apart from the aforesaid themes, "China–Pakistan" could also be found.

The themes in national and regional media

Out of 167 total editorials in the national newspapers we selected, 73 expressed concerns for "China as a Rising Power" compared to only 23 on "India–China border." Also, the concern for "China as a Rising Power" witnessed steady increase over the years with the highest number of editorials being published on it in 2014 (see Table 10.3). In this context, one can recall the moment of Chinese ascendance on global platform by 2012, in the face of financial meltdown in the West and how in the following years China increased its visibility in the international arena with reassertion of "Chinese dream" and declaration of the "One Belt One Road Project." Therefore, national media considered it was more important to discuss these emerging trends and their implications for Indian foreign policy rather than dwell on the long-standing India–China border issues. The theme of "China as a Rising Power" was quite influential and often seeped into other editorial themes like "India–China Border" or "Economy," "Ecology" and "Connectivity." For instance, border incursions were often explained in terms of aggressiveness commonly associated with great powers.

It was surprising that themes like "China–Pakistan" or "India–China Border" did not garner much editorial attention (see Table 10.3) despite their distinctly negative impact on India–China relations and occasional concern expressed by the Indian government. On the contrary, "Economy" emerged as the

TABLE 10.3 Editorials by themes by national newspaper (2012–2014)

Newspaper	China–Pakistan	India–China border	China as rising power	Economy	Ecology	Connectivity	Domestic	Total
The Indian Express	2	7	32	4	1	3	4	53
The Times of India	0	4	12	7	1	0	0	24
The Hindu	0	6	10	8	3	3	3	31
The Economic Times	0	6	12	8	0	4	4	40
The Financial Express	0	0	7	7	2	3	3	19
Total	2	23	73	34	7	14	14	167

Source: Prepared by the researchers working under the ORF project "Understanding public perception."

second dominant theme (34) distantly followed by "India–China Border" (23), "Connectivity" (14) and "Domestic" issues (14). Thus, national media was seen to be more attentive to the growing economic muscle of China and how that could benefit the lives of the people and contribute to healthier bilateral relations.

It is worth-mentioning in this context that most perception studies usually do not take into account the factor of geographical proximity in understanding perception. This chapter, however, finds that distance from/proximity to the border can have its impact on what issues are considered most urgent. Thus, examination of the regional newspapers finds that *The Arunachal Times* being published from Arunachal Pradesh, the north-eastern state bordering China, shows greater interest in India–China border issues and published 22 out of 31 editorials on "India–China Border" (see Table 10.4). Compared to India–China border theme, it published fewer editorials on ecology, economy and even on China as a rising power. *The Assam Tribune*, on the other hand, appeared highly sensitive to China's rising power in the neighbourhood for no other reason than the associated threat of muscle flexing near the border followed by its concern for border issues. This possibly was a reflection of the newspaper's sensitivity to the border incidents of 2013 and 2014 as also of the memory of 1962 conflict when its border was breached by the Chinese forces. Ecology/river as a theme has drawn some attention of *The Assam Tribune* – expectedly, due to a lot of news on China regarding the alleged diversion of the Brahmaputra waters – while remarkably little attention or interest has been shown by either of these regional newspapers to the highly talked about issue of connectivity. Apparently, given the presence of the more urgent issues like the border or China's rise as a great power, these newspapers probably felt that closer connectivity could have divergent, if not undesirable, implications for India and hence it should take a back seat for the present. Reflecting concerns specific to their state, *The Assam Tribune's* editorials

TABLE 10.4 Editorials by themes by regional newspaper

Newspaper	Themes						Total
	China as a rising power	India–China border	Ecology/river	Economy	Connectivity	China domestic	
The Arunachal Times	2 (6.45%)	22 (70.96%)	3 (9.67%)	3 (9.67%)	1 (3.22%)	0	31 (100)
The Assam Tribune	33 (56.89%)	9 (15.51%)	7 (12.06%)	4 (6.89%)	1 (1.72%)	4 (6.89%)	58 (100)
Total	35 (39.32%)	31 (37.34%)	10 (11.23%)	7 (7.86%)	2 (2.24%)	4 (4.49%)	89 (100)

Source: Prepared by the researchers working under the ORF project "Understanding public perception."

on "ecology" mostly discussed the Brahmaputra River's water sharing dispute putting it in the background of China's rising power.

Understanding editorial perception

The central question that this chapter is trying to answer is what kind of perception the print media in India was projecting about China: was it viewing China as a country friendly towards India, a country which India could approach with more trust than suspicion or was it looking at China as a threat for India? Summarily, could the media's projection of China through editorials be termed as positive or as negative?

Table 10.5 shows the distribution of the editorials for each of the selected national newspapers in terms of positive/negative projection of China. A deeper reading of the texts of the editorials under each theme for the national press revealed that 42.5% of the total number of editorials could be labelled as positively disposed towards China while 57.4% looked at China negatively. This, of course, is a binary view of perception and this way of looking at it may conceivably conceal varieties of nuances within what has been called positive and negative perceptions. One way to get around this problem was to classify each type of perception in terms of its intensity of expression, that is, how intensely a perception has been expressed.

Interestingly, the study finds (Figure 10.1) that out of 71 positive editorials in national dailies, 28% (20) could be qualified as "strongly positive," while out of 96 negative editorials only 25% (24) could be labelled as "strongly negative." That is to say, the newspapers wrote proportionally nearly the same number of editorials which could be labelled as "strong/positive" or "strong/negative." At the same time, while a greater number of editorials in national media portray China in a negative light in general, in three-fourth of such editorials the point is moderately or weakly made.

Contrary to national media's perception of China where the gap between positive and negative perception was narrow, the regional media demonstrated

TABLE 10.5 Perception by national newspapers, 2012–2014 (percentages in brackets)

Newspaper	Perception		Total
	Positive	Negative	
The Indian Express	16 (30.1%)	37 (69.8%)	53 (100%)
The Hindu	19 (61.2%)	12 (38.7%)	31 (100%)
The Times of India	8 (33.3%)	16 (66.6%)	24 (100%)
The Economic Times	19 (47.5%)	21 (52.5%)	40 (100%)
The Financial Express	9 (47.3%)	10 (52.6%)	19 (100%)
Total	**71 (42.5%)**	**96 (57.4 %)**	**167 (100%)**

Source: Prepared by the researchers working under the ORF project "Understanding public perception."

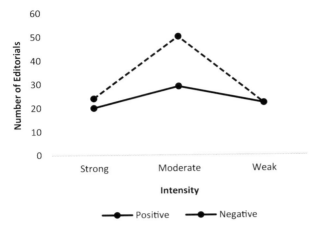

FIGURE 10.1 Perception by intensity in national newspapers, 2012–2014. *Source:* Prepared by the researchers working under the ORF project "Understanding public perception."

huge gap between its positive and negative perceptions of China (Table 10.6). Figure 10.2 shows the graphic representation of the intensity of the media perception. *The Arunachal Times* has written only 9 out of 31 editorials (29.03%) with a positive projection of China as against 22 (70.96%) editorials that are negative. *The Assam Tribune* has been even less charitable: its positive editorials constituted only 25.86% (15 out of 58) as against 74.13% (43 out of 58) editorials with a negative tone.

All of the positive editorials in *The Arunachal Times* were written with weak or moderate intensity (more weak than moderate), while 19 out of 22 negative

TABLE 10.6 Editorial perception by intensity by regional newspaper (2012–2014)

Newspaper	Intensity	Perception		Total
		Positive	Negative	
The Arunachal Times				
	Strong	0	11 (50%)	11 (35.48%)
	Moderate	3 (33.33%)	8 (36.36%)	11 (35.48%)
	Weak	6 (66.66%)	3 (13.63%)	9 (29.03%)
	Total	9 (100)	22 (100)	31 (100)
The Assam Tribune	Strong	2 (13.33%)	14 (32.55%)	16 (27.58%)
	Moderate	7 (46.66%)	18 (41.86%)	25 (43.10%)
	Weak	6 (40%)	11 (25.58%)	17 (29.31%)
	Total	**15 (100)**	**43 (100)**	**58 (100)**

Source: Prepared by the researchers working under the ORF project "Understanding public perception."

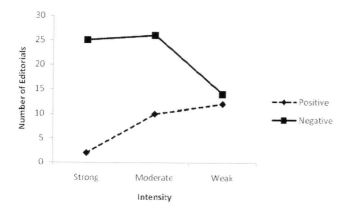

FIGURE 10.2 Perception by intensity in regional newspapers (2012–2014). *Source:* Prepared by the researchers working under the ORF project "Understanding public perception."

editorials (i.e. 86%) were strong or moderate (more strong than moderate). That is to say, when *The Arunachal Times* is writing negative editorials, it is doing so with a lot more assertion than when it is making a positive point about China. *The Assam Tribune*'s position is somewhat different: 86% of its positive editorials are moderate or weak, nearly evenly balanced, in contrast to 73% of its negative editorials which are strong or moderate. That is, its editorials, whether positive or negative, tend to be moderate and not extreme. This slight but noticeable difference between the two newspapers from these two Northeast Indian states could well be because of the existential threat posed by China to Arunachal Pradesh through official de-recognition of its belongingness to India. *The Assam Tribune*'s negativity is mostly because of historical reasons rather than due to any contemporary threat perception from China; thus, the intensity of its negative and positive editorials are relatively more evenly balanced.

Against this backdrop, it is important to see how different themes of editorials reflected the presence of positive and negative perceptions of China.

Elaboration through textual analysis

"China as a Rising Power"

As has been previously stated, "China as a Rising Power" emerged as the most dominant theme in national media during this three-year period (2012–2014). To convey China's forceful emergence on the global platform, editorials highlighted multiple aspects like China's economic growth, its strategic outreach or growing international political clout. Some editorials took a positive view of

China's global image, deeming it worthy of admiration and emulation. Yet most of them perceived China negatively and as a competitor and threat to India's geopolitical aspirations. This perception was explicit especially in editorials of 2012 where China's rise was stated as a challenge for India both economically and geo-strategically. As an editorial in *The Indian Express* argued, "China is likely to be around still and, in all likelihood, stronger than India economically and militarily."[2] *The Times of India* and *The Financial Express* were particularly vocal about the urgency of challenging China either by increasing trade ties with the Asian Tigers or by exploiting the economic space vacated due to China's increasing wage rates.[3] The impact of distrust on economic relations at the popular level was highlighted by *The Hindu* which, referring to a local feud between Indian and Chinese businessmen, argued that "trade has done precious little to remove the mistrust that pervades the relationship between India and China at the popular level."[4]

China's rise is palpably present in phrases like, "China as emerging economy," "China as economic super power," "(China) has shifted global axis of power eastwards" or "inexorable march of China." Sometimes this rise has been interpreted as a threat or at least, as cause for apprehension for India. The use of phrases like "China's rise as a challenge for India," "India's fear of offending China," "a Chinese threat should never be taken lightly," "betting against China has always been a bad idea" are excerpts that indicated China is a formidable force to be alert about. Therefore, China's rise, by and large, has been an alarming development for Indian media in 2012.

The negative perception of China's rise continued through 2013 in the national dailies and was often associated with China's mounting defence spending and the assertive projection of its power in South China Sea. This negative perception might have been a reflection of the opinion generated from border incidents at Daulat Beg Oldi and Depsang valley in the Ladakh region. It is worth-mentioning here that the term *aggressive* was used too frequently and mostly in association with China's security or military approach to India. Other related terms that portrayed China in Indian media's editorial projections are "coercive tactics," "sparked concern," "increasing assertion," "PLA's new aggressiveness," "anti-India policy," "growing military aggressiveness," "provocative acts," "costs of hostility," "growing anxieties about China's military rise," etc. Similar to the trend observed in 2012 and 2013, the national media remained deeply apprehensive of China's economic rise. *The Times of India*, especially, proposed a cautious approach, suggesting that India should be wary of China's growing economic clout.[5]

In 2014, China continued to be portrayed as an evolving "Asian Giant." As in the previous years, all the five national dailies were critical and also apprehensive of the rise of China and its implications for India. Yet there was marked difference as well. In 2014, the editorials exhibited a more pragmatic and positive style and spoke about ways to enhance trade and economic relations between the two countries. The editorials with favourable orientation towards China were increased by nearly 62% over the previous year. Terms like, "pragmatic engagement," "pragmatic approach" and "realistic plan" were used more frequently across editorials.

Like other national dailies, "China as a Rising Power" is also the dominant theme in *The Assam Tribune* as already mentioned. Phrases like "unquestioned trouble shooter of the region" or "increased influence around the globe" or "incredible economic and international stature" have been used to identify China as a rising power. There were two important sub-themes that merit discussion: India–China geo-strategic competition and China's expanding influence in India's neighbourhood. The perception of "aggressive" Chinese foreign policy ran through both sub-themes. In the context of India–China geo-strategic competition, India was urged to play a more proactive role through the Indian navy by challenging China's aggressive tendencies in Asian hotpots.[6] From 2012 to 2014, the words and phrases used were very similar and the content repeatedly emphasised China's aggressive foreign policy which was inclined more towards a display of power than of cooperation. While the perception thus projected remained negative and cautionary, India was advised to forge alliance with other countries, which have also been victims of China's power play.

Accordingly, China was accused of displaying overbearing tactics, resorting to military bullying and absolute control.[7] The suspicion expressed in regional media over China's expanding influence in India's neighbourhood was hard to miss and became prominent primarily in 2013 and 2014. An editorial published in 2013 held Indian diplomacy responsible for estrangement of neighbours,[8] although Modi's visit to Nepal was perceived as "neutralizing the gains made by China."[9]

The Arunachal Times' focus on China's rising power remained meagre and China was mentioned as an important country in themes like economy and ecology. There was no marked difference from *The Assam Tribune* in its perception of China. Unfavourable attitude towards China's rise was tacitly present in concerns expressed over environmental impact of China's increasing consumption.[10] China's strategy of expanding influence in India's neighbourhood through development aid to countries like Sri Lanka[11] was also looked upon as disagreeable.

- India–China border issues

In the national media, India–China border issues were another sector where negative perception regarding China prevailed. The year 2013 saw the highest number of publication on this theme primarily for two reasons: (a) consecutive border incidents in April–May and (b) visit of Chinese Prime Minister Li Keqiang to India in May 2013. The conflict of interest was highlighted and the tone was strongly unfavourable towards China in editorials published mostly in 2013. Intrusions at Daulat Beg Oldi and Depsang valley in Ladakh elicited strong response from the national media. While *The Times of India* criticised China's intrusion to be "provocative,"[12] *The Hindu* urged India and other Asian neighbours to join hands with the United States to counter Chinese coercive tactics.[13] It was therefore hinted that India could strengthen its position in Asia by seeking alliance with China's opponents. The editorials published in *The Indian Express* exhibited an innate sense of fear and vulnerability in Indian psyche regarding Chinese military presence on the border; the Chinese field commanders and senior officials at Beijing were accused of being "unresponsive" to India's concerns.[14] Developments such as these could possibly have provoked the national print media to project a negative image of China during the year. The year before, in 2012 and also in 2014, national media's response to India–China border issues was more evenly balanced. In 2012, one negative and one positive editorial was published leaving little room to gauge any shift in Indian media's perception of China.[15] And despite reports of Chinese incursions in the Ladakh sector in 2014, the border problem aroused less animosity than had happened in the previous year. The highlight of the 2014 editorials was "hardnosed-yet-flexible approach," where a hard stance on the border issue was balanced by a flexible approach towards enhancing trade relations with China and securing Chinese support for counterterrorism measures.[16] An editorial entitled "Combining Candour with Warmth" published in *The Hindu* cheered the Modi government for keeping India's strategic interests separate from expanding economic and trade ties.[17] Interestingly, negative perception of China's attitude towards the border issues was getting diluted by suggestions of economic cooperation with the same.

However, it is interesting to note that like other border-related issues, the national media evinced similar nature of conflict and competition between India and China on issues of river water. For instance, national media harshly criticised China's building of the Zangmu dam on the Brahmaputra River; it perceived China's actions to be insensitive and unmindful of the ecological impact it would have downstream.[18] Similarly, the context of climate change evoked comparisons between the economies of India and China. Citing China's higher CO_2 emissions, the national media sought to emphasize conflicting values and development trajectories pursued by the respective countries.

Unlike national media, the regional media's perception of China throughout these three years was consistently negative. Compared to *The Assam Tribune*'s geopolitical inclination, *The Arunachal Times* appeared more attentive towards border issues.

It is indeed interesting to note that in *The Assam Tribune*'s publication on India–China border started from the year 2013 with reporting of incursions at the Ladakh sector. In 2013, a persistent theme in the editorials is Chinese aggression denoted by phrases like "Chinese intrusions into India's border" or "aggressive Chinese expansionist tactics" and "India's weak response to Chinese aggressive agenda" reflected in developmentally backward condition in Arunachal Pradesh as opposed to the tremendous infrastructural expansion on Chinese side ("Unwarranted Delays," 18 November 2013; "Frontier Face-Off," 25 April 2013). In 2013 while editorials described the Chinese nature of incursion, in 2014 the focus shifted to

Chinese and Indian attitude towards the border. In 2014, editorials were published using phrases like "China's grumbling habit" and "India's feeble rumbling" ("Pleasant Surprise," 20 October 2014). One editorial on "Look North East" (17 September 2014) reminded India of the "thrashing" it received in the hands of Chinese army in 1962 and warned that this incident should not be repeated. The extent of persistent suspicion about Chinese intention along the border is also worth discussing, because a number of editorials mentioned 1962 war as a reminder of China's aggressive and unilateral intentions. Although in 2012 no editorials were published exclusively on India-China border, reflections of 1962 border conflict were found in some. Therefore, the theme "India-China border" primarily demonstrates a conflicting tone and during 2013–2014, media's perception of China over border issues remained negative with highest number of negative editorials published in 2013 (see Table 10.6). However, the editorials in both 2013 and 2014 chose to talk primarily about incursions at Daulat Beg Oldi in western sector. On the contrary, few editorials mention the need for upgrading infrastructure in the Northeast region of India.

In contrast to *The Assam Tribune*, where the theme "China as a Rising Power" dominated the editorials in both 2013 and 2014, the highest number of editorials published on the India-China border issues in *The Arunachal Times* during the same period focused on two aspects: border incursions and border trade. Publications on India-China border incursions started from 2013. A consistent component in the editorials had been the threat perception vis-à-vis China. Editorials used phrases like "shaken the nerve of New Delhi" or "sends chilling warning" to New Delhi or "incursion inside Arunachal territory by Chinese army had given heartache to many citizens" ("Chinese incursion in Chaglagam is a wakeup call," 22 August 2013; "Indo-China relations get better," 26 October 2013; "Beijing's Old Ploy," 2 November 2013). Some editorials also opined that the lack of border infrastructure can turn into a security threat in the long run ("Chinese incursion in Chaglagam is a wakeup call," 22 August 2013; "Don't Play with Fire," 24 December 2013). At the same time, the editorials sounded hopeful regarding improvement in relations between the two neighbours. An important feature in many of the editorials was the recommendation of border trade through Arunachal Pradesh. The editorial, "International Border cannot be redrawn" (9 November, 2013) opined that "places like Kibitho and Anjaw district and Bumla pass at Tawang can become major hub for business activity." Similar sentiments for diversifying relations on a healthier track were found in 2014 as well ("Open Arunachal Border for Trade purposes," 2 September 2014; "Relation with neighbours should be improved," 1 April 2014).

Therefore, the regional dailies while editorialising the theme of India–China border envisioned a future containing both conflictive and cooperative possibilities. Unlike *The Assam Tribune*, *The Arunachal Times* avoided declaring China as an aggressor and used phrases like "incursion" or "China's expansionist mindset."[19]

- Economic pragmatism leading to positive perception

It is worth-mentioning here that in 2014, the national media was most positive about China which helped narrow the gap between negative and positive perceptions. A pragmatic approach along with cooperative engagement was suggested in areas of trade, infrastructural development and connectivity. While the national media did not abandon concerns for India's security and defence or the uncertainties arising out of widening trade deficit, the event of Chinese president's visit to India helped side line these issues. The national media ruminated on various ways India could profit from a stronger bilateral relation with China. *The Financial Express* comparing China's economic standing with the United States and Japan argued that India should prioritise economic relations with China[20] and *The Times of India* advised India should focus on establishing independent and fruitful economic relations with both China and Japan.[21] Some editorials even suggested India should take cue from a powerful China to chart its own course of development. Both these trends were visible in editorials of 2012 and 2014. China's miraculous economic rise and domestic governance patterns were projected worthy of emulation. In 2012, an editorial published in *The Economic Times* advocated India's transition to cashless economy citing the example of emerging economies like China along with other countries such as South Africa and Mexico.[22] In 2014, with change of leadership in Delhi, renewed opportunity to forge better political and economic ties with China was ushered. Chinese e-commerce giant Alibaba was recommended as an exemplary model for India to develop its own domain of e-commerce.[23] It thus appears that with regard to emerging opportunities in areas like economy and connectivity, the national press felt that the government could experiment with a more flexible and relaxed approach independent of security concerns. However, the regional media's editorial expressions interestingly were quite in contrast. During 2013, when border tensions were running high on the western sector, the national media chose to refrain from suggesting economic cooperation; the regional media, on the other hand, published editorials promulgating close economic cooperation, confidence-building measures and diplomatic dialogue.[24] One editorial on "Indo-China trade" argued that reopening of Stilwell Road would not only be beneficial for India–China trade but also for entire South-East Asia.[25] Another editorial published on China's domestic issues projected China positively and as worthy of emulation.[26] Perhaps, in this case, the gravity of the border issue thinned out as it travelled from New Delhi to the Northeast state capitals.

- Brahmaputra River as a bone of contention

Resentment against China was expressed in matters of water sharing as well. China's building of the Zangmu dam on the Brahmaputra River was criticised by the Indian media as an instance of insensitivity, of ignoring the impact of ecological imbalance that could arise from the exploitation of river resources. Setting up of a transparent and transnational body with involvement of Bangladesh and Bhutan was called for.[27]

For the regional press, unease over Brahmaputra River water sharing also contributed towards negative projection of China. It was *The Assam Tribune* which wrote about ecological issues where the "nagging problem" of Brahmaputra River water sharing figured prominently.[28] The editorials opined China to be hostile and exploitative and argued that India was reluctant to rub the powerful neighbour in a wrong way.[29]

Conclusion

In conclusion, it needs to be admitted that while selection of national print media is more or less robust, the same cannot be said about the regional media where only two newspapers could be selected. Further, the time period covered is not long, though it is good enough for making a beginning. Despite these limitations, the chapter could come to some interesting observations. Firstly, it is quite clear from the above presentation that the print media, national or regional, perceives China predominantly negatively. It is also true that the regional media, represented by the two newspapers from two states in the bordering region of India's Northeast, as contrasted with their national counterpart, was distinctly more negative and was becoming increasingly so over these years. At the same time, it is also visible that there is an increasing tendency to be more discerning about issues and more forthright in pointing out areas where cooperation is possible and achievable. For such cooperation, the national press has identified connectivity, and collaboration on economic and environmental issues as possible arenas. The regional press apparently is less enthusiastic about such cooperation.

Secondly, it is noteworthy that not only national and regional perceptions differ; even the regional perception is internally fragmented: the print media representing the two Northeastern states differed in terms of importance given to the different themes as well as in terms of the intensity with which they projected China negatively or positively. This draws attention to the role of the specific locale and its problems in influencing, if not determining, perception of China. Arunachalee and Assamese perceptions as seen through *The Arunachal Times* and *The Assam Tribune* did happen to be different.

Thirdly, the editorials in the regional newspapers certainly conveyed the idea that even though they represented two states from the bordering areas with historical and contemporary problems with China, they were not overwhelmed by the presence of a globally muscle-flexing China. Probably this reflected the confidence that contemporary Indians generally share about the ability and skill of our diplomats and armed forces in handling issues with China or other neighbouring countries. Thus, the degree of attention paid to China by *The Assam Tribune* and *The Arunachal Times* was in the neighbourhood of what the national newspapers had done: the former exceeded the degree of attention paid by the *Indian Express* (4.84, being the highest mean score among the national dailies) by a small margin, while the latter equalled the score of *The Hindu*. The regional press did not think they needed to be overly concerned with China even though they happened to be located in the bordering regions of China.

Finally, it is also necessary to point out that broadly, the regional media's views overlapped with those of the national media. Thus, both the national and the regional media thought it appropriate to pay more attention to themes like China as a rising power and the border issue, among all the other themes or issues.

Acknowledgements

A wider version of this study has been published by Observer Research Foundation, New Delhi as special report on Understanding China Part 1: *Indian Media's Perception of China: Analysis of Editorials*, 2016, https://www.orfonline.org/research/indian-media-perception-of-china-analysis/, and Understanding China Part 2: *Indian Regional Media's Perception of China: Analysis of Select Editorials from The Assam Tribune and The Arunachal Times,* 2017, https://www.orfonline.org/research/indian-regional-media-perception-china-analysis-select-editorials-assam-tribune-arunachal-times/.)

Notes

1 Mohan Guruswamy and Zorawar Daulet Singh, "Indian and Chinese Foreign Policies in Comparative Perspective", in P. N. Haksar and Surjit Mansingh (eds), *India China Relations*, New Delhi: Viva Books, 2009, p. 115.
2 *The Indian Express*, 12 January 2012.
3 *The Times of India*, 24 December 2012; *The Finacial Express*, 19 December 2012.
4 *The Hindu*, 7 January 2012.
5 *The Times of India*, 29 March 2013.
6 *The Assam Tribune*, 16 June 2014.
7 *The Assam Tribune,* 17 September 2012, 31 May 2013; 10 October 2013, 13 May 2014; 31 October 2014.
8 *The Assam Tribune*, 28 May 2013.
9 *The Assam Tribune*, 14 November 2014.
10 *The Arunachal Times*, 4 December 2012, 9 September 2013.
11 *The Arunachal Times*, 24 May 2013.
12 *The Times of India*, 2 May 2013.
13 *The Hindu*, 3 May 2013.
14 *The Indian Express,* 24 April 2013.
15 *The Economic Times*, 23 October 2012; *The Times of India*, 2 November 2012.
16 *The Times of India*, 10 September 2014.
17 *The Hindu*, 29 September 2014.
18 *The Indian Express*, 1 December 2014.
19 *The Arunachal Times*, 18 November 2014.
20 *The Financial Express*, 28 November 2014.
21 *The Times of India*, 4 September 2014.
22 *The Economic Times*, 12 January 2012.
23 *The Economic Time*, 22 September 2014.
24 *The Assam Tribune*, 22 May 2013.
25 *Assam Tribune*, 12 November 2013.

26 *The Assam Tribune*, 30 May 2013.
27 *The Indian Express*, 1 December 2014.
28 *The Assam Tribune*, 11 March 2012
29 *The Assam Tribune*, 3 March 2012, 19 April 2013, 27 November 2014.

11
PEARL IN THE STRING

Sri Lanka–China relations in the twenty-first century

N. Manoharan

Introduction

According to China, "China–Sri Lanka bilateral relations is a time-honoured Friendship under whatever circumstances."[1] But going by the long-term trends in relations between these two asymmetrical powers situated far away from each other, one is tempted to ask: is it a "time-honoured" or a classic case of need-based ties? Though Sri Lanka recognised China in 1950, formal diplomatic relations was established only in February 1957 by the Left-of-the-Centre Sri Lanka Freedom Party-led government headed by SWRD Bandaranaike. Much before that in 1952 a need for exchange in the form of "Rice-Rubber Agreement" was signed: Sri Lanka needed rice and China needed rubber. Interestingly, Bandaranaike requested withdrawal of British naval and air bases, respectively, in Trincomalee and Katunayake at around the same time.[2] China and Sri Lanka signed an agreement on Economic and Technical Cooperation in 1962, the same year of Sino-Indian conflict. Sri Lanka voted for PRC's admission to UN Security Council in 1971. Sri Lanka–Chinese Business Cooperation Council was established in 1994 aimed at improving trade and investment relations. Colombo strongly supported China's entry into the World Trade Organization in 2001.[3] These were major flashpoints in the bilateral ties.

Although the above-mentioned milestones remained, the level of bilateral relations has picked up tremendously in the recent years due to the felt mutuality of needs for each other. Sri Lanka is strategically important for China both at global and regional levels. Of course, in return, China had been assisting Sri Lanka through infrastructural and economic aid, diplomatic support and military assistance during Eelam War IV and thereafter. The aim of this chapter is to look at the dynamics of the "need-based ties" in the present context and its impact on India.

DOI: 10.4324/9781003146223-11

Pearl in the string

"Need-based" relations between China and Sri Lanka could be illustrated by a metaphor of garland of pearl: pearl requires string and vice versa for a garland. The scope of China–Sri Lanka relations in the present context have been cast within the broad structure of the "China–Sri Lanka All-round Cooperation Partnership of Sincere Mutual Support and Ever-lasting Friendship."[4] Three broad areas of mutuality could be identified: strategic infrastructure, economic interaction and ethnic issue.

Strategic infrastructure

Since time immemorial, Sri Lanka is considered as the "oceanic cockpit of Asia," as it acted as an entry point, a midpoint meeting place, a harbour, an emporium for international merchandise and a landfall. Perhaps for its strategic location, the island attracted attention of major powers of the world from time to time. Mindful of this advantage, Colombo has been using it to further its national interests. In this regard, Sri Lanka's Board of Investments proudly says: "Sri Lanka is situated strategically at the crossroads of major shipping routes to South Asia, the Far East and the continents of Europe and America, making the country a convenient port of call for shipping lines and airfreight services."[5] In the 2019, Galle Dialogue, Minister of Media and State Minister of Defence Ruwan Wijewardene pronounced: "the strategic importance of Sri Lanka in history is much bigger compared to its small size."[6] Chinese Admiral Zheng He was reported to have visited the island in early fifteenth century while commanding his treasure fleet (*baochuan*) in the Indian Ocean area. Portuguese, Dutch and later British found the then Ceylon a convenient base for their further reach towards South and Southeast Asia. Trincomalee, considered second largest natural harbour in the world, served as a strategic oil reserve during Second War for Allies in the region. During the Cold War period, the United States called Sri Lanka an important piece of "real estate" and even attempted to establish broadcasting and listening station in the island.

On its part, China did not miss taking note of the strategic significance of Sri Lanka. Beijing, in fact, considers the island state "an important hub on the Maritime Silk Road"[7] and a key pearl in its presence in Southern Asia, which some experts call as "String of Pearls" strategy. It is in this backdrop that infrastructure development by China in Sri Lanka has to be viewed.

Some of the important infrastructure projects in Sri Lanka developed by China include Hambantota port, Colombo South Harbour expansion, Katunayake-Colombo expressway, Norochcholai coal power project, Moragahakanda multipurpose development project, Maththala airport, 661-room Shangri La hotel, the Center for Performing Arts in Colombo, Matara–Kataragama railway line and the Colombo International Financial City. China is also assisting in building a specialised hospital for kidney disease, as well as an outpatient building at the National Hospital in Colombo. Statistically speaking, funding from China accounts for more than half of Sri Lanka's construction and development loans. In value terms, it is estimated at over US$6 billion – more than to any other country.

Of these varied infrastructural projects, three of them – Hambantota port, Colombo Port City, and Colombo International Financial City – are part of China's Belt and Road Initiative (BRI). Sri Lanka agreed willingly to actively participate in China's BRI when it was unveiled in 2013 as "One Belt One Road" (OBOR). The then President Mahinda Rajapaksa, known for his pro-China stance, took greater interest in these development projects, especially after economically devastating ethnic conflict. Rajapaksa's vision was to "reposition Sri Lanka as the 'pearl of the old Silk Route'."[8] The cumulative Chinese investments on infrastructure in Sri Lanka totals to US$13.5 billion between 2006 and 2020.

Of these, the most controversial project is Hambantota port. The first phase of the port was completed in 2010 by the China Harbour Engineering Co. Ltd at a cost of $360 million. It should be noted that this was much before formal announcement of OBOR in 2013 and immediately after the end of ethnic war in Sri Lanka. The project included a high-quality passenger terminal, cargo handling, warehousing, bunkering, provisioning, maintenance and repair, medical supplies and customs clearing facilities. Sri Lanka time and again tried to convey that "the Chinese interest in the Hambantota port is purely commercial."[9] However, the harbour is strategically located not only for the Chinese merchant vessels and cargo carriers sailing to and from Africa and the Middle East to make a stopover but can also be used by any military fleet. Given the scope of facilities created at the port, there is a dual usage mode – a perfect match of both "place" and a "base." A strong Chinese foothold in Hambantota would allow them to have dominance over a vast area of the Indian Ocean extending from Africa in the west to Australia in the east, and up to Antarctica in the south. Not surprisingly, the United States sees Sri Lanka as "a beacon for a free and open Indo-Pacific" and China has been doing "predatory bad deals" violating sovereignty.[10]

Most importantly, it is easy for China to closely monitor all military and non-military ships that shuttle between east and west coasts of India encircling Sri Lanka. Colombo did propose the Hambantota port project as a joint venture with India. But as the talks got delayed, China got into the picture and grabbed the opportunity. Sri Lanka justified the move away from India by saying "China offered the best terms," and "we don't have favourites."[11] In the words of the then president and present Prime Minister Mahinda Rajapaksa, "Sri Lanka's economy is currently at an important turning point and it is our country's strategy to enhance our ports-related economy."[12] Thus, it was a perfect match of need between China and Sri Lanka on the project. Interestingly, when Sri Lanka defaulted loan payment of US$1.1 billion taken for the construction of the port, the very same port was given in for a 99-year lease to China Merchants Port Holdings Co Ltd. Many questioned this move citing violation of Sri Lanka's sovereignty.[13]

China's footprints are not seen just in Sri Lanka but in other countries in the Indian Ocean littoral as well. Beijing has for long been building maritime and other linkages with, apart from Sri Lanka, countries of eastern Africa, Seychelles, Mauritius, West Asia, Pakistan, Maldives, Bangladesh, Myanmar and Southeast Asian countries. The main objective behind this is to secure its sea lanes, especially critically needed energy supplies for its industries from Africa and West Asia. At the same time, these linkages have doubled up as virtual encircling of India, which some experts call as "String of Pearls" construct.[14]

Sri Lanka tries to balance between India and China to take benefits from both the big powers of Asia, a kind of "positive non-alignment." To distinguish India from other players, the then President Rajpaksa observed:

> We are a non-aligned country. Our neighbours are Indians. I always say, Indians are our relations. From the time of Asoka, we have had that culture ... but that doesn't mean we won't get commercial benefits from others; from China, or Japan, or whoever. They will come here, they will build and they will go back. India comes here, they will build and they will stay. This is the difference.[15]

Keeping this in mind, development projects are offered to both India and China from time to time. Yet, Colombo's Beijing tilt is palpable, especially when Rajapaksas are in power.

India's involvement in Sri Lanka's infrastructure development is also immense, ranging from the Matara–Colombo rail line, the dredging and refurbishment of the Kankesanthurai Harbor, renovation of Palaly Airport, construction of five vocational training centres for creating job opportunities, renovation of the famous Duriappah stadium in Jaffna, restoration of the Tiruketheeswaram temple, interconnection of electricity grids between the two countries, construction of a 150-bed hospital in Dickoya, setting up a coal power plant in Sampur, rehabilitation of the Atchchuvely Industrial Zone near Jaffna and construction of a new cultural centre in Jaffna. India's line of credit is about US$1.8 billion, although the figure is small compared to China's line of credit.[16] Sri Lanka's preference to China is mainly because of "no strings attached" policy of the latter, at least overtly, to any of the projects implemented or aid granted. The latest example is scrapping of the 2019 agreement with India and Japan to develop the strategic East Container Terminal (ECT) at the Colombo port due to "trade unions pressure." Of course, there are internal political dimensions to it.

Also, China is rated better in terms of timely completion of projects, cost-effectiveness and quality of infrastructure. Most importantly, Beijing places no conditions in terms of "structural adjustments, policy reforms, competitive biddings, or transparency attached to their loans" or even human rights, except bringing in some of their own labourers.[17] On the other hand, Indian companies have certain inherent disadvantages compared to their Chinese counterparts. While most Indian companies are privately owned, Chinese ones are state-owned; they are also supported by state financial institutions like China Development Bank Corporation, Industrial and Commercial Bank of China, China International Trade and Investment Corporation, China Export and Credit Insurance Corporation and China Export–Import Bank. Profit is not the primary motive, but to look towards aspects like strategic advantages, diplomatic mileage and goodwill gained through projects.[18] Most importantly, in the Indian case, the private sector and the government do not seem to complement each other's efforts and gains. Risk-averse Indian companies care less about projection of Indian "soft power" without much state support and motivation.[19] At the same time, what is not appreciated is India's multi-varied involvement in infrastructure projects aimed genuinely at the overall socio-economic development of the country. There is no strategic consideration whatsoever.

Economic

Economic relations between Sri Lanka and China have emerged quite strong guided by various bilateral arrangements: an agreement on commercial maritime relations (1963), Trade and Payment Agreement and setting up of China–Sri Lanka Joint Trade Committee (1982), Agreement on Economic and Trade Cooperation (1984), Sri Lankan–Chinese Joint Commission (1991), Sri Lanka–Chinese Business Cooperation Council (1994), Investment Facilitation Agreement (2009), MOU on Trade and Economic Cooperation (2013), completion of five rounds of negotiations on free trade agreement till 2020.[20]

Not surprisingly, China has now become a major trading partner of Sri Lanka, overtaking India on and off. But it is only a matter of time when China permanently becomes the largest trading partner of Sri Lanka. The total trade turnover between Sri Lanka and China now stands at around US$5 billion, a fivefold increase in just a decade. But the concerning aspect is the balance of trade that is hugely in favour of China (ratio of 1:19 compared to 1:10 with India in 2020).[21] Given the trend of trade movement, the deficit is going to increase further. Yet, it is surprising that the long-term consequences of such gap are not taken note of by Colombo.

Apart from the impressive bilateral trade volume, China is also one of the main donors of Sri Lanka. The latest aid was to the tune of US$500 million in March 2020 towards economic development in the light of COVID-19 pandemic.[22] Sri Lanka is also becoming an attractive destination of Chinese tourists of late. But for the ongoing pandemic, there has been increase in the arrival of Chinese tourists in the last few years, especially after the end of ethnic conflict. The Easter attacks in April 2019 did put a break, but otherwise the numbers have been on the ascendance. The growth in tourists from China was 72.5% between 2010 and 2016. In 2019 alone, despite Easter attacks and corona virus visa restrictions, 167,863 Chinese selected Sri Lanka as their tourism destination. But the annual average is 300,000.[23] Interestingly, Sri Lanka's Central Bank announced in June 2011 use of the Yuan (renminbi) for its international transactions. In comparison, the Indian rupee does not enjoy the same privilege, despite India remaining as one of the largest trading partners, donors and investors and Indian tourists the largest in the island.[24]

Ethnic issue

Ethnic issue in Sri Lanka does not figure consciously, but under broad frame of political ties between China and Sri Lanka. Juxtaposed to India, China is not in the proximity of Sri Lanka with a Tamil Nadu-like province. Sinhala-dominated governments of the island are grateful to Beijing for two reasons: military assistance during Eelam War IV to take on the LTTE; and unconditional diplomatic support in the UN Human Rights Council as and when West-sponsored strictures are made.[25]

China supplied requisite arms and ammunition to Sri Lankan troops during "Eelam War IV" to defeat the LTTE. The arms packages were delivered as if for a proper conventional war: Jian-7 fighter jets, antiaircraft guns, Type-85 heavy and Type-80 light machineguns, Type-56 rifles, 152 mm howitzer, 81 mm mortar shells, RPG-7 rockets and large quantities of ammunition.[26] Sri Lanka justified arms aid from China for two reasons: one, due to refusal from other countries citing humanitarian considerations; and two, cost-effectiveness. In the words of the then Army Chief, Gen Sarath Fonseka:

> India had told us they were not in a position to sell or send offensive weapons or even equipment like radars and basic communication equipment to meet our requirements. So we had no other option... . It was readily available and comparatively cheaper ... almost half the price compared to Russia. I think, we had no other option.[27]

The arms supply at that juncture got China tremendous goodwill both from the Sri Lankan government and the majority Sinhalese. On the other hand, India refused to supply arms, but agreed to provide "non-lethal weapons" due to domestic political implications, especially from Tamil Nadu. The long-pending Defence Cooperation Agreement was also put under suspension.[28]

Sri Lanka also appreciated China's diplomatic support against the West-led call for international investigations on "war crimes" committed during Eelam War IV. India and Russia also joined China to defeat the UN resolution that censured Sri Lankan government in May 2009. However, in March 2012, not satisfied with the Colombo's sincerity in carrying forward assurances on reconciliation and in finding long-term political settlement, India was compelled to vote in favour of the US-sponsored resolution. Sri Lanka's disappointment with India was very much conspicuous when India voted in favour of UNHRC resolution in March 2013 as well.[29] But China consistently supported Sri Lanka in the UN Human Rights Council. Although China's tenure in UNHRC ended by 2012, it tried to mobilise support in favour of Sri Lanka in 2013 and thereafter.

Beijing also extended support to Colombo for the UNHRC resolution scheduled in March 2021.[30]

In return, apart from deeply appreciating China's help, Sri Lanka has time and again reiterated its strict adherence to "one China policy": "that the Government of the People's Republic of China is the sole legal government representing the whole of China and that Taiwan is an inalienable part of the Chinese territory."[31] Sri Lanka has also supported China several times on human rights motions against China and in several international forums. It was instrumental in bringing China to SAARC as an observer and also vying to get China in forums like BIMSTEC (Bay of Bengal Initiative for Multi-sectoral Technical and Economic Cooperation) and IORA (Indian Ocean Rim Association) as partner.

Conclusion: India's concerns and responses

China–Sri Lanka relations is a classic case of "need-based" ties since 1950s. The bilateral relations have increased in its intensity in the recent years because of the increase in the mutual needs. China considers strategically located Sri Lanka an important hub for its BRI in the Indian Ocean; Sri Lanka wants China for its economic development and diplomatic support. China's infrastructure footprint in the island ranges from ports, railways, roads and airports. Of these, port-related projects are significant to note as they have strategic implications for India. In due course, some of them turned as "white elephants" for Sri Lanka to manage and literally pushed the country to what is famously called as "debt trap."[32] The island state is still in the process of getting out of this trap. Economic relations between China and Sri Lanka have been growing strong of late to the extent of China becoming the largest trading partner of Sri Lanka. However, the concern is the widening trade deficit. Increasing Chinese aid and choice of Sri Lanka as tourist destination by the Chinese is worth mentioning. China also helped Sri Lanka to defeat the LTTE by the supply of arms, and also in the form of diplomatic support at the UNHRC. The important question is: in what manner India's interests are impacted due to China–Sri Lanka bonhomie and how India has been handling it?

India is not overly concerned about China's footprints in Sri Lanka, but at the same time the strategic implications of three broad Chinese engagements – infrastructure, economic interactions and ethnic issue – in the island that would go against India's interests could not be ignored.

Firstly, on the infrastructure footprint, there is a possibility of dual-use mode of certain infrastructure projects by China, especially when conflict escalates between India and China. For instance, China is allowed to have storage and fuelling facilities at Hambantota, which could be used by military fleet as well. Similarly, the Colombo port that handles about 70% of India's shipping is being modernised with Chinese assistance. If China wishes, it can always turn these projects to India's disadvantage. Now that Eastern Container Terminal has also slipped out of India's hand, the situation is all the more concerning. Chinese attempts to develop certain energy projects in the northern Sri Lanka is seen as yet another thorn. Something like "Malacca Dilemma" for China, it could be India's "Sri Lanka Dilemma." In the Annexure of the India–Sri Lanka Accord of 1987, India and Sri Lanka have agreed that Trincomalee or any other port in Sri Lanka would not be made available for military use to any country in a manner which is prejudicial to India's interest. India trusts that Colombo would abide by this provision seriously. India is clear in its approach towards infrastructure projects:

> [C]onnectivity initiatives must follow principles of financial responsibility to avoid projects that would create unsustainable debt burden for communities; balanced ecological and environmental protection and preservation standards; transparent assessment of project costs; and skill and technology transfer to help long term running and maintenance of the assets created by local communities… . Connectivity projects must be pursued in a manner that respects sovereignty and territorial integrity.[33]

Secondly, China's deepening economic engagement in Sri Lanka is yet another concern for India. China is fast attempting to overtake India as Sri Lanka's largest trading partner. However, there is a significant difference in the nature of economic relations that is often missed by those who just see the numbers. And that difference is the balance of trade that has been shifting towards Sri Lanka from India, though gradually. But, in the case of China, it is drifting away from Sri Lanka. This is concerning.

Thirdly, China's blind support to Colombo on ethnic issue has actually hindered the process of ethnic reconciliation and long-term political settlement of the issue. India is not pleased, especially when China indirectly points out India's role in the ethnic issue as interference "with matters that are essentially internal concerns of Sri Lanka."[34]

New Delhi has indeed been taking various steps to address these concerns. In a similar situation in the 1980s, India was assertive in conveying its standpoint. New Delhi, in fact, made sure that Sri Lanka was not used by forces inimical to India's interests through the bilateral Accord of July 1987. Although the Accord stands, India has been dealing the issue in a more nuanced manner instead of being assertive and sensitive.

New Delhi has to understand its strengths and weaknesses when it comes to its role in a third country on development. It should strive to have an edge on whichever fields it could, apart from quality of its delivery. Resettlement, tourism, cultural exchange and trade are few areas that India has distinct advantage over other countries.

What is more important is to positively exploit the aspect of proximity. New Delhi should consciously build constituencies in the neighbourhood and could have series of dialogues with the concerned political, economic, social and cultural actors. If there are any apprehensions because of China's role in the neighbourhood, there is nothing wrong in dealing the issue bilaterally with China itself. India has to balance out between regional peace, its own strategic interests and that of long-term peace and development of Sri Lanka. The key is to sustain bilateral ties with Sri Lanka in the long run and make up for the lost ground.

Notes

1. "China-Sri Lanka Relations an All Weather Partnership – Vice President of China", 12 February 2014, https://www.mfa.gov.lk/ta/4419-china-sri-lanka-relations-an-all-weather-partnership-vice-president-of-china/, accessed 12 July 2020.
2. On the withdrawal of bases Prime Minister SWRD Bandaranaike remarked: "The last remnants of colonialism in this country have been removed; the bases will no longer exist … . That will be one more step towards full freedom – the removal of rather stubborn remnants of colonialism." Cited in Lucy M. Jacob, *Sri Lanka –– From Dominion to Republic: A Study of the Changing Relations with the United Kingdom*, Delhi: National Publishing House, 1975, p. 76.
3. Grace Asirwatham, "Overview of Sri Lanka-China Relations", *The Prospector*, 24 December 2018, https://lki.lk/blog/overview-of-sri-lanka-china-relations/, accessed 18 June 2020.
4. Came during the visit of Chinese Premier Wen Jiabao in April 2005, the four-point proposal included: "promoting traditional friendship and expanding exchanges between governments, parliaments and parties; exploring new areas for economic and trade cooperation; expanding cooperation in such fields as agriculture, fishery and tourism; and enhancing coordination in international and regional issues." See "China, Sri Lanka Set Up All-Round Cooperative Partnership", *People's Daily*, 9 April 2005, http://english.peopledaily.com.cn/200504/09/eng20050409_180198.html, accessed 21 June 2020.
5. "Sri Lankan Board of Investment", http://investsrilanka.com/services/strategic-location/, accessed 23 June 2020.
6. Ruwan Wijewardene, "Keynote Address,' Galle Dialogue on 'Refining Mindset to Address Transnational Maritime Threats; A Review of the Decade", http://galledialogue.lk/assets/files/2019/paper/honourable_ruwan%20_wijewardene.pdf, accessed 25 June 2020.
7. Remarks made by the visiting Chinese State Councillor and Minister of National Defence General Liang Guanglie at the Defence Services Command and Staff College (DSCSC) at Sapugaskanda (Sri Lanka). For full text, see http://www.army.lk/detailed.php?NewsId=5176, accessed 25 June 2020.
8. Ashok Kumar Mehta, "Not so Hidden Agenda", *Hindustan Times*, 18 August 2011, https://www.hindustantimes.com/india/not-so-hidden-dragon/story-gdej8Sq9cFdTXaIIAdPAeJ.html, accessed 25 June 2020.
9. Speech delivered by the then Sri Lankan Defense Secretary Gotabaya Rajapaksa at the "Galle Dialogue 2012 Maritime Conference", the Light House Hotel, Galle, 13 December 2012, for full text of the speech see http://www.galledialogue.com/index.php?id=20, accessed 27 June 2020.
10. US Department of State, Secretary Michael R. Pompeo, Remarks to the Press, 28 October 2020, https://2017-2021.state.gov/secretary-michael-r-pompeo-and-sri-lankan-foreign-minister-dinesh-gunawardena-at-a-press-availability//index.html, accessed 15 February 2021.
11. Sri Lankan Ambassador to the United States, Jaliya Wikremasuriya, cited by Vikas Bajaj, "India Worries as China Builds Ports in South Asia", *The New York Times*, 15 February 2010, https://www.nytimes.com/2010/02/16/business/global/16port.html, accessed 27 June 2020.

12 Bao Chang, "China Merchants to Invest $500 m in Sri Lankan Port", *China Daily*, 16 August 2011, http://www.chinadaily.com.cn/cndy/2011-08/16/content_13119362.htm, accessed 28 June 2020.
13 Dipanjan Roy Chaudhury, "Chinese Investments in Sri Lanka Compromises Colombo's Sovereignty", *Economic Times*, 26 December 2019, https://economictimes.indiatimes.com/news/defence/chinese-investments-in-sri-lanka-compromises-colombos-sovereignty/articleshow/72975247.cms?from=mdr, accessed 28 June 2020.
14 Nilanthi Samaranayake, "Are Sri Lanka's Relations with China Deepening? An Analysis of Economic, Military, and Diplomatic Data", *Asian Security*, vol. 7, no. 2, 2011, pp. 120–21.
15 "India's Views Matter, Don't Care about the World: Rajapaksa", *The Times of India*, 28 June 2010, https://timesofindia.indiatimes.com/india/Indias-views-matter-dont-care-about-the-world-Rajapaksa/articleshow/6099633.cms, accessed 29 June 2020.
16 High Commission of India, "India-Sri Lanka Development Partnership", http://www.hcicolombo.org/index.php?option=com_pages&id=73, accessed 30 June 2020.
17 Patrik Mendis, "The Colombo-Centric New Silk Road", *Economic and Political Weekly*, vol. 47, no. 49, 8 December 2012, p. 69.
18 Some refer the working relation that exists between Chinese companies, the state and quasi-commercial lending institutions as the "Golden Triangle" that provide the Chinese companies with cheap finance to undercut their Western competitors. See, in the African context, Executive Research Associates, China in Africa: A Strategic Overview (China: Institute of Developing Economics & Japan External Trade Organization), October 2009.
19 Some of the Indian companies present in Sri Lanka are IOC, Tatas, Bharti Airtel, Piramal Glass, Life Insurance Corporation of India (LIC), Ashok Leyland, Larson & Tubro (L&T), ICICI Bank and Taj Hotels.
20 Embassy of Sri Lanka in People's Republic of China, "Sri Lanka-China Trade Relations", http://www.slemb.com/third.php?menu_code=38&lang=en, accessed 14 February 2021.
21 Trading Economics, "Sri Lanka Balance of Trade", https://tradingeconomics.com/sri-lanka/balance-of-trade, accessed 17 February 2021.
22 PTI, "Sri Lanka Gets USD 500 million Loan from China as Financial Aid", *The New Indian Express*, 18 March 2020, https://www.newindianexpress.com/world/2020/mar/18/sri-lanka-gets-usd-500-million-loan-from-china-as-financial-aid-2118472.html#:~:text=COLOMBO%3A%20China%20has%20provided%20USD,official%20reserves%20of%20the%20country, accessed 1 July 2020.
23 "China Drops out from SL's Top 10 Tourist Source Markets", *Daily Financial Times*, 6 March 2020, http://www.ft.lk/front-page/China-drops-out-from-SL-s-top-10-tourist-source-markets/44-696982, accessed 2 July 2020.
24 Informally, Indian rupees are accepted freely as a currency in some pockets of capital Colombo. But, this is not enough.
25 Ananth Krishnan, "China Backs Sri Lanka on UNHRC Resolution", *The Hindu*, 22 March 2012, https://www.thehindu.com/news/international/china-backs-sri-lanka-on-unhrc-resolution/article3088478.ece, accessed 3 July 2020.
26 Jonas Lindberg, Camilla Orjuela, SiemonWezeman, and Linda Åkerström, *Arms Trade with Sri Lanka: Global Business, Local Costs*, Stockholm: Swedish Peace and Arbitration Society, 2011, p. 46.
27 "India's Refusal to Supply Arms Turned Us to China: SL", *The Indian Express*, 25 May 2009, https://indianexpress.com/article/news-archive/print/indias-refusal-to-supply-arms-turned-us-to-china-sl/, accessed 4 July 2020.
28 PTI, "India Calls Off Annual Defence Talks with Sri Lanka", *The India Today*, 18 March 2013, https://www.indiatoday.in/india/north/story/sri-lankan-tamil

-issue-india-calls-off-defence-talks-with-lanka-156475-2013-03-18, accessed 5 July 2020.
29 The then Sri Lankan Defence Secretary observed: "[T]hose wanting Sri Lanka to satisfy the global community should realise that they were adopting double-standards. In fact, they would never have tolerated external intervention in domestic issues, though Sri Lanka was being asked to give into an investigation on the basis of unsubstantiated allegations. Would India address its accountability issues to the satisfaction of Western powers or the UN?". See Shamindra Ferdinando, "Gotabhaya Deeply Disappointed with India's Stand," *Lankasiri News*, 22 March 2013, http://www.island.lk/index.php?page_cat=article-details&page=article-details&code_title=75220, accessed 7 July 2020.
30 Syed Shafiq, "Human Rights Champion China Promises Support to 'Ally' Sri Lanka in Defending Allegations of War Crimes", *The Eurasia Times*, 28 October 2020, https://eurasiantimes.com/human-rights-champion-china-promises-support-to-ally-sri-lanka-in-defending-allegations-of-war-crimes/, accessed 18 February 2021.
31 See Joint Communique between China and Sri Lanka issued in Colombo at the end of Premier Wen Jiabao's official visit on 9 April 2005. For full text of the Communique, see http://www.china.org.cn/english/2005/SouthasiaTour/125353.htm, accessed 8 July 2020.
32 Kinling Lo, "Sri Lanka Wants Its 'Debt Trap' Hambantota Port Back. But Will China Listen?", *South China Morning Post*, 7 December 2019, https://www.scmp.com/news/china/diplomacy/article/3040982/sri-lanka-wants-its-debt-trap-hambantota-port-back-will-china, accessed 9 July 2020.
33 Government of India, Ministry of External Affairs, "Official Spokesperson's Response to a Query on Participation of India in OBOR/BRI Forum", 13 May 2017, https://mea.gov.in/media-briefings.htm?dtl/28463/Official+Spokespersons+response+to+a+query+on+participation+ of+India+in+OBOR BRI+Forum, accessed 9 July 2020.
34 PTI, "China Wouldn't Allow 'Outside Interference' in Sri Lanka's Internal Affairs: Wang Yi", *The New Indian Express*, 14 January 2020, https://www.newindianexpress.com/world/2020/jan/14/china-wouldnt-allow-outside-interference-in-sri-lankas-internal-affairs-wang-yi-2089555.html, accessed 10 July 2020.

12
CHINA'S DEEPENING ENGAGEMENT WITH BANGLADESH

Sreeradha Datta

> The two countries have supported each other and made progress together. Today, both countries are at a crucial stage of revitalization and development. The Chinese dream of great national renewal can well connect with the "Sonar Bangla" dream.
>
> Chinese President Xi Xingping[1]

Introduction

It is ironic, the China dream of national renewal and Bangabandhu Mujibur dream of Sonar Bangla are presently being viewed through similar prism, given that China did not recognise Bangladesh in its early days, despite its first Prime Minister's Mujibur Rahman's outreach to try and win their confidence. However, the changing dynamics of geopolitics have determined a revised policy. Undoubtedly, China sees South Asia as its immediate neighbourhood and as a zone of influence, and Bangladesh has assumed criticality in its South Asian policy. Prolonged relations with Pakistan within the context of containing India gradually gave way to more assertive policy towards the region. China's economic ascendance and growing political clout since the mid-1980s and presently poised as the second largest economy in the world, estimated to overtake the United States sooner than expected within this decade, has lent China with a confidence and support that has grown in the past decade. Almost all states of South Asia, barring Bhutan, enjoy strong economic and political relations with China.

Much of China's agenda in South Asia has an Indian context and it has managed to make significant inroads in countries that were once seen as India's sphere of influence. Besides managing to retain its traditional sway over Pakistan, in recent years it has made significant gains in countries such as Myanmar, Nepal

DOI: 10.4324/9781003146223-12

and Bangladesh. In so doing, it has eroded some of the historic advantages that India enjoyed in these countries. China's rising global status and massive economic clout were tactfully used to overcome some of the historic hangovers that these countries had towards Beijing. In the process, China has established itself as their friendly neighbour and largest source of funds to underwrite some of the major projects undertaken in the region.

In the contemporary context, Bangladesh has assumed greater salience given its access to the Bay of Bengal, and with it, a larger access to the Indian Ocean. It was not unexpected that the landlocked Yunnan province of China will seek to establish economic engagement with Bangladesh to access the Bay of Bengal. Understandably, China's inroads in the Indian Ocean region is without any pretension and its growing naval presence has increased over time and gathered a momentum and partnership with Bangladesh has proved valuable.

The Sino-Bangladesh relations formally took off with the visit of President Ziaur Rahman to China in 1977. Coming within months after Chinese recognition, this visit put the bilateral relations firmly on place and both sides quietly buried the uneasy and unfriendly phase. The Chinese non-recognition of Bangladesh and its opposition to UN membership was explained away "within" the Cold War context and both sides began to expand and intensify bilateral ties. Thus, Bangladesh presently enjoys the most comprehensive and robust ties with China straddling a wide spectrum of areas, including political ties, economic cooperation and defence assistance. Within a span of five decades, China has moved from its non-recognition position and became Bangladesh's closest ally.

This chapter attempts to trace the nature of the Sino-Bangladesh relations and the imperatives that dictated the dynamism of the bilateral ties. The foreign policy of post-Mujibur Bangladesh was dictated by its desire to reposition itself in the international community and alongside ease out its previous close ties with India. The first section examines the political dynamics that brought the two powers together. The next section on economic cooperation explains how China offered the scope for infrastructural development, including the Belt and Road Initiative (BRI). The next section highlights the defence and strategic issues. This chapter finally argues that in the contemporary context, given the increasing regional activity, China is viewing the relationship through a regional perspective of growth and development, and Bangladesh is a critical factor in its ambition in South Asia and in the Indo-Pacific.

The recognition and political convergence

Bangladesh won its liberation from West Pakistan in December 1971 and within few years dramatic changes occurred in Bangladeshi politics caused by the assassination of Sheikh Mujibur Rahman in August 1975 having a direct and far-reaching impact on its domestic and foreign policy. More than any other arena, these changes were visibly manifested in Bangladesh's relations with the People's Republic of China.

At the time of the Liberation War of 1971, the global order was deeply divided over Bangladesh. Indeed, rival blocs of the Cold War took opposing sides during this South Asian crisis. India and Soviet Union supported efforts by the people of the then East Pakistan to gain independence from the clutches of the military-ruled West Pakistan, while the other bloc led by the United States was strongly against the division of Pakistan. During this period, the latter played a pivotal role in the rapprochement that was taking place between the United States and China. Interestingly, China which entered the United Nations in September of 1971 blocked Bangladesh's membership of the UN in 1972. Despite the initial opposition and reservations from many quarters in the West and the Islamic world, Mujib was able to establish ties with most of the detractors, including Pakistan and the United States. He, however, was unable to appeal to the Chinese intransigence.

At the same time, the critical importance of China was never lost on Bangladesh. Despite its non-recognition, Prime Minister Mujibur Rahman made several attempts to reach out to China but in vain. Thus, the erstwhile links that East Pakistan shared with China was briefly snapped when Mujib was at helms of affairs. The Chinese disapproval of Bangladesh coming into existence was sharp with the immediate closure of the Chinese consulate in Dhaka. Unlike its western counterpart, ironically, the eastern wing had drawn heavily from Mao's ideological moorings. The deepening of this strand eventually led to a split in the Awami League, the leading political party of East Pakistan. At the Lahore summit meeting of the Organisation of Islamic Conference in 1974, also attended by Mujib, Bangladesh was successful in securing the recognition of the Islamic countries, including Pakistan. The progress on the China front did not happen during his lifetime.

Conscious of the Chinese policy of non-interference, Bangladeshi leaders do not try to make political capital from Beijing. No Bangladeshi political party has been accused or perceived as pro-Chinese to the point of being harmful to Bangladesh. There is a subtle rivalry among mainstream parties to promote closer political and economic ties with Beijing. Correspondingly, China is not a battleground for Awami League – Bangladesh Nationalist Party (BNP) rivalry, something India–Bangladesh's other large and critical neighbour has come to symbolize. Every Bangladeshi leader has reached out to China and hence visits to China by government and opposition figures do not generate negative responses but are seen part of a wider national consensus towards Beijing. As a sharp contrast to its relations with other countries, Bangladesh enjoys the most tension-free friendship with China.

While the Bangladeshi military leaders were in the forefront of normalising the relations, there has been a wide political acceptability of China as an important and friendly neighbour. Notwithstanding the divisive politics of Bangladesh, political leaders have all coveted and courted China. Despite the contrasting position on various foreign policy issues, the BNP and the Awami League, the two main political parties, have adopted identical views towards closer cooperation with China. The non-controversial nature of the bilateral relation has facilitated the growth and interlinkages of Bangladeshi–Chinese ties. The "ever-growing and multifaceted" ties were aptly summed up by Prime Minister Zhu Rongji. According to him, China is always committed to remaining "Bangladesh's trustworthy and reliable friend and partner for development" irrespective of "whatever changes may occur in the international landscape."[2]

When it comes to China, therefore, there is no difference between the BNP and the Awami League as both are committed to improving ties with Beijing. Indeed, there existed a subtle rivalry among mainstream parties to promote closer political and economic ties with Beijing.[3] Reflecting the national consensus, the Awami League is equally keen to promote closer ties with China, something India could not expect from Khaleda Zia even when she was in power. Both Sheikh Hasina and Khaleda have been visiting China, both as prime minister and as leader of opposition, and Hasina latest trip to China was in July 2019. The third prominent leader in Bangladesh, H.M. Ershad also appreciated the need to strengthen ties with Beijing and while in office he visited China as many as five times.[4] Even Jama'at-i-islami, known for its religious agenda, has not made any unfriendly noises towards China.

One of China's endearing qualities has been its strict policy of non-interference and non- partisanship in the domestic Bangladeshi politics. Irrespective of the domestic developments taking place within Bangladesh, Beijing has always refrained from issuing any public statements regarding Bangladesh. It has consistently refrained from taking any position or attempting to influence the Bangladeshi politics in favour of or against any one particular party or group. Unlike other powers, China has never shown any preference towards a particular leader or political party. Such an attitude in turn has given enormous political comfort to all the political forces within Bangladesh and their willingness to promote closer ties with Beijing. This is amply reflected by the large number of bilateral visits that have been taking place for over the last three decades.

The political comfort shared between the two sides manifests though various symbolic actions China initiates, such as commemoration events marking Bangladeshi–Chinese normalisation (2000), year-long friendship celebrations (2005) and numerous other special events. In fact in keeping with 2021 being the Mujibur Rahman centenary year, China is also showcasing its respect to the greatest Bengali of all time, Father of the Nation Bangabandhu Sheikh Mujibur Rahman in his birth centenary this year, which also corresponds with the celebration of the 45th anniversary of Dhaka–Beijing.[5] The Chinese Embassy in Dhaka has also presented the Bangladeshi Prime Minister Sheikh Hasina with a brass mural of Bangabandhu Sheikh Mujibur Rahman.

The frequent reference to "one China policy" underscores the importance that Bangladeshi leaders accord to China. The small incident over opening up of the trade office of Taiwan, with whom Bangladesh enjoys flourishing trade ties, is case in point. Not only was the inaugural of the centre cancelled, but also the commerce minister responsible for the move was immediately sacked for his insensitive decision. Despite its other large trade partners, Bangladesh has never lost sight of China's pivotal role in its state.

Economic and developmental partnership

Having overcome the recognition hurdle, both Bangladeshi and Chinese leaders lost no time to prioritise their common interests arising out of an understanding of mutual needs. From the very outset, both sides were keen to establish close economic ties and beginning with the Zia period (1975–1981), the Sino-Bangladesh cooperation began on various economic, technical and trade matters. The first ever visit by the Chinese leadership took place in March 1978 when Vice Premier Li Xiannian visited Dhaka. During the visit, both sides signed the Agreement for Cooperation in Economy, Science and Technology. Over the next few decades, various Bangladeshi leaders, officials and delegations have been periodically visiting China and many similar agreement were signed. Beginning from the H.M. Ershad period (1982–1990), China has also emerged as the largest player in the FDI sector in Bangladesh. Bangladesh has keenly encouraged both public and private sectors in China for introducing modern technology and to develop its communication infrastructures.

China has become one of Bangladesh's strongest trade partners too. The long-term trade agreement concluded in 1984 still forms the basis of the growing trade partnership between the two countries. In 1975 when China recognised Bangladesh, the bilateral trade stood at the meagre amount of US$13.75 million. Quarter of a century later, in 2001, it touched US$918 in 2001 and US$1.14 billion in 2003–2004 and crossed the US$3.4 mark in 2007. China exports raw cotton textile and textile goods, machinery and mechanical appliances, electrical equipment, base metals and vehicles to Bangladesh and it buys garments, textiles, frozen foods, leather, jute, jute goods and plastics from Bangladesh. In the last 15 years, China has emerged as Bangladesh's largest trading partner, overtaking India which enjoyed that status until 2005.

From the very beginning, the trade has been heavily loaded in favour of China. In 2004, the deficit stood at little over a $1 billion, crossing to US$ 2billion mark in 2006. China trade with Bangladesh has been increasing annually by almost 30%. Many Chinese companies appear interested in investing in the special economic zones that Bangladesh is setting up.

Earlier, Bangladesh proposed a free trade agreement with China given its concern over its inability to bridge the growing trade gap. While that never got signed, China gave a tariff exemption for 97% of Bangladeshi products effective from 1 July 2020. This accorded Bangladeshi zero duty access to Chinese market to 8256 products from the earlier 3095 Bangladeshi products.[6] Sino-Bangladesh trade has grown exponentially to be around US$18 billion from US$12.4 during 2016–2017.[7] While in 2006, Bangladesh's imports from China grew by 39% to US$1.66 billion in the same period, widening the trade gap further to over US$1.2 billion. Subsequently, Chinese imports grew at an 82.1% growth from

2013 to 2018. The trade deficit between Bangladesh and China stood at an all-time high of US$12,808 million in FY 2019 from the earlier rate of the trade deficit during FY 2015–2016 and FY 2017–2018 at 19%.[8] In 2015, China became Bangladesh's top trading partner, knocking India out of the position it had held for 40 years.[9]

But this trade gap never became a controversial issue in Dhaka unlike its trade gap with India. Indeed, accepting the asymmetrical structure of the two economies, China has recognised and often expressed in public that the problem of trade imbalance could be resolved only through measures such as Chinese investments in Bangladesh. Towards this end, China has sought and encouraged a business-friendly environment for their investors to invest in Bangladesh. In 2016, President Xi Jinping visited Bangladesh, after a gap of 30 years that resulted in 27 agreements and MoUs during the visit, involving an amount of over US$20 billion. China has for long been involved in various infrastructural projects in Bangladesh and 13 of these bilateral agreements covered infrastructure, construction, energy and transportation.

Clearly, while it has emerged as one of Bangladesh largest trading partners, China has also taken over as one of its largest development partner. The Chinese investment in Bangladeshi infrastructure has been conspicuous and sustained. While there has been a lot of buzz over the BRI, on the ground not many of the projects have been initiated. The BRI continues to be a subject of discussion in Bangladesh. Some of the visible projects funded by China include the following:

- The China–Bangladesh Friendship Centre that was initially built with a US$24 million interest-free loan, which was subsequently converted into a grant.
- Seven China–Bangladesh Friendship Bridges have been built. The eighth, Bekutia of Barisal–Khulna regional highway on the Kocha River, is under construction, scheduled for completion in 2021.[10]
- Barapukuria coal-fired power plant and Khulna thermal power plant: the total cost of these projects is estimated at $500 million and they are seen vital for the energy sector in Bangladesh.[11]
- Installation of digital telephone countrywide as well as for the Pagla Water Treatment Plant and North Dhaka (East) Sewerage Treatment Plant and Associated Sewerage System through concessional loan. China also committed to provide supplier's credit for the Greater Dhaka power project.
- It has set up three complete ownership and six joint venture companies in Export Processing Zones (EPZ) areas and have been jointly tapping the resources of Taiwan and Hong Kong in forming 23 more such joint ventures in Bangladesh.[12]
- China is building the 6.15 km rail link project of the Padma Multipurpose Bridge, which is in its last stages of completion now, although there has been rumours of fund crunch for this project. Once completed, it will connect Bangladesh's principal sea ports and link it to the Dhaka–Chittagong

Highway. The bridge will connect multi-lane expressways and railway lines with Dhaka to Bangladesh's largest deep-sea port at Payra which can then be accessed easily from northeastern India, Bhutan and eastern Nepal.[13] Apart from connecting nearly 30 million people in Bangladesh's southwest region to the rest of the country, the bridge will enhance regional trade and collaboration along the Asian highway No. 1 and the Trans-Asian railway network.[14]

- During Xi's visit in 2016, the Sino-Bangladeshi joint venture, the 1224 MW thermal power plant at Banshkali, was formally inaugurated on this visit.

From the Bangladeshi perspective, China's cooperation and assistance as a development partner and friend are important ways and means to mitigate Bangladesh's poverty levels and increase its self-reliance.[15]

It has been pointed out that "this vast web of projects and deals around the world is less about China attempting to attain global domination than about desperately promoting, among Chinese people, Xi and the Chinese Communists party's right to rule."[16] As part of the BRI, China has founded 81 education establishments and 35 cultural centres and spent around US$39.3 million on Silk Road scholarships in the first half of 2018.[17] And specifically for Bangladesh, beyond creating large-scale infrastructures for transport and energy sectors, BRI also provides opportunities for further engagements with governments, private sector and civil society entities as well as think tanks and academia.[18] Development of the Confucius Institute at Dhaka University and the Tier-4 National Data Centre in Gazipur's Kaliakoir were some of the projects decided under BRI.

Not only has Bangladesh expressed its willingness to be part of the BRI, Premier Sheikh Hasina has urged India to join the project. According to her, "being such a big country and big economy, India should not worry about it [OBOR]. Rather, they can also join so that all the countries can benefit economically."[19] This statement issued within weeks of Awami League winning the election in 2019 needs to be understood in the context of growing China's importance to Bangladesh. Undoubtedly, BRI is largely viewed positively in Bangladesh. Accordingly, "BRI has significant impact on Bangladesh from an economic and connectivity perspective and the Chittagong Port can act as a central hub to connect Northeast India, Myanmar, Southeast China, Bhutan, Nepal, and Bangladesh."[20] Bangladesh through its land and water routes forms a natural corridor between South Asia and South East Asia, making it a critical player in interregional integration. Thus, China initiated a "Strategic Partnership of Cooperation," leading to a new chapter in the BRI.[21] It needs to be noted that while the strategic context of BRI is understood, the trade and commerce aspects are yet to be fully known.

The two sides signed 27 agreements and MoUs totalling to a projected value of US$24.45 billion, making China the biggest investor for Bangladesh. Additionally, China offered US$13.6 billion investment for joint ventures, thereby making it a total of US$38.05 million in Chinese assistance.[22] As per another study, the figure would stand at US$42 billion given the private sector investments from China.[23] These figures as yet have not set the alarm bells in Dhaka, but many do suggest caution. Bangladeshis possibly hope that China would be easy on the loans as in the past when China had waived off US$24 billion loans.

Contrary to the situation unravelled in Colombo and elsewhere, the prospects of BRI will apparently lead to greater financial integration that may lead to greater Chinese portfolio investment in the Bangladesh Stock market. Indeed, Bangladesh will also have an opportunity to access China's equity (globally second largest) and bond markets (globally third largest) through this initiative.[24] Most of the Chinese investment in Bangladesh comes through soft Chinese loans, with interest rates of 2% and repayment periods of 20 years.[25] The Chinese investments stand at US$85.94 million dollars, and US$380 million in terms of stock in 2018 with engineering contracts signed between Bangladesh and Chinese companies reaching US$10.4 billion.[26] While Bangladesh's external debt now stands at about US$25 billion with a debt-to-GDP ratio of about 27%, Bangladeshis presently seem sanguine about the BRI project. Experts have also argued that although "Bangladesh carries about US$8 billion in Chinese debt but has a close military relationship, purchasing many of its latest weapons systems from China," it will be an unlikely source of anxiety.[27] But a note of caution is introduced about connectivity facilitating greater movement of goods from China to Bangladesh, invariably impacting on the existing trade imbalance.[28] However, it is too early to say that Bangladesh is falling into a debt trap, some experts argue. Bangladesh's total external debt at the end of 2018 stood at around US$33.1 billion, and the share owed to China does not seem big.[29]

As per some reports, under the BRI projects, Bangladesh will receive US$26 billion for BRI projects and US$14 billion for joint venture project, together totalling to a US$40 billion package.[30] While there exists some amount of trepidation regarding the long-term implications of the loans, there is as yet no further clarity about the details of the projects and "the financial implications for Bangladesh in agreeing to China's BRI will depend primarily to what extent Bangladesh chooses to be involved in the project overall experts suggests weighing the real cost–benefit ratio carefully with a long-term view before Bangladesh decides whether it should get involved in this project and to what extent.[31] Some of these include:

1. Proposed China and Bangladesh tentatively agreed to construct a road and railway system linking Kunming and Chittagong (Chinese concessional loan US$1.5 billion). The proposed transportation route, called the Chittagong-Kunming Road and Railway Link, provide a cheaper alternative of only 250-km railway lines than is presently available for shipping through 900 kms highway linking Chittagong to Kunming.

2. The Karnaphuli Multi-Channel Tunnel Project in southern Bangladesh is now well under way. Due to be completed in 2020, ease the heavy congestion on the existing two bridges across the river, while also connecting-up with the Korean Export Processing Zone and Shah Amanat International Airport. It will also feed into two other projects that are currently under way – the Asian Highway and the Dhaka-Chittagong-Cox's Bazar Highway. With a total length of 9 km – of which 3.4 km will run below the river – it will be the first tunnel in Bangladesh to facilitate simultaneous road and rail transit.[32] Once completed, the tunnel will connect the port city of Chittagong, to the Asian Highway and the Dhaka–Chittagong–Cox's Bazar Highway.[33]
3. The port modernisation plans include that of Chittagong port, which handles around 92% of the country's import–export trade. Dhaka, however, cancelled China's proposal to the deep-water port facility at Sonadia, located near Cox's Bazar, 140 km south of Chittagong, proposed to connect to Kunming, citing lack of commercial viability in 2016.[34]
4. China's interest in the port area is evident and for the first time Bangladesh has also agreed to China's proposal to build a 750-acre industrial park in Chittagong. Bangladeshi sea ports will be used by China for its exports to other markets, befitting Bangladesh in a meaningful way.[35]
5. China will finance the construction of a 170-km-long Marine Drive Expressway connecting to Sitakunda–Chittagong–Cox's Bazar is estimated US$2.68 billion, The project will be carried out with Chinese soft loans and without any competitive bidding. According to the proposal, the Marine Drive Expressway and Sitakunda–Chittagong–Cox's Bazar Coastal Protection Works would cost US$2.8 billion.[36] This expressway will be connected with the Asian Highway No. 41 and the Bangladesh–China–India–Myanmar (BCIM) Economic Corridor.

As yet, there has been no recorded progress in many of the projects except for the Karnaphuli tunnel in Chittagong and a 1000-MW thermal power plant in the Payrasea-port of Patuakhali, many are in various stages of implementation. On the whole, while the BRI projects hold high promises for economic development, the outcome will be determined by the way Bangladesh plans and executes these high-value projects.[37]

Indeed, while there was some disruptions due to the COVID-19 pandemic, but many Chinese nationalists resumed work for the various ongoing projects.

Defence cooperation

China in the last three decades has emerged as the main supplier of military hardware and training to Bangladesh. Bangladesh's armed forces are predominantly equipped with Chinese military hardware. The army uses Chinese tanks and light tanks. The Bangladesh navy's frigates and patrol crafts are mostly Chinese.

Similarly, Bangladesh air force's combat aircrafts are almost exclusively Chinese. It was during Khaleda Zia's visit to China in 2002 that the two countries signed the most comprehensive defence cooperation agreement. The agreement, the only of its kind that Bangladesh has signed with any country, includes cooperation in the field of training, exchange of information on defence and production and maintenance of materials and in other sectors. What for long remained a piecemeal arrangement in the defence sector has now become "a broad-based agreement."[38] China also caters to capacity-building of internal security forces, including the police.

In fact, earlier one exception was when the then Prime Minister Sheikh Hasina (1996–2000) decided to acquire 8 MiG29 fighters from Russia, since Bangladeshi–China relations were established in the post-Mujib period. Among others, Bangladesh has acquired 65 fighter planes, 39 helicopters and a number of coastal patrol boats, tanks and artillery systems. The only munitions factory in Gazipur was built with Chinese assistance. Most of them were given to Bangladesh either as military aid or at friendly prices. Bangladesh has been useful for China to discard its ageing and obsolete soviet weapons as it embarked upon military modernization. In 2002, both countries signed an agreement whereby China would provide Bangladesh with military hardware and training.

- Bangladesh stocked up on, 122 mm guns and a host of small arms such as pistons, sub-machine guns and 82 mm mortars, 65 large calibre artillery system, 16 combat aircrafts and 114 missiles and related equipment from China.
- It also gifted a large quantity of equipment to the Bangladeshi police.
- In February 2007, the neutral caretaker government decided to purchase 16 fighter planes from China at the cost of US$94 million.
- In 2011, Bangladesh procured 44 Chinese MBT-2000 main battle tanks worth US$162 million.
- In 2016 Bangladesh took delivery of the first of the two submarines purchased from China at a cost of US$203 million. Beijing will also help Bangladesh construct its first submarine base, but Chinese submarines will not use the facility.[39]
- To strengthen its naval forces, Prime Minister Hasina had also commissioned a Chinese Corvette named BNS Sangram.[40] Clearly, the Bangladeshi military has been strongly supported by China.
- Bangladeshi air force received 16 F-7BGI fighter jets from China by 2013.[41]

However, it is widely believed that the Bangladesh army is unsatisfied with the quality of weapons received from China. But given the "friendly prices" of such supplies, it is unlikely that Bangladesh would be able to replace China's position as the largest supplier of military hardware in the near, or even distant, future, although the Indo-Bangladeshi defence cooperation has grown in last five years, but China continues to be a dominant player in this sector.

Assuming new roles

The one aspect that China had limited presence in Bangladesh was in the public health sector; however, the recent COVID-19 pandemic introduced the new element to the bilateral ties. The recent offer of Beijing to send 100,000 doses of Chinese coronavirus vaccine to Bangladesh for emergency use on 16 March 2021 was following up on its promise of Bangladesh being given priority when it had discovered COVID-19 vaccine. In Bangladesh, a Chinese company has been allowed to run the third phase trial of the Sinovac coronavirus vaccine, although it did not agree to co-fund the trial. Earlier Bangladesh has sent medical accessories, including masks, gowns, caps and gloves to China, while China sent a medical expert team to guide the pandemic control measures, patients' treatment and laboratory tests, and also training for Bangladeshi medical professionals. China has also provided Bangladesh with over 3 million surgical and N-95 masks, over 110,000 sets of personal protective equipment and a large number of test kits, thermometers, ventilators and sanitisers. Bangladesh was promised USD100 million by the Asian Infrastructure Investment Bank to deal with the pandemic conditions.[42]

This apart, China has carved out a niche for itself when it publicly stood up for Bangladesh over the Rohingya refugee crises. According to Li Jiming, the Chinese Ambassador in Dhaka, 'Beijing will do whatever they can to help alleviate the situation and push forward early repatriation.' … Beijing is playing a role in finding a sustainable solution to the Rohingya crisis as China shares Bangladesh's concerns regarding the issue. For its part, China has been supportive of Bangladesh, especially when it reiterated that "China is trying to persuade Myanmar all the time that the eventual solution of the Rohingya issue will be beneficial to both the countries (Bangladesh and Myanmar), and I believe that the Rohingya issue will be settled in the end."[43] This supportive role of Beijing and mediating its deep crises won the hearts of Bangladeshis. Bangladesh has been deeply affected by the millions of Rohingya refugee influx from Myanmar and has been struggling to provide for them. While Bangladesh's relationship remains tenuous with Myanmar, China has been the only power that has unhesitantly given some assurance of possible conflict resolution.

Without a doubt, limited cultural-historic background has not impeded Bangladesh from developing close and comprehensive relations with China. Since the normalisation, the relations remained non-controversial and enjoy widespread political support and public endorsement. Without a doubt, in recent years, China has emerged a strategic partner for Bangladesh, accompanied by strong political cooperation, economic interaction and military partnership.[44]

At one level, Bangladesh does not fear from Chinese culture emerging as a dominant factor in bilateral relations and, secondly, China has not been too closely identified with a particular political force in Bangladesh. The determination of China to strictly follow non-interference in the domestic affairs of Bangladesh resulted in a bipartisan support for closer friendship with Beijing. And while Bangladesh is becoming an important regional partner, it is assuming a relevance that is ensuring that all its neighbours deepen its engagement and China is certainly leaving no stone unturned to lend its hand of partnership. The graduation of Bangladesh into a middle-income country graduation and to developing country from the group of least developed country status substantiated by its sustained economic growth and its geographical situation at an increasingly important theatre of international jostling makes Bangladesh a valuable partner that China will wish to nurture. The years ahead will see further deepening of Sino-Bangladesh partnership.

Notes

1 "Chinese President Xi Jinping Marking the Celebration of Mujib Borsho and the Golden Jubilee of the Independence of Bangladesh", *Dhaka Tribune*, 17 March 2021, https://www.dhakatribune.com/bangladesh/foreign-affairs/2021/03/17/chinese-president-will-strengthen-development-strategies-with-bangladesh, accessed 17 March 2021
2 "Bangladeshi FM Calls China 'Active Development Partner on Eve of Visit'", *FBIS-NES-2002-1222*, 22 December 2002.
3 Sreeradha Datta, "Bangladesh's Foreign Policy", in S. Narayan and Sreeradha Datta (eds), *Bangladesh at 50: Development and Challenges*, Hyderabad: Orient BlackSwan, 2020.
4 1 November 1982, July 1985, July 1987, November 1988 and June 1990.
5 Nafees Sakhawat, "China-Bangladesh Relations Stronger than Ever Before", *Asia Times*, 6 October 2020, https://www.thedailystar.net/opinion/news/china-bangladesh-relations-stronger-ever-1972993, accessed 17 March 2021.
6 PTI, "China Offers Bangladesh Tariff Exemption for 97% of Exports from Dhaka Amid Tensions with India", *Business Insider*, 20 June 2020, https://www.businessinsider.in/policy/foreign-policy/news/china-offers-bangladesh-tariff-exemption-for-97-of-exports-from-dhaka-amid-tensions-with-india/articleshow/76482640.cms, accessed 17 March 2021
7 "Bangladesh China Trade to Hit $18 Billion by 2021", *The Independent*, 17 March 2021, https://m.theindependentbd.com/arcprint/details/191922/2019-03-188, accessed 17 March 2021
8 "China Bangladesh Trade: New Prospects Opening Up for Bangladesh", *Data BD*, 2 July 2020, https://www.lightcastlebd.com/insights/2020/07/china-bangladesh-trade-war, accessed 17 March 2021
9 Anu Anwar, "How Bangladesh Is Benefiting from the China-India Rivalry", *The Diplomat*, 12 July 2019, https://thediplomat.com/2019/07/how-bangladesh-is-benefiting-from-the-china-india-rivalry/, accessed 17 March 2021.
10 "8th Bangladesh-China Friendship Bridge to Be Built in Pirojpur", *Daily Sun*, 5 April 2019, https://www.daily-sun.com/arcprint/details/382773/8th-BangladeshChina-Friendship-Bridge-to-be-built-in-Pirojpur/2019-04-05, accessed 17 March 2020.
11 Aminul Islam, "Chinese Co to Produce Brakpuria Coal by April", *New Age*, 31 January 2005, http://www.newagebd.com/2005/jan/31/front.html, accessed 17 March 2005.
12 Mashiur Rahaman, "S Korea Largest Investor in Bangladesh", *The Nation*, 3 February 2008, http://nation.ittefaq.com/issues/2008/02/03/news0683.htm, accessed 7 March 2009.
13 Probir Pramanik, "Bangladesh Inches Closer to Tame Padma, Bridge Economic Gap", *Outlook*, 19 November 2018, https://www.outlookindia.com/website/story/bangladesh-inches-closer-to-tame-padma-bridge-economic-gap/320396, accessed 3 April 2020.

14 "4th Span of Bangladesh's Padma Bridge Installed Successfully", *The China Daily*, 13 May 2018, http://www.chinadaily.com.cn/a/201805/13/WS5af7fb83a3103f6866ee807b.html, accessed 1 March 2019.
15 Sreeradha Datta, "Bangladesh China Growing Ties and Impact on India", in Satish Kumar (ed.), *India's National Security: Annual Review 2013*, New Delhi: Routledge India, 2014.
16 MerridenVarrall, "Belt and Road Initiative, China's Biggest Brand That Is Too Big to Fail", *Channel News Asia*, 14 September 2018, https://www.channelnewsasia.com/news/commentary/belt-road-initiative-china-biggest-brand-cannot-afford-to-fail-10671460, accessed 17 March 2021.
17 A. N. M. Muniruzzaman, "Belt and Road Initiative: The Hurdles along the Way", *The Daily Star*, 13 December 2018, https://www.thedailystar.net/opinion/global-affairs/news/the-hurdles-along-the-way-1672738, accessed 17 March 2020.
18 Authors interview with Prof. Munir Khusru, Dhaka University, 3 November 2019.
19 "India Shouldn't Worry about China Led One Belt One Road", *Daily Star*, 23 January 2019, https://www.thedailystar.net/frontpage/news/india-shouldnt-worry-about-china-led-one-belt-one-road-1691632, accessed 7 March 2020.
20 Authors interview with Prof. Munir Khusru, see n. 18.
21 "Chinese Ambassador Proposes Belt and Road Mechanism for Bangladesh", *Bdnews24.com*, 11 September 2018, https://bdnews24.com/neighbours/2018/09/11/chinese-ambassador-proposesbelt-and-roadmechanismfor-bangladesh, accessed 17 March 2019
22 T. V. Paul, "When Balance of Power Meets Globalization", *Politics*, vol. 39, no. 1, 2019, p. 53.
23 "Chinese Investment in Bangladesh Rings Alarm Bells in India", *Financial Times*, 7 August 2018, https://www.ft.com/content/1ab2ebe6-85c3-11e8-96dd-fa565ec55929, accessed 17 March 2020.
24 Authors interview with Prof Munir Khusru, see n. 18.
25 Serajul Quadir, "China to Develop Bangladesh Industrial Zone as Part of South Asia Push", *Reuters*, 4 April 2018, https://www.reuters.com/article/us-bagnladesh-china/china-to-develop-bangladesh-industrial-zone-as-part-of-south-asia-push-idUSKCN1HB1M2, accessed 17 March 2019
26 "Chinese Ambassador Proposes Belt and Road Mechanism for Bangladesh", *Bdnews24.com*, 11 September 2018, https://bdnews24.com/neighbours/2018/09/11/chinese-ambassador-proposesbelt-and-roadmechanismfor-bangladesh, accessed 17 March 2020.
27 "China's 'Debt Trap' Economics Will Likely Result in It Gaining Greater Access to Nations around India: US Think-Tank", *Financial Express*, 18 May 2018, https://www.financialexpress.com/economy/chinas-debt-trap-economics-will-likely-result-in-it-gaining-greater-access-to-nations-around-india-us-think-tank/1172743/ (statement by Richard D. Fisher, Senior fellow at International Assessment and Strategy Centre), accessed 17 March 2019.
28 Authors interview with Amb. Shamsher Chaudhury, former Foreign Secretary to the Government of Bangladesh, 3 November 2019.
29 "Is the Strategic Partnership with China Luring Bangladesh into a Debt Trap?", *The Wire*, 12 July 2019, https://thewire.in/south-asia/china-bangladesh-relationship-debt-trap, accessed 17 March 2020.
30 "Belt and Road Initiative: Perspective from Bangladesh", *Daily Star*, 7 August 2019, https://www.thedailystar.net/round-tables/news/belt-and-road-initiative-perspective-bangladesh-1782928, accessed 17 March 2020.
31 Authors interview with Amb Shamsher Chaudhury, see n. 28.
32 HKTDC news release 8 May 2018, https://hkmb.hktdc.com/en/1X0ADVB4/market-spotlight/China-Helps-to-Upgrade-Bangladesh%E2%80%99s-Infrastructure-for-Belt-and-Road, accessed 17 March 2019.

33 Indrani Bagchi, "Dhaka Cancels Port to Be Built by China, India Eyes Another", *Times of India,* 8 February 2016, http://timesofindia.indiatimes.com/articleshow/50894554.cms?utm_source=contentofinterest&utm_medium=text&utm_campaign=cppst, accessed 17 March 2016.
34 *Ibid.*
35 Authors interview with Amb Shamsher Chaudhury, see n. 28.
36 Jagran Chakma, "Sitakunda-Cox Bazar Marine Drive, China to Finance Expressway", *The Independent*, 8 July 2017, http://www.theindependentbd.com/arcprint/details/102803/2017-07-08, accessed 17 July 2017.
37 Fahmida Khatun and Syed Yusuf Saadat, "How Can Bangladesh Benefit from the Belt and Road Initiative?", *Dhaka Tribune*, 19 November 2020, https://www.dhakatribune.com/opinion/op-ed/2020/11/19/op-ed-how-can-bangladesh-benefit-from-the-belt-and-road-initiative, accessed on 17 March 2020.
38 "Broad-Based Defence Deal with China on Agenda Khaleda Leaves for Beijing Today", *The Independent,* 20 December 2002.
39 Arshad Mahmud, "New Bangladesh Sub Base Could Revive Indian Tension", *Asia Times*, 23 July 2019, https://asiatimes.com/2019/07/new-bangladesh-submarine-base-could-revive-tensions-with-india/, accessed 17 March 2020.
40 "China Fast-Tracks Key Defence Projects in Bangladesh", *South Asia Monitor*, 23 July 2020, https://southasiamonitor.org/china-watch/china-fast-tracks-key-defence-projects-bangladesh, accessed 17 March 2021.
41 Bina D'Costa, "Bangladesh in 2011 Weak Statebuilding and Diffident Foreign Policy", *Asian Survey*, vol. 52, no. 1, January/February 2012, p. 153.
42 Nafees Sakhawat, "China-Bangladesh Relations Stronger than Ever Before", *Daily Star*, 6 October 2020, https://www.thedailystar.net/opinion/news/china-bangladesh-relations-stronger-ever-1972993, accessed 17 March 2021.
43 "Envoy: China Plays Unique Role in Resolving Rohingya Crisis", *Dhaka Tribune*, 24 November 2019, https://www.dhakatribune.com/bangladesh/rohingya-crisis/2019/11/24/chinese-envoy-china-will-remain-neutral-over-rohingya-issue, accessed 17 March 2021.
44 Sreeradha Datta, "Bangladesh's Relations with China and India: A Comparative Study", *Strategic Analysis*, vol. 32, no. 5, 2008, pp. 755–72.

13
CHINA'S ENGAGEMENT AND MANAGING SECURITY DILEMMA IN SOUTH ASIA

A Nepali perspective

Kosh Raj Koirala

Introduction

Like in other South Asian countries, China's engagement with Nepal has increased manifold, mainly after this Himalayan nation witnessed major political changes, including the formal end of a decade-long Maoist insurgency and the abolition of the 240-year-old institution of monarchy in 2008. Lately, China seems to have used its Belt and Road Initiatives (BRI) as an important tool to increase its influence and engagements in Nepal as well as other countries in the region. While China seems to have taken Nepal as a gateway to South Asia, Nepal sees this as an opportunity to diversify its "dependence" and also as an alternative source to finance its mega infrastructure projects. Surrounded by India on its three sides of the border, Nepal currently relies heavily on India for trade, investment and infrastructure development. But with the growing aspiration of people for the development and prosperity, this Himalayan nation is currently negotiating with China to bring in investment in various mega infrastructure projects such as railways and industrial parks, despite some displeasure from India, the United States and Japan. Not surprisingly, China's growing engagement and willingness to put investment in major railways, roadways, industrial parks and port cities in various South Asian countries has drawn "security dilemma" to many countries in the region and beyond. China's assertive foreign policy towards South Asia coincides not just with its economic rise but also with changes in strategic environment in South Asia, with India gradually aligning with the United States. It is thus important now to manage brewing "security dilemma" many countries face, encouraging China to ensure transparency and quality of its investment. They can also work on some confidence-building measures to avoid their suspicions and doubts with each other. Traditional realism guided primarily by geopolitical and strategic consideration cannot be proper response to China's growing engagements in South Asia, but a liberal approach that upholds the values of cooperation and interdependence. There are a number of areas China and South Asia can work together for peace, stability and development of the region.

Background

Nepal is a small country sandwiched between the two giant neighbours, India and China. Historically, this Himalayan nation has maintained closer relation with India due to cultural and linguistic affinity, political links and the unique open border regime that exists between the two countries. While India remains the major trading and development partner of Nepal,[1] it is also deeply involved in Nepal's internal politics. All major political changes, including the introduction of democracy for the first time in 1951, and restoration of this system later in 1990 in Nepal took place with direct or indirect involvement of India.[2] It was India that helped to broker peace between the Maoist rebels and the mainstream political parties back in 2006 and end the decade-long Maoist insurgency. The relation at the level of people between the two countries is equally deep-rooted as the Peace and Friendship Treaty reached in 1950 legitimatised free movement of people across the borders. The cross-border marriages are common, especially among people living in the southern part of the country.[3] Until recently, India was the main destination for higher education and foreign employment to Nepalese nationals. While Nepalese students constitute about 19% of the total international students India receives each year,[4] nearly six million Nepalese nationals live and work in India even today.[5]

On the contrary, Nepal has had a very limited interaction with China for centuries.[6] It does not share common language, culture and religion except for a small size of population that lives in the bordering districts with the modern-day Tibet Autonomous Region (TAR). Although Nepali traders used to walk across treacherous mountains and trade their goods in the TAR, Nepal did not have direct contacts with China until the latter took over Tibet in 1951. The limited cross-border movement that existed between the two counties was subsequently restricted further despite the fact that China helped build a 113-km Kodari highway that links Nepal's capital city Kathmandu with the TAR in 1960s.[7] Except for its assistance to build a few key pride projects like road, government buildings and factories, China's engagement with Nepal was largely confined to occasional exchanges of high-level visits between the two countries.[8]

However, the dynamics of Nepal–China relation witnessed meaningful transformations after 2008. There was a visible reorientation in China's foreign policy towards Nepal as Kathmandu witnessed a major political transition in 2006, marking the end of the decade-long Maoist insurgency. Two years later, the 240-year-old institution of monarchy was abolished, and the country was declared a federal democratic republic. Also, Tibetan refugees living in Nepal since China took over TAR in 1950s stepped up "anti-China" protest activities in Nepal ahead of Beijing Olympics in 2008.[9] These developments came amid India's strategic alignment with the United States, especially after the civil nuclear deal between the two countries in 2008.[10] India also began increasing its engagements in various Southeast Asian countries – something China traditionally considered its strategic backyard. In the wake of these developments, China appears to have begun pursuing assertive foreign policy towards Nepal, growing manifold its engagements with both state and non-state actors to create its influence and neutralise, if not offset, the near total influence of India in Nepal. Over the years, the engagements of China have grown so much that Indian policymakers and strategic thinkers seem already nervous.[11]

An overview of Chinese foreign policy

The founding of the People's Republic of China in 1949 marked the end of the century of humiliation China faced under colonial rule. It was with the humiliating events of the past in mind Mao Zedong as the founding leader of the PRC announced that China would never again be an insulted nation. Mao held beliefs that China must not leave itself vulnerable to abuse as foreign powers want to weaken, and deny due respect despite China becoming a country with traditionally great civilisation. Mao also believed that it is not possible to overcome the legacy of humiliation until Beijing regains control of all historically Chinese territory, especially Taiwan.[12]

Although China became a founding member of the non-alignment movement that sought to unite third-world countries based on the Five Principles of Peaceful Coexistence,[13] the policy of self-reliance enunciated by Mao greatly constrained Beijing's foreign contacts for long.[14] This isolationist foreign policy witnessed changes after new Chinese Premier Den Xiaoping in 1978 renounced Mao's disastrous economic model, and adopted "open door" policy, giving greater play to market forces, and encouraging foreign trades and investment.[15] This paved way for increased interactions of China with foreign countries.

However, the Tiananmen incident in which CPC leadership brutally suppressed mostly peaceful demonstration in and around Tiananmen Square in 1989 had important consequences on China's foreign relations.[16] While this incident created crisis of its image at international level, the PRC's stunning economic growth and military modernisation also started courting anxieties in its immediate neighbourhood and beyond in the following years.[17] Some scholars even floated "China threat" theory (Mearsheimer, 2001), suggesting that China is a "smart revisionist" power.[18]

It was against this context that China adopted a policy of reassurance, and even employed "charm offensive"[19] towards its neighbours as well as other countries. Chinese leadership realised that it was absolutely necessary for China to pursue accommodating stance "to avoid clashes with other countries that could derail the economic growth and threaten the CPC's hold on power."[20] While the use of hard power resources like aid, investment and military support dominated Chinese foreign policy since a long time, China now began using soft power resources as well to achieve its foreign policy goals to improve its international image and meet the conditions necessary to keep its economy afloat. Some of the foreign policy measures employed to achieve them included accommodating neighbours, assuming role of a team player in multilateral organisations and using economic ties to make friends. Beijing also promoted high-level diplomatic exchanges, trade initiatives, investment agreements, tourism and cultural understandings.[21]

The most visible manifestation of China's soft power in the realm of education and culture was the establishment of Confucius Institutes, which serve as a tool for "China's commercial, cultural, and linguistic proselytization."[22] China also adopted a policy of organising large-scale international events such as Beijing Olympic in 2008 and Shanghai World Expo and Asia Games in 2010 to bolster its benign image at international level.[23] A number of scholars have tried to examine China's use of soft power resources in its foreign policy in different perspectives. While Joshua Kurlantzick[24] has dealt with the threats, this may pose to the United States, other scholars have focused largely on its efficacy and the degree to which it presents threats to the standing of the United States or other countries.[25] Likewise, Kingsley Edney[26] suggests that China's use of soft power is basically aimed at building national cohesion, and achieving domestic legitimacy.

Scholars maintain that Chinese foreign policy after 2008 witnessed changes mainly in three fronts: enhanced regional cooperation, deviation from non-interference policy in internal affairs of other countries and increased assertiveness.[27] After his appointment as the president in November 2012, Xi Jinping announced China's goals of becoming a strong maritime power, and developing a new type of China–US Great Powers relations. Formulation of new periphery diplomacy, setting the goal of building two "Silk Roads," increasing great power responsibility, including through the participation in the UN peacekeeping, adopting more flexible pragmatism in its foreign policy and combining a "carrot and stick" approach[28] are some of his foreign policy innovations. All these policy measures have "three primary and enduring goals: power, wealth and status"[29] as the PRC's founding leader Mao sought to achieve.

Chinese policy towards South Asia

China shares common border with five South Asian nations, namely Nepal, India, Pakistan, Afghanistan and Bhutan. Although some informal trade relations between South Asia and the modern-day TAR as well as China mainland persisted since ancient times, China remained isolated from much of South Asia by the formidable Himalayas. This isolation increased further after China took over TAR in 1950s. Following a brief war with India in 1962, "China formed a close relationship with Pakistan, and even sold its nuclear and missile technology in order to balance India, which was then under the patronage of the then Soviet Union."[30] However, other small countries in the South Asian region, including

Nepal, Bangladesh (achieved independence from Pakistan in 1971), Sri Lanka and Maldives, figured much less in Chinese foreign policy radar until Beijing sought to develop warm relations with all its neighbours, including India, as an "early part of its omni directional good-neighbor policy in 1979."[31]

China's South Asia policy is largely dictated by its strategic rivalry with India, and its desire to keep its border safe. Although the visit of then Indian Prime Minister Rajiv Gandhi to Beijing in 1988 paved way for the improvement in the relations between the two countries, this did not yield much result in restoring normalcy in their relations. As China sought to enhance its ties with South Asian countries to create political influence in the aftermath of Cold War,[32] New Delhi felt uncomfortable with Beijing's advances in the areas deemed as its spheres of strategic influence. Much to the chagrin of New Delhi, Beijing further increased its assertive foreign policy towards the region after Bush administration began cultivating India as China's counterweight in the region through civil nuclear deal.[33] Policymakers in Beijing believe that the Indo-US nuclear deal and India's exclusive right as a non-party to the Non-Proliferation Treaty to engage in nuclear trade would create imbalance in South Asia, given no comparable arrangement for Islamabad, which is Beijing's strategic partner in South Asia.[34] As such, China has chosen to keep its border disputes with India in status quo, while it has no major border disputes with other South Asian countries. Territorial dispute between India and China, therefore, seem less likely to be resolved as long as Beijing considers New Delhi as the strategic ally of the United States and other Western powers. It is a positive development for all small countries in South Asia, including Nepal, that China and India have agreed to amicably settle their months-long bitter border dispute in the Eastern Ladakh. But there is no guarantee that this border dispute will not revive in the future, given the fact that India has heavily thrown its weight behind the United States and its allies in their strategic goal to keep China, which is growing strong both in terms of its economy and military powers, in check in recent years.

China's engagements with South Asian countries appear to have increased further in recent years despite the United States and its allies in the region have devised various strategies to thwart China's ever-expanding influence in the region. China's foreign policy overtures to increase its influence in the South Asia are less likely to recede as Beijing sees the South Asia as strategically important region. Some of the important foreign policy goals of China towards South Asia include ensuring regional peace and stability through diplomatic influence and balance of power, countering the US policy of containment of China, engaging regional countries, including India, through friendly relations, maintaining multidimensional cooperation and economic ties and securing sea lanes of communication in the Indian Ocean for uninterrupted supply of energy and raw materials to its economy. China's South Asia policy also includes supporting the US-led anti-terrorism campaign in Afghanistan without getting intractably involved in order to avoid terrorism spilling across its borders to restive Xinjiang and TAR.[35] With ascendance of Xi Jinping in power in 2012, China has pursued a policy of enhancing connectivity with South

Asian countries through initiatives like the BRI and Maritime Silk Road. While introducing the concept of community of shared destiny, the PRC has in recent years shown willingness to sign friendship treaties with neighbouring countries to build trust. The PRC, for example, expressed its readiness for China–Nepal–India trilateral cooperation and China–India–Sri Lanka trilateral cooperation to address security concerns of India.[36] China has been creating its influence in India's small neighbours through various measures such as increased grant assistance, investment in major infrastructure projects such as hydropower plants, airport, port city development, scholarship to students, military aid as well as training to security personnel, military exchange and high-level visits.[37]

China has been able to make a good footprint in South Asia as most small neighbours of India see China as a viable alternative to balance India's so-called hegemonic behaviour (both perceived and real). They want to give some space to China to resolve their own "security dilemma." Unprecedented economic growth that China has been able to achieve over the past few decades has also attracted many of these small countries towards China. This economic success story has made China able to project itself as economic and political alternative. Among other things, rulers, especially those with authoritarian ambition, in many different countries around the world, including those in South Asia, have chosen to ally with China, mainly because China makes no issues of human rights. It does not even choose to interfere or put pressure of any forms to these countries to establish democracy or safeguard human rights as long as its interests are met.

Chinese policy towards Nepal

Nepal and the restive TAR of China share a common boundary of over 1400 km.[38] The two countries maintained modest interactions ever since the formal diplomatic relations was reached in 1955. Although the mass exodus of Tibetan protestors to Nepal after their failed uprising against PRC's rule in TAR in 1959 drew heightened concern of China towards Nepal, the interaction between the two countries was still limited largely to Chinese economic and technical assistance to a few key pride projects, and the occasional exchange of visits on the part of top leadership of China, and Nepal's monarch until 1990, and later prime ministers.[39]

But with the major political change that brought Maoist rebels into mainstream politics, and subsequently abolished the 240-year-old institution of monarchy in 2008, China's policy of limited interactions with Nepal appears to have seen a major change. This foreign policy departure also coincided with anti-China protest activities on the part of Tibetan refugees in Kathmandu streets just ahead of Beijing Olympics, and India's strategic alignment with the United States following civil nuclear deal in 2008.

Chinese foreign policy towards Nepal after 2008 appears to have a key objective to neutralise India's near-total influence in Nepal's internal affairs through economic and political engagements. Beijing has been employing various strategies such as aid, trade, investment, exchange visits, people-to-people contact and support in the areas of education, culture and sports in Nepal in order to achieve these foreign policy objectives. Among other things, China has announced to connect Rasuwagadhi near capital city Kathmandu with its train service by 2020, and open up more border points, including one in Hilsa in western Nepal,[40] in a bid to boost connectivity between the two countries.

Unlike India, China maintained a pretty low-key presence in Nepal until recently. The abolition of monarchy in 2008 made a point for China to cultivate relation with all major political forces, and security agencies in Nepal, keeping in view of the possible anti-China activities by Tibetan refugees – something China believed was incited by India and Western countries active in Nepal.[41] As such, China started providing huge amount of financial assistance and logistic support to Nepalese Army, which until 2008 relied solely on India. A large number of senior Chinese army officials visited Nepal these years apparently to deepen their relations with Nepal's security agencies. The desire of China to cultivate better relations with army is aimed at finding a reliable force, which could effectively curb anti-China activities in Nepal. Besides it engagements with the army, Beijing also increased its engagements with Nepal Police and Armed Police Force (APF) in Nepal. While it has handed over APF Training Academy building to Nepal Government, Beijing provided a large number of logistics such as riot gears, water cannons and other transport vehicles to Nepal Police.

Chinese foreign policy towards Nepal after 2008 is also aimed at deepening economic interaction. In recent years, China stands as the largest donor and the FDI source country to Nepal, leaving behind even India. Most recently, China is pushing to make investment in major infrastructures in Nepal under its ambitious BRI project. President Bidya Devi Bhandari of Nepal was among the high-level delegates attending in the second Belt and Road Forum for International Cooperation in Beijing in April 2018. China is keen to invest in cross-country railway line, transmission line and various other road and industrial projects under BRI. Equally, China has increased its cooperation in education, culture and other areas in Nepal. While it has substantially increased scholarship quotas to Nepalese students, China has been funding Confucius Institutes and a variety of cultural fairs to promote Chinese language and culture in Nepal. Unlike its long-standing policy of non-interference in other country's internal affairs, China has started influencing internal politics of Nepal as well.[42] China is now engaged in almost all areas in Nepal, from security to economic cooperation to cultural exchanges to people-to-people contacts.

Nepal's BRI dilemma

Nepal signed China's BRI in May 2017 amid discomfort of India and major Western powers. Subsequently, two separate committees led by foreign and finance secretary identified various 35 projects to be developed under BRI. But with the sluggish progress in negotiations in the following months, Chinese side suggested Nepali side to bring down the number to less than ten. Government is currently negotiating on nine different projects related to connectivity and energy under the BRI. These include three road projects, two hydroelectricity projects, one cross-border railway project and one cross-country transmission line project. One technical institute named after late NCP founding leader Madan Bhandari is also in the Nepal's wish list. Two key projects – Nepal–China Trans-Himalayan Multi-Dimensional Connectivity Network and Nepal–China Cross Border Railway – have been incorporated in the joint communique issued after the conclusion of the second Belt and Road Forum for International Cooperation held in Beijing in April 2019.

As a small landlocked country between India and China, Nepal has always maintained friendly relations with both the countries, inclining a little more towards India because of geographical proximity, linguistic and cultural affinity and open border regime. However, Beijing's current attempt to jostle with New Delhi for its influence is now forcing policymakers in Kathmandu to confront a difficult choice – whether to go with India or China, which is now heavily investing in the country to enhance the connectivity and infrastructure. One of the worst casualties of this dilemma has been Nepal's mega infrastructure projects, including those related to hydropower. The country's major political players – Nepal Communist Party (NCP) and Nepali Congress (NC) – have contributed towards the casualty. Over the past few years, the two have governed Nepal alternatively and seek to appease one neighbour over the other. While NCP is widely seen as being close to Beijing, the main opposition party, NC, is considered to be a traditional ally of New Delhi. It has been a trend in recent years for both India and China to nudge their "favourable" government in Nepal to revoke or reward contracts of any major development project of their interest, thereby turning the development of major hydropower projects into a victim of geopolitical calculation of the two big powers.

One such example is a reservoir-based 1200 MW Budhi Gandaki hydro project in central-western Nepal. In June 2017, the then Nepal government led by Pushpa Kamal Dahal awarded the contract to China's state-owned China Gezhouba Group Corporation (CGGC). This not only courted controversy back home but also caused a flutter in India, which considers Nepal as its strategic backyard. New Delhi nudged the subsequent government led by Nepali Congress and eventually, the Sher Bahadur Deuba-led cabinet decided to unilaterally withdraw the Memorandum of Understanding (MoU) reached with the Chinese company to build the project in November 2017, citing that the US$2.5 billion project was awarded without a competitive bidding process. Controversy surrounding the Budhi Gandaki project began again after the NCP government, led by K.P. Sharma Oli, revoked the decision of Deuba government in September. A cabinet meeting on 21 September decided to give back the project to CGGC on EPCF (Engineering, Procurement, Construction, and Finance) model at the personal interest of Prime Minister Oli himself. With such flip-flop decision on the part of each subsequent government, the project expected to bring economic and social transformation of the entire country is now put in limbo. Since the exercises to form a new government has begun again in Nepal after the country's top court overturned the decision of Prime Minister K P Oli to dissolve the parliament and hold mid-term elections on 30 April and 10 May, many in Nepal still see the fate of this mega hydropower project uncertain.

Although Nepal is currently in negotiation to launch various projects under BRI, there is visible dilemma on the part of Nepal's policymakers how do they negotiate projects under BRI as Nepal's major donors, including the United States, Japan and India are advising Nepal against taking loan under the BRI. In all their meetings with Nepali officials, diplomats of these countries have been reminding Nepal of China's debt-trap diplomacy. The Donald Trump administration in the United States called the BRI project predatory, and thus discouraged its allies to be part of BRI. Nevertheless, Nepal's Communist Party-led government is bent on taking loan from China even to fulfil its election pledges. In an interaction with journalists in Kathmandu in April 2019, Foreign Minister Pradip Gyawali dismissed suggestions that Nepal could fall into a Chinese debt trap if it chose to take loans under the BRI. Arguing that such suggestions were motivated by bias, Gyawali said Nepal was aware what it should do and what it should not do to fulfil its national interests. He instead asked those expressing worries about Nepal's future to give information about charitable organisations that extend loans at zero interest. Giving examples that Chinese debt was not behind serious economic crises many Latin American countries, including Argentina, passed through back in the 1990s and 2000s, Gyawali said that debt trap would be no issue if projects are selected properly on the basis of their possible returns and proper pay back plan. He also argued that it is not possible to bring in development in the country by closing doors to immediate neighbours.[43]

Managing security dilemma

While China's willingness to invest in mega infrastructures such as roadways, railway, industrial parks and port cities in various South Asian countries is a welcome move, this has equally invited security concerns to some of the countries in the region and beyond. Indeed, China's assertive foreign policy towards South Asia coincides not just with its economic rise, but also the changes in strategic environment in South Asia, with India gradually aligning with the United States. Concerns that are being raised by India, Japan and the United States over growing engagements of China in South Asia and elsewhere appear to have come from security dilemma they face with China mainly after Beijing's unprecedented rise in the past one decade. In fact, Nepal itself faces security dilemma as major Western countries, including India and China, jostle each other to ensure their influence in this Himalayan nation to fulfil their geopolitical and strategic interest. As Beijing has been able to heavily increase its influence in the national polity, there are concerns that small countries like Nepal could eventually lose their strategic autonomy when it comes to taking crucial decision for the country. The controversy surrounding the projects under the Millennium Challenge Corporation (MCC) grant of the US government in Nepal is a case in point. While a section of political parties seen close to India and the United States in terms of their political ideology have stood in favour of implementing MCC projects in Nepal, the leftist parties, including the ruling Nepal Communist Party (NCP), remain sharply divided over whether to accept the MCC projects.

The most important thing, therefore, is to manage brewing "security dilemma" many countries face. For a small and resource-hungry country like Nepal, a policy of cooperation with both China and India (United States and other major Western powers included) is not only the only viable but also a pragmatic option. This calls for Nepali policymakers to be guided not by realist but by liberalist principles.

As a matter of fact, each subsequent government in Kathmandu seems to have realised that China as a major power, if not the superpower already, is a reality and that it cannot afford to ignore any of the big players such as India, United States and China. As such, Nepal has carefully chosen not to bandwagon with any of the two big powers in its backyard. Since Nepal has already become part of BRI and Indo-Pacific strategy propounded by the United States, it is now a sword's edge walk for Nepal in terms of its foreign policy. In fact, Nepalese policymakers have already started setting their own red lines in their foreign policy conduct with China or India or the United States or any other country around the world. This is in line with the government's "amity with all and enmity with none" foreign policy. Instead of seeing Beijing as a threat alone, it is high time that other South Asian countries also worked together with China by encouraging Beijing to ensure transparency and quality in its investment as well as in its other engagements. They can also work on some confidence-building measures to avoid their suspicions and doubts with each other.

Conclusion

China's miraculous economic rise over the past few decades is a reality. While it is poised to be the world's number one economy within a decade, China is already the world's major military power with its massive military modernisation drive in the recent past. With its economic and military rise, China is now in position to wield its influence not just in South Asia but in any parts of the world. It is natural in international system that a country with such resources at its disposal tries to increase its sphere of influence. Thus, it is unrealistic to expect China to confine itself within its domestic issues pursuing again the isolationist foreign policy. There is, however, no unanimity among countries as to how they should respond to China's growing assertiveness. Some countries have seen China's rise as a threat, while others see this as an opportunity. But for a country like Nepal, traditional realism guided primarily by geopolitical and strategic consideration cannot be proper response to China's growing engagements in South Asia. A liberal approach that upholds the values of cooperation and interdependence could be the best policy option when it comes to the engagements with China. Nepal expects to see other countries in the region also upholding the same approach in their interaction with China. In the geopolitical and strategic calculation, whether a country stands to gain or lose, it is important for countries in the region not to ignore the fact that their aspirations to achieve peace, stability and development in the region can be realised only if they stand ready to join hands with China.

Notes

1 MEA, *India and Neighbours*, 2012, http://mea.gov.in/nepal-in.htm, accessed 20 April 2019.
2 Ramjee P. Parajulee, *The Democratic Transition in Nepal*, Oxford: Rowman and Littlefield Publishers Inc, 2000.
3 MEA, *India-Nepal Relations*, 2013, https://mea.gov.in/Portal/ForeignRelation/Nepal_Brief.pdf, accessed 20 April 2019.
4 Government of India, *Status of International Students in India for Higher Education*, 2014, http://aishe.nic.in/aishe/viewDocument.action?documentId=173, accessed 25 April 2019.
5 Sunil Raman, "Nepal-China Agreement: Why India Needs to Work on Some Foreign Policy Issues without Delay", *First Post*, 2016, http://www.firstpost.com/world/nepal-china-agreement-why-india-needsto-work-on-some-foreign-policy-issues-without-delay-2697610.html, accessed 30 April 2019
6 Vijay Kumar Manandhar, *A Comprehensive History of Nepal China Relations up to 1955*, New Delhi: Adroit Publishers, 2004.
7 Pushpa Adhikari, *Ties that Bind: An Account of Nepal-China Relations*, Kathmandu: Sangam Institute, 2010.
8 EoN in Beijing, *Nepal-China Relations*, 2016, http://nepalembassy.org.cn/nepal-china-relations/dimensions-of-currentrelations/#, accessed 10 August 2016.
9 Reuters, "Tibetan Refugees Protest Ahead of Beijing Olympics", *Times of Malta*, 2008, http://www.timesofmalta.com/articles/view/20080311/world/tibetan-refugees-protestahead-of-beijing-olympics.199921, accessed 19 August 2016.
10 Jayshree Bajoriya and Esther Pan, "The US-India Nuclear Deal", *Council on Foreign Relations*, 2010, http://www.cfr.org/india/us-india-nuclear-deal/p9663, accessed 24 August 2016
11 Dasarathi Bhuiyan, "China's Growing Pace in Nepal a Threat to India: Nepal's Policy Options between Principles and Pragmatisms", *International Journal of Academic Research*, vol. 2, no. 1, 2015, pp. 7–18.
12 Denny Roy, *China's Foreign Relations*, London: Macmillan Press Limited, 1998.
13 John W. Garver, *China's Quest: The History of Foreign Relations of People's Republic of China*, Oxford: Oxford University Press, 2016.
14 Marc Lanteigne, *Chinese Foreign Policy: An Introduction*, London: Routledge, 2013.
15 Roy, n. 12.
16 Dan Twining, "How Tiananmen Changed China—And Still Could", *Foreign Policy*, 2009, http://foreignpolicy.com/2009/06/04/how-tiananmen-changed-china-and-still-could/, accessed 22 July 2016.
17 James F. Paradise, "China and International Harmony: Role of Confucius Institutes in Bolstering Beijing's Soft Power", *Asian Survey*, vol. 49, no. 4, 2009, p. 647.
18 Jonathan Holslag, "The Smart Revisionist", *Survival*, vol. 56, no. 5, 2014, pp. 95–116.
19 Joshua Kurlantzick, *Charm Offensive: How China's Soft Power Is Transforming the World*, London: A New Republic Book, 2007.

20 Susan L. Shirk, *China: Fragile Superpower*. Oxford: Oxford University Press, 2008, p. 139.
21 Kerry Dumbaugh, "China's Foreign Policy: What Does It Mean for US Global Interests?", in Alice V. Monroe (ed.), *China's Foreign Policy and Soft Power Influence*, New York: Nova Science Publishers Inc., 2010, pp. 1–25.
22 Jean-Marc F. Blanchard and Fujia Lu, "Thinking Hard about Soft Power: A Review and Critique of the Literature on China and Soft Power", *Asian Perspective*, vol. 36, 2012, p. 572.
23 Yu-Nu Lu, "The Representation of the 2008 Beijing Olympic Games: The Rise of China's Soft Power", in Baogang Guo and Chung-chian Teng (eds), *China's Quiet Rise: Peace Through Integration*, Lanham: Rowmann & Littlefield—Lexington, 2011, pp. 29–40.
24 Kurlantzick, n. 19.
25 Christopher B. Whitney and David Shambaugh, *Soft Power in Asia: Results of a 2008 Multinational Survey of Public Opinion*, Chicago: Chicago Council of Global Affairs, 2008; S. Suzuki, "Chinese Soft Power, Insecurity Studies, Myopia, and Fantasy", *Third World Quarterly*, vol. 30, no. 4, 2009, pp. 779–793; S. Ding, "Analyzing Rising Power Perspective of Soft Power", *Journal of Contemporary China*, vol. 19, no. 64, 2010, pp. 255–272.
26 Kingsley Edney, "Building National Cohesion and Domestic Legitimacy: A Regime Security Approach to Soft Power in China", *Politics*, vol. 35, nos. 3–4, 2015, pp. 259–272.
27 Chen Qi, Paul Haenle, Patrick Cronin, and Ely Ratner, "China's Evolving Foreign Policy and Implications for US-China Relations", *Carnegie Tsinghua*, 2013, http://carnegietsinghua.org/2013/11/04/china-s-evolvingforeign-policy-and-implications-for-u.s.-china-relations/gvud.html, accessed 18 July 2016.
28 Wang Yizhou, "China's New Foreign Policy: Transformations and Challenges Reflected in Changing Discourse", *The Asan Forum*, 2014, http://www.theasanforum.org/chinas-new-foreign-policy-transformationsand-challenges-reflected-in-changing-discourse, accessed 18 July 2015.
29 Roy, n. 12, p. 215.
30 Shirk, n. 20, p. 117.
31 Shirk, n. 20, p. 397.
32 Khalid Saleem, "China's Policy towards South Asia: An Appraisal", *Defence Forum*, 2013, http://www.cdsndu.org/userfiles/file/00001/00001-20141231084839/1%E4%B8%AD%E5%9B%BD%E7%9A%84%E5%8D%97%E4%BA%9A%E6%94%BF%E7%AD%96-%E8%8B%B1.pdf, accessed 10 April 201.
33 Shirk, n. 20.
34 Nora Saalman (ed.), *The China-India Nuclear Crossroads*, Washington: Carnegie Endowment for International Peace, 2012.
35 Saleem, n. 32.
36 D. S. Rajan, "China: President Xi Jingping's South Asia Policy: Implications for India", *South Asia Analysis Group*, 2015, http://www.southasiaanalysis.org/node/176, accessed 11 August 2016.
37 Lisa Curtis, "China's South Asia Strategy", *The Heritage Foundation*, 2016, http://www.heritage.org/research/testimony/chinas-south-asia-strategy, accessed 19 July 2016.
38 Vijay Sakhuja, "China's Strategic Advantage in Nepal", *James Town Foundation*, 2011, http://www.jamestown.org/single/?no_cache=1&tx_ttnews%5Btt_news%5D=38070#.V6YHCdIrLIV, accessed 26 March 2019.
39 EoN in Beijing, n. 8.
40 MoFA, *Joint Press Statement between People's Republic of China and Nepal*, 2016, https://www.mofa.gov.np/jointpress-statement/, accessed 8 August 2016.
41 *International Forces Fuelling Anti-China Activities in Nepal: Chinese Envoy*, The Kathmandu Post, 16 October 2011, http://kathmandupost.ekantipur.com/news/2011-10-16/intl

-forces-fueling-anti-chinaactivities-in-nepal-chinese-envoy.html, accessed 29 July 2016.
42 Prashant Jha, "Chinese Advice behind Prachanda's U-Turn on Support to Nepal Government?", *The Hindustan Times*, http://www.hindustantimes.com/india/the-chinese-advice-behind-prachanda-s-uturn-on-support-to-nepal-govt/story-4sdNKxZxTu3QRMDdfcnjlN, accessed 8 August 2016.
43 Republica, *Debt Trap Warnings over BRI Projects Motivated by Bias: FM Gyawali*, https://myrepublica.nagariknetwork.com/news/debt-trap-warnings-over-bri-projects-motivated-by-bias-fm-gyawali/, accessed 30 April 2019.

14
THE DRAGON'S EMBRACE

The contours of China–Pakistan strategic relations

Reena Marwah

Introduction

China and Pakistan share age-old ties, from the time when Chinese traders travelled through Pakistan en route to Pakistan and to the Middle East, Europe and the rest of the world through the ancient Silk Route. It is well known that the Indian subcontinent (prior to India and Pakistan being partitioned by the British) hosted famous travellers and monks, including Fa Xian and Xuan Zang.

China arrived early in Pakistan's orbit of bilateral relations. Pakistan and China have enjoyed close and friendly relations since the establishment of diplomatic relations on 21 May 1951. In the 1950s, there were visits of significance among both countries. In 1955, Vice President of China Song Ching Ling's visit to Pakistan marked the first high-level visit from Chinese side. In 1956, first high-level visit from Pakistan to China was that of H. S. Suhrawardy. In the 1960s, the two countries settled their border issue and Pakistan International Airlines (PIA) started its flights to Beijing, becoming the first non-Communist country airline to fly from Beijing.

It was in 1978 that the Karakoram Highway, a part of the ancient Silk Road, and a construction miracle, linked mountainous Northern Pakistan with Kashgar in Western China. It was opened for the public in 1985 and remains an important conduit for the movement of goods and people.

Pakistan has always viewed China as a guarantor of its security, even when it was and continues to be seen by India and the United States as an exporter of terrorism. While China continues to give Pakistan constant support at international forums, it refrains from commenting on its internal challenges.

Over the years, the relationship has blossomed into an "All-Weather Strategic Cooperative Partnership," with the China Pakistan Economic Corridor (CPEC) at its core. Pakistan considers China as one of its closest friends and partners, and

China considers Pakistan as its "Iron Brother."[1] Moreover, the relationship has forged ahead through economic, cultural, political and strategic engagement. Educational exchanges have also fortified the relationship, providing a fillip to people-to-people exchanges.

Hence, the bedrock of Pakistan–China relations can be portrayed as "Iron brothers, time tested and All-weather friends." According to the Chinese saying, "good neighbours cannot be traded for gold."[2]

Roots of the relationship

It is essential to understand that the seeds of the relationship germinated as a result of the Kautilyan dictum, "Your enemy's enemy is your friend," that was well put to practice by China and Pakistan.

It was none other than Pakistan which became the facilitating country for the visit of Henry Kissinger's secret ice-breaking visit to China in 1971, laying the base for a visit by President Richard Nixon the following year. This was considered its huge victory in international diplomacy. However, China's apathetic attitude to its friend during the 1971 war is well known. Pakistan lost its territory in the war, resulting in the creation of Bangladesh. However, this fact was soon eclipsed and relegated to pages of forgotten history.

Moreover, China–Pakistan became close friends particularly due to Pakistan's role in China–US rapprochement in 1972, also known as PingPong diplomacy, which helped to change China's ideological position in the world.[3]

For the present-day China, according to Mohan Malik, economics constitutes an important component of its strategic outreach. While for China, with its accumulated surpluses, its deep pockets have replaced Maoism as the tool for gaining global influence, there is no other country where this strategic tool has been better deployed, especially as it engineered to keep India, a rising neighbour, in check. Bandwagoning with an economic juggernaut transforms the fortune of nations, and Pakistan's handholding by China is a perfect manifestation.[4] In trade and commerce, nations do not take sides but play all sides, as is evident from China's Belt and Road Initiative (BRI), which apparently is for building economic partnerships. For conflict-torn countries with autocratic regimes that cannot get funding from global financial institutions, China's aid and investment comes in handy. Being part of the Chinese sphere of influence may well be, or seem, a small price to pay for economic success.[5]

Pakistan's economic woes can also be attributed to its affinity with China. In 2017, Pakistan's total GDP was roughly US$305 billion, but was expected to grow to $340 billion in 2020. On 16 June 2017, the IMF had warned of re-emerging "vulnerabilities" in Pakistan's economy. Although it praised the country's GDP growth of above 5% a year, it noted the missed fiscal targets and a ballooning current account deficit.[6] It is no surprise that Pakistan which sought aid from the IMF in 2013, at a time of the global financial crisis, had once again approached it in 2018 for funds. As underlined by Atif Mian, in an article on the dismal state of the Pakistan economy, "government engaged in an import-led growth strategy by borrowing from abroad to finance large-scale infrastructure projects – the China–Pakistan Economic Corridor (CPEC) being the most prominent example."[7]

Given the deleterious impacts of the pandemic across all countries and fragile economies in particular, Pakistan's real growth rate for 2020 has been projected by the World Bank to go into the negative, between −1.3% and −2.2% in 2020, thus bringing to a halt any optimism. Pakistan's Planning Commission estimated that Pakistan's economy will shrink by 0.39% in the 2019–2020 financial year, which ends on 30 June 2020 because of the additional impact of the coronavirus pandemic.

A broad overview of current bilateral relations

It was in 2003 that the two countries signed the Preferential Trade Agreement (PTA) to provide market access to Pakistani exports. The relationship got a fillip when 2005 Chinese Premier Wen Jiabao visited Pakistan, during which the "Treaty of Friendship, Cooperation, and Good Neighborly Relations" was signed between the two countries. This was followed by the visit of the Chinese President Hu Jintao to Pakistan in 2006. The PTA was then extended to a Free Trade Agreement (FTA) to strengthen the partnership.

The first phase of the FTA between the two countries was signed in 2006. By 2015, trade between the two countries was US$16 billion. The second phase of China Pakistan Free trade Agreement (CPFTA) was initiated from 1 January 2020. According to a Chinese spokesman, the CPFTA,

> stipulates the proportion of the tariff lines with zero tariff products between China and Pakistan will gradually increase from 35 per cent to 75 per cent. In addition, both parties will implement 20 per cent reduction in taxes on other products that account for 5 per cent of their respective tariff lines. The tariff elimination measures have been implemented from 1 January 2020.

The second phase of the FTA permits the Pakistani manufacturers and traders to export almost 313 new products on zero duty to the Chinese market, taking the total products to 1047, as reported by Pakistan's state-run APP news agency. Pakistan's trade deficit with China has further widened to US$9.7 billion in 2018 in about US$13 billion total trade, according to official data.[8]

This rising trade deficit is not surprising given the fact that Pakistan, with a low manufacturing base, does not have substantial opportunities for expanding exports to China. In 2018, while Pakistan's exports to China were US$1.95 billion, its imports from China were US$16.3 billion.[9] The huge trade deficit with China, a result of imports being almost eight times that of exports, underlines the point that even with FTA-related concessions by the Chinese, the scope for reducing the deficit remains untenable. Hence, China has become Pakistan's largest trading partner and important source of investment for many years, with bilateral trade value amounting around US$20 billion.

In terms of investments from China, it was when Chinese President Xi Jinping during his visit to Pakistan in 2015, signed several key agreements, including the agreement on CPEC outlining projects worth US$46 billion. The pledged investment has already increased to US$62 billion, though the amount received is about a third of this.

There are several projects for which agreements have been signed. In 2018, an agreement to establish the first SEZ as Rashakai Special Economic Zone (RSEZ) was signed. This RSEZ is expected to cover an area of 778 acres in Nowshera district and is to be developed in three phases over a period of six years.[10] Faisalabad Special Economic Zone is another such SEZ being established under the CPEC.

There are several other initiatives as well launched recently, including the celebration of 2019 as the year of sister-city/province. Fourteen pairs of friendly provinces and cities have been established, and the friendship between China and Pakistan has been deeply rooted in the hearts of the people. "Higher than the mountain, deeper than the ocean, harder than steel, sweeter than honey" has become a vivid portrayal of China–Pakistan friendship. In 2014 and 2015, a survey conducted by the Pew Research Center at the global level showed that 78–82% of Pakistanis are pro-China.[11] Besides, there are nearly 200,000 people-to-people exchanges between the two countries each year, with thousands of students from Pakistan receiving opportunities to study in China. It is also interesting to note how Pakistani students studying in China expressed their appreciation of the Chinese handling of the pandemic and further expressed their desire to be engaged with China's BRI. This communication to President Xi Jinping has been broadcast widely, even as China is seen to expect letters of solidarity and gratitude from its partner countries.

Marking a strategic milestone, Pakistan hosted the Third China–Afghanistan–Pakistan Trilateral Foreign Ministers Dialogue in Islamabad, in 2019, ushering in a diplomatic effort to resolve the Afghan crisis. This further entrenches Chinese interests in the region.

Cooperation in crises

During 2008 when an earthquake struck China, Pakistan responded to help its neighbour with its transport aircraft to ship its entire reserve of tents to China. Pakistan reached out to China for help when it was hit by a severe flood in 2010. Moreover, building the Karakoram Highway brought to test the courage and capacity of all those involved in that challenging terrain.

When, at first COVID-19 struck China, it was the Government of Pakistan which promptly expressed its solidarity with the people of China and underlined the importance of standing by each other. Not only did Pakistan donate face masks and other materials, it also firmly opposed the stigmatization of China. Similarly, when Pakistan was struck with the pandemic in March 2020, China sent medical teams and donated many medical goods to Pakistan, including more than 300,000 test kits, 7 million masks, more than 400,000 sets of medical protective clothing and over 500 ventilators, and assisted in the construction of quarantine hospitals. Private Chinese companies also reached out with essential supplies for the people of Pakistan.

Moreover, given the fact that CPEC projects have not laid off any staff or stopped functioning, adds to their contribution in supporting people's livelihoods. The energy projects guaranteed one-third of the electrical supply in Pakistan during the pandemic and provided reliable energy for the continuous operation of hospitals. The Gwadar port and infrastructure projects ensured the normal supply of living materials for the people of Pakistan. China will continue to promote the construction of the CPEC together with Pakistan on the premise of preventing and controlling the epidemic and ensuring the safety of personnel, so as to provide motivation for Pakistan to overcome the epidemic and develop the economy.

Strategic engagement

It is well known that Pakistani military has been very closely aligned with the Chinese military, for many decades, particularly since the 1960s. During this period, Chinese military has provided weapons armaments, ammunition, as well as naval vessels to Pakistan. Instructors from China regularly provide training to the military personnel of Pakistan. Although the Pakistan army had close ties since the 1960s, it is later in the twenty-first century that the Airforce and Navy also started sourcing equipment, fighter aircrafts, submarines and frigates from China.

Pakistan's geo-strategic location in the Indian subcontinent not only helps China to keep India constantly engaged on its western and northern borders, but also provides it with opportunities to navigate towards the Arabian Sea. This is further delineated by Ayesha S. Agha as she stated in an interview, "It sees the project beneficial in establishing Beijing's long-term stakes in Pakistan's security and indirectly committing to strengthening Pakistan against traditional rivals like India or new confrontational relations like with the US."[12]

For several decades, Pakistan's largest donor has been the United States, granting around US$70 billion in aid. In 2015, China, as part of its One Belt One Road (OBOR) global ambitions, promised Pakistan US$46 billion (revised to US$60 billion) for a road running from its border to the port of Gwadar. The CPEC is being seen as a "fate-changer" for Pakistan.[13]

In recent years, China–Pakistan relations have maintained a steady and rapid development at a high level. President Xi Jinping paid a historic visit to Pakistan in 2015, and China–Pakistan relations have been upgraded to an all-weather strategic cooperative partnership. Since assuming office, Prime Minister Imran

Khan has visited China three times and met President Xi Jinping four times. Political mutual trust has been continuously consolidated.

It suits the Chinese to continue supporting Pakistan's terrorism moves in India. In fact, despite the global community having criticised Pakistan for its support to havens of terrorists on its soil, China has continued to shield its friend, as long as the link with the Uighurs in Xinjiang is kept at bay. Beijing's myopic policy and selective approach in this regard is dangerous for the stability of the region.[14] China desires better performance from Pakistan in combating Uighur militancy. As a quid pro quo, China provides Pakistan with serviceable weapons that embolden it to remain the revisionist power in its security competition with India. Then there is the nuclear programme which is very much tied to help from Beijing.

Moreover, China has helped Pakistan to protect terror suspects like Masood Azhar of Jaishe Muhammad, an organization that has links with Pakistan's intelligence, from being declared as terrorist through a UN resolution.[15]

China's charm offensive: Dragon's captive diplomacy through CPEC

Without a doubt, in the present, it is the CPEC which is defining the multi-layered and multifaceted partnership between the two countries. This has its roots in an agreement signed in 1963, soon after the China–India war. It was under this agreement that China gave 1942 km^2 to Pakistan; in turn, Pakistan recognised Chinese sovereignty over thousands of square kilometres in northern Kashmir and Ladakh. India terms this area as Pakistan Occupied Kashmir.

After President Xi Jinping assumed position in March 2013, he was quick to launch the OBOR project. In the same year, the Chinese Premier Li Keqiang visited Pakistan; the visit resulted in a Joint Statement on Deepening Comprehensive Strategic Cooperation, which became the basis of CPEC. This initiative is embedded in China's BRI (the term OBOR changed in 2016 to BRI), under which it builds infrastructure and provides connectivity with roads, railways and ports. As a result of the strong support of the two governments, the construction of the CPEC has achieved a lot of "early harvest." Sixteen projects have been completed and 16 projects are under construction. The CPEC has become a model for high-quality development of BRI.

The Gwadar Port in Pakistan is referred to as a pearl in the "string of pearls" that China is weaving in South Asia to keep India in check.[16] The making of Gwadar as central to Chinese security and as a deep sea port that would be useful to China provides Beijing with an important base in the Indian Ocean. The development of the port of Gwadar on the Arabian Sea is expected to become the economic hub of world trade and economic activities by 2030. The economic and strategic significance of the port emanates from the fact that it is expected to shorten China's existing route to the Persian Gulf by more than 10,000 km. With this trade route becoming operational, it would take Chinese imports and exports only 10 days to reach its potential destination instead of 45 days. This would not merely help to save costs, but would also circumvent the navigational issues in the proximity of countries: Vietnam, Indonesia and India.[17]

There are other projects in the offing, including the China Three Gorges Corp for the US$2.5 billion Kohala hydropower project, which would generate 1124 MW of electricity. Work has also started for the building of a US$230 million airport at Gwadar. In addition, a second motorway route through western Pakistan, connecting the Karakorum Highway to Quetta to improve overland transit connectivity between Gwadar and China's Xinjiang province has picked up pace.

However, given Pakistan's precarious economic situation, soon after assuming office in August 2018, Imran Khan reduced the overall size of CPEC to US$50 billion, from the earlier level of US$64 billion. There was also an endeavour to shift the focus of the investments to more employment-generating activities as manufacturing zones, agriculture and social sector development, instead of the huge erstwhile committed infrastructure projects.

In mid-May, another project of US$2.75 billion was awarded to Power China and Frontier Works Organisation, the latter being in control of the Pakistan military, to build infrastructure of the Diamer–Bhasha Dam and its reservoir. The project's funding details have not been made public, but it is known that Power China has a 70% stake in it. It could not be included under CPEC, because of security concerns related to control of the waters of the Indus River.[18]

Arms transfers: advantage China!

The arms transfers from China to Pakistan have been significant from the mid-1960s. The trigger emanated from the US sanctions – first, in 1965 and then, after the initiation of Pakistani nuclear programme in 1979. Driven towards China, Pakistan's reliance on the United States gradually declined. Hence, by the early 1980s, almost 75% of tanks and 65% of the aircraft were of Chinese origin, highlighting the fact that China then assumed a significant role in the technology transfer to Pakistan for its nuclear and missile programmes.

To understand the extent to which transfer of arms have taken place over ten years (2009–2018), it would be useful to employ data sourced from SIPRI. The data for the period 2009–2018 provides evidence of China continuing to be the largest source of arms for Pakistan.[19] Consequently, the US–Pakistan arms trade has gradually declined during 2009–2018, and has declined significantly during the last three years (2016–2018). This is largely due to the change in the White House, where President Trump has castigated Pakistan for its inability to weed out terrorists. In September 2018, the United States went further and reduced aid to Pakistan worth US$300 million.[20]

In terms of the weapon-wise classification of total arms imported by Pakistan from all countries in 2009–2018,[21] the following can be highlighted:

a. Pakistan has sought to improve its air capabilities which involves procurement of varied weaponry like light combat aircraft, helicopters, and airborne early warning systems. This together comprised almost 48% of the imports.
b. Almost 24% of total imports constitute missiles.
c. Artillery and engines for ground warfare comprise the least share in percentage terms.

Hence, it is evident that more than two-thirds of arms imports are from China. Despite the fact that Pakistan–China share a comprehensive defence partnership, it is obvious that the terms of trade are dominated by China in this highly "unequal" or "asymmetric" partnership.[22]

Challenges in China–Pakistan relations

Andrew Small seeks to explain the underlying motivations for one of the most important bilateral relationships in Asia. Small questions the reasons for the remarkably resilient relationship between these two countries given that it lacks the "cultural affinity or common values that so often underpin friendships and alliances."[23] His explanation is that for one, China generally has not asked Pakistan to do anything divergent from what it would do if its ties with China were not strong.

Given that CPEC is a Chinese project for protecting and expanding Chinese interests, and Pakistan just happens to be part of the geographical terrain, apprehensions of Chinese debt trap diplomacy, coupled with instances of officials and politicians being manipulated, have surfaced. To quote Senator Tahir Mashhadi, chairman of the senate standing committee on planning and development, who warned, "Another East India Company is in the offing."[24] On the flip side, it is important to question, whether China can continue to sustain its debt-driven investments in countries as Pakistan. According to Malik, China may lose almost 80% of its investments in Pakistan.[25]

It is interesting to note that the Imran Khan government conducted an enquiry into the anomalies of CPEC project. This enquiry revealed that six China-funded power projects under CPEC had resulted in excessive profits for Chinese firms, which had set up the plants through over invoicing. *Economic Times* had reported that government-to-government deals signed under CPEC had unduly favoured Chinese investors. One of the six power projects was found to be 234% expensive than a similar project in India, the study revealed. Another revelation of the report was that the $1.7 billion power transmission line project of the CPEC was 234% more expensive than a similar project in India with superior technology. These are some examples of the irregularities that were highlighted. A similar series of allegations have also been detected with regard to non-coal-based projects. Wind power projects by Hydro China and Three Gorges have also come under scanner of the committee. While senior officials of Pakistan are aware of these discrepancies and underlying corrupt practices, these are being kept guarded from the public eye, for fear of damaging ties with China.[26]

Although there is a great hype and enthusiasm for the US$46 billion CPEC that will ultimately link Kashgar, in China's Xinjiang Province, with Gwadar, in Pakistan's Balochistan Province, the fact that it hinges upon critically in the Karakorum Highway (KKH), in the north, itself makes the project almost uneconomic. The KKH, a highway that took almost 20 years to build does not have much traffic to boast of. As Small says, even though the KKH is the "most potent symbol of China–Pakistan relations,"[27] one can see very little of on the KKH is actual traffic. Moreover, the highway actually increases tensions within India as its hopes to control the part of Kashmir with Pakistan are almost grounded.

According to Small, the Gwadar port project (which inevitably has India on its guard) also does not fit into the economic viable calculations of any discerning investor. The project is often the target of nationalist groups in Balochistan, who are wary of the port project. By 2008, "Gwadar stood virtually isolated." Part of the problem is that the entire project is targeted by Baloch nationalist groups who fear that the massive project will render them a "minority in their land."[28] Hence, to what extent the port would be functional enough to serve the interests of both China and Pakistan is anybody's guess. The costs, however, would continue to weaken Pakistan's fragile economy.

The large presence of Chinese in most Pakistani cities has added to the security problem as Chinese are provided security, even those that are in the country on private business. In the words of a former senior bureaucrat, "it is a China-Pakistan Economic Corridor and not a Pakistan-China Economic Corridor" hinting at the ownership of the project.[29]

As Agha writes, Pakistan's hybrid "civilian-military" government has weakened the already weak democratic forces, much needed to ensure accountability of projects as also to ascertain their viability.[30] Given that CPEC is seen as Pakistan's only hope for economic growth and development, there is scant analysis of the costs and benefits of the projects. While inevitability dictates that China will gain in the long run, undergirded by the fact that, for example, some public sector infrastructure and energy development projects in Punjab are tax exempt. This implies that raising money for the Chinese loans is impossible, making repayments to China difficult. However, several experts have cautioned Pakistan about how Chinese terms and investment turned sour in Sri Lanka, Tajikistan and several parts of Africa. In both Sri Lanka and Tajikistan, with rising costs and debts incurred by the host countries, large chunks of land were handed over to the Chinese in lieu of unpaid funds. There are fears that Pakistan could become a "vassal state."[31]

Although CPEC comprised investment of almost US$60 billion, by 2019, the investment was limited to US$26 billion. It is believed that the terms on which Chinese debt is received are tougher than those from financial institutions.

On 3 March 2020, the World Bank committed US$200 million for the Punjab Human Capital Investment Project intended to strengthen health services and social protection for poor and vulnerable households in select districts in Punjab.[32] It is evident that while the World Bank would provide funding on easy terms for social sector projects, it would take a different approach to funding projects it deemed unnecessary. The IMF supported Pakistan through aid of US$6 billion in July 2019. However, the ability of the Imran Khan Government to revive the economy has been limited.[33]

Conclusion

Undoubtedly, China and Pakistan have a long history of camaraderie together going back to the early 1960s. The origin of their "all-weather" relationship is now firmly embedded in their perceptions of seeing a competitor in India. While India and China fought a border war in 1962, India and Pakistan fought wars in 1965 and in East Pakistan crisis in 1971. China's territorial dispute with India continues to simmer, even as the former has entered into several agreements for handling of the border dispute. The latest standoff that continues from May 2020 is even more aggressive. China is also objecting to India's abrogation of Article 370, terming it as a bid to change the status of Jammu and Kashmir. What worries New Delhi today is the increasing Chinese presence in Gilgit–Baltistan. Another element of contemporary China–Pakistan ties that irks India is the strengthened three-way partnership between Pakistan, Afghanistan and China.[34]

It is a foregone conclusion that China has enveloped Pakistan into its design and manoeuvres both on land and on sea. Its substantial support to Pakistan for the CPEC not only endeavours to completely change the status quo between India and Pakistan, but also to ensure that India's sovereignty is challenged. The port of Gwadar which is being invested in by China is a move to gain access to the Arabian Sea and use the port for economic and strategic purposes.

Moreover, regional integration efforts in the shape of South Asian Association of Regional Cooperation (SAARC) has been derailed substantively due to the involvement of China in the region.

While China continues to beef up its trade surplus through economic ties as well as through its cooperation with India at multilateral forums, its strategic engagement with Pakistan, in particular, always raises concerns in Delhi. Additionally, China shields Pakistan from international pressures to end cross-border terrorism.

Even as China and Pakistan celebrated the 69th anniversary of the establishment of diplomatic relations on 21 May 2020, according to the Chinese Ambassador in Islamabad, Yao Jing, "China-Pakistan relations have grown from strength to strength, since 1951. As the first country in the Islamic world to enter into diplomatic relations with China, Pakistan has always provided valuable assistance to China."[35] Undoubtedly, it is China that is winning in this "win–win" partnership. While there is enough evidence to show that the two-way relationship between Pakistan and China is an asymmetric one, with the latter's vision stretching far beyond the benign, it suits Pakistan as long as it continues to receive support for its proxy warfare with India. The motivation for welcoming Chinese investment into infrastructure and connectivity sectors is some job creation, infrastructure development and an increase in GDP. Much of the costs that do not get publicised are what Pakistan does not count.

An Islamabad-based expert, Mustafa Hyder Sayed, executive director of the Pakistan–China Institute, who works closely with the Chinese and Pakistani governments to promote cooperation between the "iron brothers," underlined that the CPEC would be critical to reviving Pakistan's moribund economy in the post-pandemic phase. In his words,

> As the world braces itself for a 2008-like or worse recession, we see a renewed importance of CPEC projects in Pakistan, as it emerges as an island of prosperity that provides hope, jobs and tangible foreign direct investment in a sea of economic uncertainty.[36]

He further added that there were concerns in Pakistan about the US' reliability as an economic partner, because of President Donald Trump's response to the coronavirus pandemic. "The contrast between the US and China is stark,"[37] Sayed said. "And China is, thanks to Trump, assuming global leadership by standing up and being counted, which in the pre-Covid and pre-Trump period, would have always been the role of the US."[38] These statements reiterate that Pakistan is tightly in China's embrace, both as an economic and a strategic partner.

Notes

1 Zamir Ahmed Awan, China-Pakistan: A Journey of Friendship (1950–2020), *Global Times*, 21 May 2020, https://www.globaltimes.cn/content/1189007.shtml, accessed 12 June 2020.
2 S. M. Hali, T. Shukui, and S. Iqbal, "One Belt and One Road: Impact on China Pakistan Economic Corridor", *Strategic Studies*, vol. 34, no. 4, 2015, pp. 147–164.
3 Mohan Malik, "One Belt One Road: Dimensions, Detours, Fissures, and Fault Lines", in *What China Wants*, vol. 13, no. 5, May/June 2018, Asia-Pacific Center for Security Studies, Honolulu, HI, accessed 14 June 2020.
4 *Ibid*.
5 *Ibid*, p. 30.
6 "Pakistan's Old Vulnerabilities Persist", *The Economist*, 29 June 2017, https://www.economist.com/finance-and-economics/2017/06/29/pakistans-old-economic-vulnerabilities-persist, accessed 14 June 2020.
7 Mian Atif, "Why Pakistan Is Back in Trouble with Balance of Payments", *Herald*, 9 August 2018, https://herald.dawn.com/news/1398616, accessed 14 June 2020.
8 "Second Phase of China Pakistan Free Trade Agreement Becomes Operational", *News 18*, https://www.news18.com/news/world/second-phase-of-china-pakistan-free-trade-agreement-becomes-operational-2449717.html, 7 January 2020, accessed 14 June 2020.
9 Observatory of Economic Complexity (OEC); https://oec.world/en/profile/country/pak/, accessed 12 June 2020.
10 *The Nation*, https://nation.com.pk/17-Mar-2020/rashakai-sez-to-be-inaugurated-by-june, 17 March 2020, accessed 12 June 2020.

11 Mahesar Pervaiz Ali, "Scholarship and Friendship: How Pakistani Academics View Pakistan-China Relations", in C. Shih, P. Manomaivibool, and R. Marwah (eds), *China Studies in South and Southeast Asia: Between Pro-China and Objectivism*, Singapore: World Scientific, 2018, p. 128.
12 Port Technology International Team, Q & A with Dr. Ayesha Siddiqa, 30 August 2018, https://www.porttechnology.org/news/cpec_qa_with_dr_ayesha_siddiqa/, accessed 12 June 2020.
13 S. Akbar Zaidi, "A Road through Pakistan, and What This Means for India", *Strategic Analysis*, vol. 43, no. 3, 2019, pp. 214–226. doi: 10.1080/09700161.2019.1601408, accessed 11 June 2020.
14 Srikanth Kondapalli, "Kashmir Issue: China Treading Dangerously", *The Deccan Herald*, 17 August 2019, https://www.deccanherald.com/opinion/in-perspective/kashmir-issue-china-treading-dangerously-755010.html, accessed 8 June 2020.
15 C. Raja Mohan, "With Global Institutions in Turmoil, India Needs to Be Pragmatic and Fleet-Footed", *The Indian Express*, 11 April 2020, https://indianexpress.com/article/opinion/columns/world-health-organisation-coronavirus-crisis-india-delhi-china-un6356921/, accessed 7 June 2020.
16 In 2004, the US consulting firm Booz Allen Hamilton came up with the "string of pearls" hypothesis, which posits that China will try to expand its naval presence by building civilian maritime infrastructure along the Indian Ocean periphery.
17 N. Christ and M. J. Ferrantino, "Land Transport for Export: The Effects of Cost, Time, and Uncertainty in Sub-Saharan Africa", *World Development*, vol. 39, no. 10, 2011, pp. 1749–1759.
18 "Scope of CPEC to Be Enhanced in 2nd Phase", *The Economic Times*, 9 April 2020, https://economictimes.indiatimes.com/news/defence/scope-of-cpec-to-be-enhanced-in-2nd-phase-pakistani official/articleshow/75064819.cms?utm_source=contentofinterest&utm_medium=text&utm_campaign=cppst, accessed 14 June 2020.
19 SIPRI Arms Transfer Database 2019, cited in Ambuj Sahu, *Analysing the Trends in China-Pakistan Arms Transfer,* Observer Research Foundation, 14 June 2019, https://www.orfonline.org/expert-speak/analysing-trends-arms-transfer-china-pakistan/, accessed 7 June 2020.
20 Memphis Barker, "US Military Confirms $300m Cut in Aid to Pakistan", *The Guardian*, 2 September 2018, https://www.theguardian.com/world/2018/sep/02/us-military-confirms-300m-cut-in-aid-to-pakistan, accessed 14 June 2020.
21 See n. 19.
22 Ambuj Sahu, *Analysing the Trends in China-Pakistan Arms Transfer,* Observer Research Foundation, 14 June 2019, https://www.orfonline.org/expert-speak/analysing-trends-arms-transfer-china-pakistan/, accessed 7 June 2020.
23 Andrew Small, *The China-Pakistan Axis: Asia's New Geopolitics*, New York: Oxford University Press, 2015, p. 2.
24 Snigdhendu Bhattacharya, "CPEC: Pakistan Prostrating before Chinese Imperialist Designs, Pak Scholar Says in Kolkata", *Hindustan Times*, 13 June 2017, https://www.hindustantimes.com/kolkata/cpec-pakistan-prostrating-before-chinese-imperialist-designs-pak-scholar-says-in-kolkata/story-qt9ZdydBVjcoiOYAHFDLtK.html, accessed 10 June 2020.
25 Malik, n. 3, p. 31.
26 Dipanjay Ray Choudhary, "Pakistan's Internal Report Indicts China for Corruption in CPEC Power Sector", *Economic Times*, 20 May 2020, https://economictimes.indiatimes.com/news/international/business/pakistans-internal-report-indicts-china-for-corruption-in-cpec-power-sector/articleshow/75823762.cms?utm_source=contentofinterest&utm_medium=text&utm_campaign=cppst, accessed 8 June 2020.
27 Small, n. 23, p. 99.
28 Small, n. 23, pp. 101–102.
29 "Q&A with Dr. Ayesha Siddiqa", n. 12. https://www.porttechnology.org/news/cpec_qa_with_dr_ayesha_siddiqa/, accessed 8 June 2020.

30 Ayesha Siddiqa, *Pakistan's Hybrid Civilian Government Weakens Democracy*, 21 January 2020, https://www.eastasiaforum.org/2020/01/21/pakistans-hybrid-civilian-military-government-weakens-democracy/, SOAS, accessed 8 June 2020.
31 Zaidi, n. 13.
32 World Bank commits 300 million to support human capital and livelihoods in Pakistan, https://www.worldbank.org/en/news/press-release/2020/03/03/world-bank-commits-300-million-to-support-human-capital-and-livelihoods-in-pakistan, accessed 13 June 2020.
33 IMF Press Release, https://www.imf.org/en/News/Articles/2019/07/03/pr19264-pakistan-imf-executive-board-approves-39-month-eff-arrangement#:~:text=On%20July%203%2C%202019%2C%20the,the%20authorities'%20economic%20reform%20program.; Press Release No. 19/264; 3 July 2019, accessed 13 June 2020.
34 Happymon Jacob, "China, India, Pakistan and a Stable Regional Order", in François Godement, *What Does India Think*, 2015, https://www.ecfr.eu/what_does_india_think/analysis/china_india_pakistan_and_a_stable_regional_order; pgs 90–95, accessed 13 June 2020.
35 Ambassador Yao Jing, 21 May 2020, http://pk.chineseembassy.org/eng/zbgx/t1781487.htm, accessed 9 June 2020.
36 Tom Hussain, "As Coronavirus Bites, Pakistan Looks to China for Belt and Road Economic Boost", 24 May 2020, https://www.scmp.com/week-asia/economics/article/3085523/coronavirus-bites-pakistan-looks-china-belt-and-road-economic, accessed 12 June 2020.
37 *Ibid*.
38 *Ibid*.

15
PEACE AND STABILITY IN AFGHANISTAN

China's role

Sadaf Mohmand

Introduction

After 9/11, China's relation with Afghanistan is extended. China is pursuing the goal of a stable and prosperous Afghanistan and it does not want to align or be or close with the United States. Beijing is positioning itself to work with whoever controls Kabul. China and Afghanistan are developing their relation on two important aspects: bilateral and regional levels. It is mainly based on economic and security aspects. The most recent cooperation between China and Afghanistan is medical assistance for fighting against COVID-19 pandemic. COVID-19 is an infectious disease that started in the later months of 2019 in the Wuhan city of China. Gradually it reached to almost all of the countries of the world. At the moment, the cases of coronavirus are at its peak and increasing day by day. Being short of resources to fight the pandemic, Afghanistan needs humanitarian assistance. China is the first neighbouring state that extended its medical support to Afghanistan. Chinese doctors shared their medical experiences with Afghan doctors and counterparts through a four-hour video conference.[1] About cooperation between China and Afghanistan, Ambassador Wang said:

> China and Afghanistan as brothers, will work together to overcome all difficulties. We believe that when the epidemic is over, the friendship between China and Afghanistan will surely be stronger, the pragmatic cooperation between the two countries will be more solid, and the practice of the community of shared destiny between us will also reach a new level.[2]

The medical supplies include protective clothes, ventilators, test kits, goggles, infrared thermometer and face masks. The medical donation is the latest cooperation of China to Afghanistan to fight the pandemic virus and it also shows the strong friendship or brotherly friendship of Sino-Afghan relation.[3] Chinese enjoy a more positive relationship with Afghanistan, making their investments less likely to be targeted by insurgents. Especially, the presence of China is felt more in Afghanistan after handing over the security and full Afghan sovereignty to local security forces by NATO in 2014.

However, lack of sufficient international support in case of assisting the security in Afghanistan and the uncertain and destabilized situation in Afghanistan have made the countries of the region to become involved with the problems. In that sense, China is trying to be more active in era of security and economy. On the other hand, Afghanistan's natural resources and geopolitical position are important for China to initiate its One Belt One Road (OBOR) policy in Asia. Afghanistan signed the Memorandum of Understanding in 2016 for the development and promotion of BRI. Since Afghanistan is a developing country, it needs investments for its reconstruction. Thus, BRI is one of the ways that Afghanistan can be benefited through projects such as Sino-Afghan Special Rail Way Transportation that is for five nations railway corridor. Silk Road cable project is also a potential avenue.[4] Afghanistan is a gate to Central Asia and it is much more important for China's connectivity projects. Hence, China is trying more to not only enhance its interest in Afghanistan itself but also it has security concerns for the instability in Afghanistan.

A stable and free terror Afghanistan would play an important role in economic spectrum for China through its infrastructure projects and energy corridors. The Aynak copper mine is the biggest Chinese project in Afghanistan; China has invested around US$3.5 billion in this project. State-owned Chinese corporation are uniquely risk tolerant and can help in the future investments.

China's security concerns of Afghanistan

Afghanistan shares 76 km of the Wakhan Corridor with China. This is a mountainous area which is difficult to pass.[5] Afghanistan's instability hampers the security of its neighbouring countries. China being one of the neighbours of Afghanistan is also concerned about instability in Afghanistan. With the withdrawal of Soviet Union, the civil wars emerged in Afghanistan and disturbed the security of China's western Xinjiang province. The instability in Afghanistan has spanned the way to drug smuggling, weapons trafficking, cross-border terrorism and terrorist activities in China through Xinjiang province.[6] Beijing believes that Uighur separatists are trained to fight for an independent Xinjiang by East Turkestan Independence movement, Turkistan Islamic Party and Taliban in Afghanistan.[7] Uighur separatists are an ethnic group that lives in western province of China bordering Afghanistan who claims independence for Xinjiang-Uighur Autonomous Region. Xinjiang has abundant raw materials and the home of nuclear weapons test base. It became the part of China in 1884.[8] Moreover, Beijing also has concerns about the presence of ISIS in Badakhshan province of

Afghanistan. Beijing claims that ISIS is inducing the growing number of ETIM terrorist group to gather there. It is also believed by the United States that there are Uighur militants in Badakhshan that pose security threats to Xinjiang.[9]

Drug trafficking is among one of the major concerns for China in Xinjiang province. Opium production from 2016 to 2017 reached to 87% with most of this expansion taking place in Helmand province of Afghanistan.[10] China never wants Afghanistan to be under control of Taliban as China thinks that Taliban shelter East Turkestan Islamic Movement which is led by Uighurs.[11] On the other hand, opium cultivation and drug trafficking have become the major revenue for Taliban. Iran, Russia and China are the countries that have the largest markets for opium trade.[12] This clearly shows that drug trafficking is not only the major security concern for China but for the world as well. The first victim of Afghan narcotics is Xinjiang. According to Xinjiang police, China detected 15 cases of drug trafficking from Afghanistan.[13]

Economic relation between China and Afghanistan

Afghanistan needs foreign direct investments for its reconstruction. In this regard, China is one of the countries that have interests to stabilize Afghanistan through investments. China's economic intervention is seen as a solution to Afghanistan's stability. The relation between China and Afghanistan was seen more effective in the post 9/11. China gave economic assistance to Afghanistan on various projects. In 2002, China gave US$150 million for the reconstruction of Afghanistan.[14] Furthermore, from 2001 to 2013, it provided US$240 million.[15] Chinese involvement is felt more since 2014; the withdrawal of NATO troops from Afghanistan has made China to be more concerned and extend its economic aids to Afghanistan aiming for the stability of the country. In 2014, China provided US$80 million aid to Afghanistan and pledged to provide another US$240 million during 2015–2018.[16] Chinese government offered tariff-free treatment to 278 commodities in 2006 in Afghanistan's exports to China and set up Sino-Afghan Economic Committee to increase the bilateral trade. Afghanistan is keen to increase its bilateral trade and focused on the fields of agriculture, engineering and infrastructure that would pave the way for stabilization of Afghanistan.

In the recent years, due to the continuous conflict, corruption, drug trade, drought and lack of investments, Afghanistan's economy is shattered experiencing hardships especially in the export-led growth. Afghan government launched national export strategy in 2018 and took several initiatives to grow the exports. The China–Afghanistan air corridor was launched in November 2018. The corridor was initiated for the purpose of boosting pine nut industry. The pine nut industry had losses due to smuggling through Pakistan. The local traders found China–Afghanistan air corridor profitable because of the government subsidies.[17] The corridor project was initiated in agriculture sector. It does not solve the economic problem of Afghanistan because through the China–Afghanistan air corridor, the export of raw material is done. This air corridor would be more beneficial if the recently opened pine nut processing factory in Kabul becomes active.[18]

Afghanistan is rich in terms of having natural resources like copper, iron, marble, precious metals, lithium, gemstones and hydrocarbons, some of which are unexplored. China has so far initiated three major projects in the sectors of mining/extraction, transportation infrastructure and agriculture.[19] The best example of Chinese investments in Afghanistan's natural resource is the Aynak copper and Amu Darya oil in the northern part of the country.

Aynak copper is one of the important economic projects in Afghan history. It can produce 6 million tons of pure copper that is worth of over US$100 billion. Since the place is in high altitude, it needs infrastructure development.[20] China's Metallurgical Company won the tender for Aynak copper in 2007. China's total investment in this project is US$10 billion. Through the contract, China agreed to build railways, exploit coal mines and construct a 400-MW coal-fired power plant and 1 million ton steel works. The project was signed for 30 years. The tax for Afghan government is US$60 million per year and can earn US$808 million by granting the exploiting rights.[21] On the other hand, the internal security situation in Logar province of Afghanistan has created obstacles towards the implementation of the project. Though the Aynak project has 1500 security guards, still it has been attacked 19 times during 2012–2013.[22] The project is pending completion because of the security scenario. President Ghani was trying to solve the issues of the delays in Aynak saying that "the friendly country of China who has won the contract is concerned about security of the mine" and in order "to start the mine's extraction at the soonest time possible, it is necessary for Afghan security forces to ensure protection of this key mine."[23] On the other hand, President Ghani cancelled the Mes Aynak copper mine project in December 2019 because the companies could not meet the financial commitments to the projects.[24] The shattered economy of Afghanistan is in severe need of investments. The Chinese company had agreed to three up-front payments of US$808 million to Afghan government (US$80.8 million upon award of the contract; US$161.6 million when the feasibility study was approved – these have already been paid – and 565.6 million when commercial copper production starts). It has also promised funds for a railway line that is supposed to connect Aynak via the Khyber pass to New Silk Road comprising of roads, railways and pipelines with the markets of the region.[25] However, little has been done on the ground. The 400-MW coal-fired power plant option has been cancelled by MCC; thus, the Afghan government is not happy with the proposal and insists to continue with the existing terms.[26] This could also highlight the reason behind the long-stalled Aynak copper project. Aynak copper would create 70,000 jobs in supply and services and 5000 directly at the mine. Creating the job opportunities to the people would be a positive step in preventing people joining terrorist groups. Most of the times, people join the terrorist groups for getting incomes to sustain their families.

Similarly, China also won the tender for Amu Darya oilfield in the northern part of Afghanistan that has reserves of more than 87 million barrels, a huge investment in oil and gas resources of Afghanistan. China National Petroleum Corporation along with the local Watan Group won the tender in 2011 for 25 years. The investment for this project is US$400 million and the estimated revenue will be US$7 billion. Annually the project will provide US$304.35 million to the Afghan government.[27] This project can help the local people to get jobs and prevent them in engaging in illegal activities like drug smuggling and joining terrorist groups. It would also help the Afghan government in ensuring peace and stability in the region. Moreover, Afghanistan imports oil products from Russia, Turkmenistan and the UAE.[28] The implementation of this project will decrease Afghanistan's energy independence and enhance the revenue for the country. The extracted oil will be sent for the refinery in Turkmenistan until CNPC built a refinery in Afghanistan. The contract terms show that CNPC will pay 15% royalty on oil production, 20% corporate income tax and 50–70% of its profit to Afghan government.[29] According to the articles related to the Amu Darya basin oil extraction, the CNPC and Watan group should train and employ qualified Afghan nationals in the hydrocarbon operations. It is also stated that as long as it's possible, it should use the goods that are produced or are available in Afghanistan and services rendered by Afghan national companies. The government shall endeavour to provide security within the contract area and any other areas in Afghanistan, where hydrocarbons operations involved, according to the laws of Afghanistan.[30]

To sum up, both the projects are vital in terms of making the country economically prosperous. The huge investments from the project could be used for the reconstruction of the country. The successful implementation of both the projects will encourage foreign investors to increase and improve the prospects for other projects in the region.

China–Pakistan economic corridor

China–Pakistan economic corridor is a regional connectivity and a part of China's BRI. It will have a positive impact on Iran, Afghanistan, India, Central Asian countries and the region. It will also improve

> road, rail, and air transportation system with the free exchange of growth and people-to-people contact enhancing understanding through academic, cultural and regional knowledge and culture, activity of higher volume of flow of trade and businesses, producing and moving energy to have more optimal businesses and enhancement of cooperation by win–win model will result in well connected, integrated region of shared destiny, harmony and development.[31]

CPEC has been projected as the win–win model for countries of the region. It is the collection of the infrastructure projects worth US$54 billion that aims to connect China's Xinjiang province to Pakistan's Gwadar port. Afghanistan also expressed interest to join CPEC.

Benefits for Afghanistan

When Afghanistan joins the CPEC, it will have several benefits. Pakistan has taken the initiatives to build roads, for example the 75-km Torkham–Jalalabad road increasing connectivity to Pakistan and in return Afghanistan gaining access to CPEC. Pakistan constructed two roads leading from D.I. Khan to Angoor Adda and Ghulam Khan, linking with the Khost and Paktika provinces of Afghanistan. This will have positive impact on Afghan investors and also reduce the costs of imports. Moreover, by becoming a part of CPEC, Afghanistan will get access to Chinese markets, Central Asia and parts of Europe that currently Afghanistan does not trade.[32]

Benefits for China

Afghanistan's strategic location linking South Asia to Central Asia is an important aspect for China. China will be benefited from untapped resources of Afghanistan worth US$1 trillion. Nevertheless, Afghanistan's instability and insecure situation deters the investment opportunities. Thus, China has made contributions in supporting peace talks with Afghanistan and encouraged the Taliban to join the peace negotiation. Ensuring security will also pave the way for China's investments and prevent insecurity in its Xinjiang province.[33]

Benefits for Pakistan

Joining CPEC is a step towards the stability of Afghanistan and a stable Afghanistan would ease the economic burdens of hosting Afghan refugees by Pakistan. The improvement of economic status of Afghanistan will allow millions of Afghan refugees return back to their country. CPEC will create a cooperative situation and open up the easiest ways of trade to Pakistan with Central Asian countries. The economic cooperation will also develop the mutual collaboration towards the security. It will be a win–win situation for both the countries. Similarly, it will also have a positive impact on resolving the cross-border relations.[34]

China's role in regional cooperation for Afghanistan's security

The relationship between China and Afghanistan gained more attention in 2014 since China had apprehensions from increasing instability in Afghanistan with the withdrawal of NATO troops. In Kabul, Chinese foreign minister Wang Yi showed his strong support for Afghanistan in achieving smooth political, economy and security. Afghanistan's president Ashraf Ghani scheduled his first official trip to China stating that "We count on the active engagement of the People's Republic of China in promoting peace, prosperity, and stability in Afghanistan and in the region."[35] This led to several bilateral initiatives between China and Afghanistan. Regarding China's role in Afghanistan's stability and security, former ambassador of Afghanistan to China, Sultan Ahmad Bahin, says,

> China's role is important for Afghanistan's peace, reconstruction and other sectors. It is also important for Chinese people, as their country is one of the biggest economic countries in the world. A more secure region will be crucial for further development of that country.[36]

China and Afghanistan signed several security and economic agreements in 2012. One of these agreements was to send 300 Afghan police officers to China for training.[37] Further, in the same year, agreements on strategic partnership between Kabul and Beijing, US$150 million agreement on aid with ministry of finance and with the Afghan interior ministry in giving trainings to the police officers were signed.[38]

At multilateral level, China continues to engage in multiple levels – regional and international – for example, Shanghai Cooperation, the Heart of Asia Istanbul, the Conference on Interaction and Confidence Building Measures in Asia (CIGA); or through subregional groupings like hosting Pakistan–Afghanistan–China trilateral bilateral engagements.[39]

Shanghai Cooperation Organization (SCO)

The SCO was built to establish ties with Central Asian countries to fight against terrorism, increase stability and promote economic development. Afghanistan obtained the observer status in 2012. The Shanghai Cooperation was originally for the settlement of the border disputes and enhances border security by China, Kazakhstan, Kyrgyzstan, Russia and Tajikistan in 1996. The 9/11 incident accelerated the formation of SCO and its main purpose is to fight against terrorism, separatism and religious extremism.[40] As the two regional powers – Russia and China – are involved in the forum, they can assist the countries in the region effectively. Disagreement between Central Asian countries can also be brought to settlement through cooperative framework of SCO. As most of the Central Asian countries are neighbouring Afghanistan and they have concerns about spillover effect of Afghan turmoil, SCO's contribution on stabilization of Afghanistan could grant a greater sphere of influence for China. Regarding the role of SCO members, President Xi Jinping said:

> We need to strengthen the foundation for shared peace and security. We need to actively implement the 2019–2021 program of cooperation for combating three evil forces: terrorism, separatism and extremism, continue to conduct the "Peace Mission" and other joint counter-terrorism

exercises, and enhance cooperation on defense security, law enforcement security and information security.[41]

The president of China also said that "China offers to train 2,000 law enforcement officers for all parties in the next three years through China National Institute for SCO International Exchange and Judicial Cooperation and other platforms to enhance law enforcement capacity building."[42] The SCO members want Afghanistan to become a permanent member so that they can easily tackle the terrorism issue. The SCO can pave the way for greater cooperation between India and Pakistan as they are members.[43]

Heart of Asia: Istanbul

Another multilateral framework that can provide ground for security cooperation between Afghanistan and China is the Heart of Asia – Istanbul Process that was initiated by Afghanistan in November 2011.[44] The first declaration of this multilateral process was on "Regional Security and Cooperation for a Secure and Stable Afghanistan" issued in November 2011.[45] Clause 13 of the declaration professes: "We declare our readiness to engage in sincere, result-oriented cooperation at all levels, which will not just help Afghanistan, but will also be beneficial to security and prosperity in the region as a whole."[46] Other declarations of the process that emphasise on security and counterterrorism cooperation are Beijing Declaration Deepening Cooperation for Sustainable Security and Prosperity of the "Heart of Asia" Region issued in October 2014; the Islamabad Declaration on Enhanced Cooperation for Countering Security Threats and Promoting Connectivity in the Heart of Asia Region issued in December 2015; the Amritsar Declaration on Addressing Challenges, Achieving Prosperity issued in December 2016; and the Baku Declaration Security & Economic Connectivity towards a Strengthened Heart of Asia Region issued in December 2017.[47]

China's role in Afghanistan's peace process

A peace agreement between the United States and Taliban was signed on 29 February 2020 and the United States agreed to withdraw its troops within 14 months. Taliban also agreed not to allow any extremist militant group to operate in the territory they control. But the peace with Afghan government is still under the process and dispute is over the release of 5000 Taliban prisoners.[48] The United States and NATO have decided to withdraw from Afghanistan in a situation when the terrorists attacks and activities are reduced and the country is stable. In such an environment, neighbouring countries' or regional countries' role becomes significant for Afghanistan's peace, security and economy. Peace and security are also of mutual concern for both China and Afghanistan. China enjoys a firm relation with Pakistan and Iran both, the countries that are important for Afghanistan's peace and stability. For instance,

China has also played an important role in Afghan-led Afghan-own process. In 2015, China engaged in peace talks between Taliban and the Afghan government.[49] Active involvement of China and the United States had begun in early 2016 when they initiated the Quadrilateral Coordination Group with Afghanistan and Pakistan to create the environment for talks between the Afghan government and Afghan Taliban. At the 5th summit that was held in May 2016, China expressed its commitment to Afghan-led Afghan-own peace reconciliation process to bring lasting peace and stability in Afghanistan.[50] In 2017, Beijing hosted trilateral dialogue including China, Pakistan and Afghanistan and invited Taliban to join peace process. In October 2018, Maulana Samiul Haq who is known as the father of Taliban called on China to play a bigger role in the peace process.[51] Similarly, Chinese foreign minister in a negotiation with Afghan foreign minister proposed two essential points: firstly, Taliban should join the peace negotiation and, secondly, China would agree to be as a mediator between Kabul and Islamabad. In September 2019, a Taliban delegation travelled to Beijing to discuss with China's special envoy on Afghanistan affairs. Meanwhile, in November, China showed its interest for hosting peace talks.[52] Furthermore, Chinese efforts in facilitating Afghan peace dialogue with Taliban shows that stability and security is an important factor for the development of its BRI project. Besides, Chinese peace envoy for Afghanistan, Deng Xijun, also met with India's Foreign Secretary and Iran's Deputy Foreign Minister for Political affairs on 11 May 2019 to discuss about cooperation in the Afghan peace process and agreed on common mechanisms for lasting peace in Afghanistan.[53]

Moreover, Yun Sun, the director of the China programme and co-director of the East Asia programme, sees China's role in Afghan security in three ways: (a) China is a great power in the region and its role cannot be ignored; (b) China's investments are much more important for Afghanistan's future post-conflict reconstruction and its economic development; (c) though China is not a primary party in the conflict, it is seen marginal in that sense.[54]

These highlight the status of China's relations with Taliban and, if China plays its actual role in Afghan's peace negotiation process, it will pave the way towards stability of the country. In the recent peace talks also, China persuaded Pakistan to help push the peace process forward.[55]

Conclusion

Withdrawal of NATO forces in 2014 raised China's security concerns and made it necessary to be more involved in taking the country towards stability. With Afghanistan, it has always had a keen interest in economic relation. On the other hand, continuing civil war and existence of terrorism in Afghanistan have made China worry about two main issues: cross-border terrorism with its concerns of escalating internal challenges in western Xinjiang province and cross-border drug trafficking. Thus, the perceptions on insecurity created by these concerns provide a ground for joint efforts to ensure common interests, including economic ties, stability and security by these two countries.

For several reasons, China can play a vital role in bringing security and stability to Afghanistan. The bilateral and multilateral cooperation frameworks provide solid ground for security cooperation between the two neighbours. China is the world's second largest economy and it can play a vital role in promoting stability of Afghanistan through its economic and security assistance. SCO and Heart of Asia – Istanbul apparently provide institutional frameworks for addressing the issues faced by Afghanistan for mutual gains.

Observations:

1. The future of Afghanistan and China are linked and it is based on mutual interests. By making investments in private sectors, their cooperation would provide avenues for political settlement of the conflict and consultation.
2. Poverty and lack of job opportunities enable the environment for drug production and drug-trafficking. Thus, the Chinese government along with Afghan government should give support to aid programmes to develop alternative crops. This way, direct producers might be kept away from poppy cultivation.
3. The implementation of the Aynak copper project as well as Amu Darya basin river would play an important role in Afghanistan's stability and economic growth. Thus, China should work with Afghan government for mutual benefit.

Notes

1 Hujatullah Zia, "China and Afghanistan Join Hands Closer to Fight COVID-19", *MENAFN*, 5 February 2020, https://menafn.com/1100104271/China-and-Afghanistan-Join-Hands-Closer-to-Fight-COVID-19, accessed 27 May 2020.
2 *Ibid.*
3 Huaxia, "China Hands Over the Medical Supplies to Afghanistan to Fight COVID-19", *XINHUANET*, 2 April 2020, http://www.xinhuanet.com/english/2020-04/02/c_138941306.htm, accessed 27 May 2020.
4 Barbara Kelemen, "China's Economic Stabilization Efforts in Afghanistan: A New Part to the Table?", *Middle East Institute*, 21 January 2020, https://www.mei.edu/publications/chinas-economic-stabilization-efforts-afghanistan-new-party-table, accessed 29 May 2020.
5 Justyna Szcsudlik, "China's Evolving Stance on Afghanistan: Towards More Robust Diplomacy with Chinese Characteristics", *Strategic File*, vol. 22, 2014, pp. 1–2.
6 Sayed Waqas, "The Role of China in Economic Stabilization and Reconstruction of Afghanistan", *Maryala Papers*, 2012, pp. 39–40.
7 Szcsudlik, n. 5, p. 1.
8 Szcsudlik, n. 5, p. 1.
9 Angela Stanzel, "Fear and Loating on the New Sil Road: Chinese Security in Afghanistan and Beyond", *European Council on Foreign Relations*, 2018, pp. 6–7.
10 Venda Brown, "Afghanistan's Opium Production Is through the Roof: Why Washington Shouldn't Overact", Brookings, 21 November 2017, https://www.brookings.edu/blog/order-from-chaos/2017/11/21/afghanistans-opium-product

ion-is-through-the-roof-why-washington-shouldnt-overreact/, accessed 24 April 2019.
11 Waqas, n. 6.
12 Daniel Nguyen, "Who's Behind the Dark Money Bankrolling or Politics", *Open Democracy*, 24 November 2012, www.opendemcracy.net, accessed 26 April 2019.
13 Zhai Huasheng, "China and Afghanistan: China's Interests, Stances, and Prospects", Center for Strategic and International Studies, 26 March 2012, https://www.csis.org/analysis/china-and-afghanistan, accessed 4 July 2020.
14 Waqas, n. 6, pp. 34–35.
15 Raja Mohammad, "Chinese Economic and Strategic Interests in Afghanistan", *Journal of Social Sciences*, vol. 1, 2015, p. 3.
16 Waqas, n. 6.
17 Kelemen, n. 4.
18 Kelemen, n. 4.
19 Kelemen, n. 4.
20 C. James, "China's Interest in Afghanistan: Current Projects and Future Prospects", *Calhoun*, 2013, pp. 60–61.
21 Huasheng, n. 13.
22 James, n. 20.
23 Thomas Rutting, "Copper and Peace: Afghanistan's Dilemma", *Afghanistan Analysts Network*, 11 July 2015, https://www.afghanistan-analysts.org/copper-and-peace-afghanistans-China-dilemma/, accessed 3 May 2019.
24 Kelemen, n. 4.
25 Rutting, n. 23.
26 Amin Mohsin, "The Story Behind China's Long-Stalled Mine in Afghanistan", *The Diplomat*, 7 January 2017, https://thediplomat.com/2017/01/the-story-behind-Chinas-long-stalled-mine-in-afghanistan/, accessed 3 May 2019.
27 Rahman Tahiri, "Afghanistan and China Trade Relationship", Uroj University: Munich Personal RePEc Archive, 2017.
28 Intelligence Unit, "CNPC Begins Oil Production", *The Economist*, 23 October, 2012, http://country.eiu.com/article.aspx?articleid=589715243&Country=Afghanistan&topic=Economy&subtopic=Forecast&subsubtopic=Economic+growth, accessed 4 May 2019.
29 Tahiri, n. 27.
30 See https://www.resourcecontracts.org/contract/ocds-591adf-2547744131, accessed 10 April 2019.
31 Government of Pakistan, "China Pakistan Economic Corridor", http://cpec.gov.pk/introduction/1, accessed 10 April 2019.
32 A. Chandran, "Why Afghanistan Should Join CPEC", *The Diplomat*, 5 May 2017, https://thediplomat.com/2017/05/why-afghanistan-should-join-cpec/, accessed 2 May 2019.
33 *Ibid.*
34 *Ibid.*
35 Baisali Mohanty, "China in Afghanistan: Security, Regional Standing, and Status", *ORF Occasional Paper*, no. 126, 2017.
36 Tolo News, "Afghanistan, China to Sign Security, Economic Agreements", *Tolo News*, 10 May 2016, https://www.tolonews.com/business/afghanistan-China-sign-security-economic-agreements, accessed 5 May 2019.
37 Priyanka Boghani, "China and Afghanistan Sign Security and Economic Agreements", *PRI*, 24 September 2012, https://www.pri.org/stories/2012-09-24/China-and-afghanistan-sign-security-and-economic-agreements, accessed 2 May 2019.
38 Tolo News, "China, Afghanistan Sign Agreements", *Tolo News*, 23 September 2012, http://prod.tolonews.com/afghanistan/China-afghanistan-sign-agreements, accessed 6 May 2019.

39 Raffaello Pantucci, "Commentary: China's Expanding Security Role in Afghanistan", *Reutetrs*, 1 March 2017.
40 J. Tatar, "China's Evolving Stance on Afghanistan: Towards More Robust Diplomacy with Chinese Characteristic", *Strategic File*, vol. 22, 2014.
41 Sharif Amiri, "China's Leader Proposes SCO-Afghanistan Contact Group", *Tolo News*, 10 June 2018, https://www.tolonews.com/afghanistan/China%E2%80%99s-leader-proposes-sco-afghanistan-contact-group, accessed 6 May 2019.
42 *Ibid*.
43 Boghani, n. 37.
44 The Heart of Asia – Istanbul Process, http://hoa.gov.af/#move-top, accessed 2 May 2019.
45 Declaration of the Istanbul Process on Regional Security and Cooperation for a Secure and Stable Afghanistan on the Heart of Asia – Istanbul Process, http://hoa.gov.af/files/2-Nov-Declaration.pdf, accessed 30 March 2019.
46 *Ibid*.
47 For declarations of the Heart of Asia – Istanbul Process, see http://hoa.gov.af/335/declarations, accessed 2 May 2019.
48 Noman Akhtar, "The Importance of China's Role in Afghanistan Peace Talks", *Modern Diplomacy*, 28 April 2020, https://moderndiplomacy.eu/2020/04/28/the-importance-of-china-s-role-in-afghanistan-peace-talks/, accessed 28 May 2020.
49 Current Affairs Correspondent West Asia, "The Significance of China's Role in Afghan Peace Talks", *Belt and Road News*, 25 March 2020, https://www.beltandroad.news/2020/03/25/the-significance-of-chinas-role-in-afghan-peace-talks/, accessed 27 May 2020.
50 Mohanty, n. 35.
51 Kristin Huang, "China may 'Push Forward' Peace Process to Protect Belt and Road Interests", *South China Morning Post*, 29 January 2019, https://www.scmp.com/news/China/diplomacy/article/2184155/China-may-try-push-forward-afghanistan-peace-process-protect, accessed 6 May 2019.
52 *Ibid*.
53 Akhtar, n. 48.
54 Waqar Ahmad, "Chinese Role in Afghan Peace", *The International News*, 2 May 2020, https://www.thenews.com.pk/print/652967-chinese-role-in-afghan-peace, accessed 28 May 2020.
55 Ajmal Sahms, "China Has a Role in Afghanistan Peace Process", *Global Times*, 5 November 2018, http://www.globaltimes.cn/content/1126002.shtml, accessed 6 May 2019.

INDEX

AAGC 65
Abdulla Yaameen 32, 133, 136
Act East 4, 108, 144
ADB 50, 54, 77
Adluri Subramanyam Raju 1, 4, 28
Afghanistan 2, 5, 7, 13, 14, 20, 22, 33, 48, 54, 65, 79, 80, 130, 140, 207, 211–220
Africa 21, 31, 36, 42, 53, 60, 87, 129, 162, 163, 206
AICS 79
AIIB 60, 65, 68
al Qaeda 14
Anindiya Jyoti Majumdar 5, 97
Anasua Basu Ray Chaudhury 6, 143
Antonio Guterres 61
APTA 118, 121–124
Arabian Sea 48, 203, 207
ARF 1
ASEAN 1, 4, 5, 47, 61, 79, 81, 108
Ashminder Singh Bahal 4, 72
Ashraf Ghani 216
Asia 2, 34, 35, 53, 60, 87, 105, 127, 129, 163, 205
Asia–Africa Economic Corridor 78
Asia–Africa Growth Corridor 36
Asia-Indo-Pacific 2
Asian Giant 152
Asia-Pacific 1, 2
Australia 67, 78, 105, 108

Bangladesh 5, 6, 7, 14, 15, 20–22, 30, 54, 65, 85, 90–92, 128, 130, 136, 138, 140, 163, 171–182, 189, 199

Bay of Bengal 91, 92, 105, 172
BBIN 4, 5, 15, 80, 81, 84, 85, 90–93
BCIM 15, 34, 54, 59, 99, 108, 179
BCIM EC 14, 64, 102
BDCA 35
Bhutan 20, 44–46, 54, 85, 90–92, 101, 128, 134, 140, 171, 177
BIMSTEC 15, 54, 62, 65, 80, 81, 90, 93, 108, 166
BRI 2–5, 7, 11–14, 16, 17, 19, 20, 21, 28, 32, 34–36, 41, 42, 47, 48, 52–55, 58–67, 72, 74, 84–90, 92, 93, 106, 107, 128, 138, 144, 162, 166, 172, 176, 177–179, 185, 190–194, 199, 201, 203, 212, 215
BRIC 103
BRICS 12, 34, 67, 68
British 46

CAR 73, 79, 81
Central Asia 36, 41, 42, 60, 62, 63, 81, 215, 216
China 1, 3–7, 11–19, 21, 28–37, 42, 43, 45–55, 58, 59, 62–66, 68, 72–79, 82, 84–87, 89, 92, 93, 97–99, 100–109, 111, 112, 114–118, 121–124, 127–129, 131–141, 143–147, 149–158, 160–168, 171–182, 185–195, 198–203, 205–208, 211–215, 217, 219, 220
Chindia 103, 104
Chou En Lai 31
CIS 47
CLMV 79

CMEC 74
Cold War 1, 98, 104, 133, 161, 172, 173, 189
Connectivity 4
COVID-19 55, 76, 79–81, 85, 90, 93, 106, 123, 124, 140, 164, 179, 181, 201, 211
Cox's Bazaar 179
CPEC 4, 7, 15, 17, 18, 28, 36, 42, 54, 59, 62–64, 66, 74, 75, 88, 99, 198, 200–203, 205–208, 215, 216
CPFTA 200

Dalai Lama 45
Deng Xiaoping 12, 49, 72, 187

EAS 1
East Asia 60, 219
Eurasia 36
Europe 21, 41, 62, 63, 76, 81, 198
European Union 60

FDI 79, 191
Ferdinand Braudel 52
France 67
FTA 200

G7 60, 88
GATT 51
GDP 35, 41, 73, 74, 199, 208
Germany 67
Ghani 214
GNP 59
Gotabaya 133

H.M. Ershad 174, 175
Hu Jin Tao 92

IMF 50, 54, 61, 121, 199, 207
Imran Khan 204, 205
India 1, 5, 15, 20, 22, 23, 30, 31, 33–37, 42, 58, 62, 64–68, 72, 74, 78, 79–81, 84–86, 88–93, 97–103, 105, 106, 108, 109, 111–118, 121, 123, 124, 127–130, 132–141, 143–147, 149, 151–157, 165, 167, 168, 172, 173, 177, 186–192, 194, 204, 208
Indian Ocean 2, 3, 34, 35, 41, 74, 79, 98, 104, 139, 161, 162, 172, 189
India–Pakistan war 1965 29
Indonesia 36, 204
Indo-Pacific 2, 7, 61, 72, 75, 76, 78, 105
Indo-Pacific Economic Corridor 78
Indra Nath Mukherji 6, 111

International Monetary Fund 111
IOR 42
IORA 67, 166
Iran 48, 213, 215
ISIS 213
Islamic State 42

Japan 2, 65, 74, 75, 78, 105, 108, 123, 129, 156
Jawaharlal Nehru 31

K P Oli 133, 139, 193
Kazakhstan 47, 217
Khaleda Zia 174, 180
Kosh Raj Koirala 7, 185
Kyrgyzstan 47, 217

Ladakh 45
Li Keqiang 153, 203
Look East 144
LTTE 135, 165, 166

Mahinda Rajapaksa 133, 162
Malacca Dilemma 92, 167
Maldives 16, 30, 73, 101, 133, 134, 136, 163
Mao Zedong 44
Maritime Silk Road 2, 3, 87, 190
Maritime Silk Route 42
Mauritius 163
MFN 118
Michael Vlahos 130
Michel Foucault 53
Middle East 42, 43, 48, 60, 87, 139, 162, 198
MNC 50, 51
Mohamed Nasheed 16
Mohammad Nashid 136
MSR 58, 63, 65
Mujibur Rahman 171, 173
Myanmar 14, 63, 67, 73, 75, 80, 105, 140, 171, 177
Myanmar 163

N. Manoharan 6, 160
Narender Modi 35, 54, 86, 90, 98, 100, 101, 105, 134, 153
NATO 212, 213, 216, 218, 219
Nawaz Sharif 61
Neighbourhood First 21
Nepal 5, 7, 16, 17, 20–22, 30, 32, 44–46, 54, 63, 65, 85, 86, 89–92, 100, 128, 131, 134, 138, 139, 140, 153, 171, 177, 185–187, 189, 190–195

Nine Dash Line 78
NTB 122
Nuclear programme 29
Nuclear proliferation 30

OBOR 58, 61, 62, 68, 72, 87, 162, 177, 202, 203, 212

Pacific Ocean 2
Pakistan 3, 5, 7, 13, 17, 18, 20–22, 30, 32, 33, 52, 62, 66, 67, 73, 81, 82, 93, 99, 105, 108, 130, 132, 137, 146, 163, 171, 189, 198–208, 213, 215
Pearl in the string 160
PTA 200

Quad 1, 35, 65, 78, 105

R. Srinivasan 4, 41
Rajiv Gandhi 189
Rakhahari Chatterji 6, 143
Ranil Wickremesinghe 19
RCEP 1
Reena Marwah 7, 198
Richard McGregor 49
Richard Nixon 199
Robert Kaplan 36
Russia 14, 41, 43, 47, 66, 80, 165, 213, 217

SAARC 2, 4, 5, 29, 65, 73, 77, 80–82, 89, 90, 93, 100, 107, 166, 207
Sadaf Mohmand 7, 211
SAGAR 65
SCO 47, 54, 61, 62, 67, 79, 217, 218, 220
Second World War 77
Seychelles 163
Sheikh Hasina 180
Sheikh Mujibur Rahman 172, 174
Sikkim 44, 46
Sino-Indian war 29
SIPRI 21, 204
Smruti S Pattanaik 6, 127
South Asia 2–4, 11, 12, 19, 20, 22, 28–34, 36, 37, 41, 42, 52, 54, 55, 59, 65–67, 73, 75, 77, 79, 81, 82, 84, 89, 97–101, 106–108, 127–133, 137, 139, 141, 171, 177, 185, 186, 188–190, 193–195
South China Sea 31, 36, 74, 75, 78, 152
South Korea 129

Southeast Asia 21, 63, 73, 86, 177
Soviet Union 173, 188
Sreeradha Datta 6, 171
Sri Lanka 5, 6, 18–22, 30, 36, 52, 53, 73, 89, 93, 101, 105, 130, 131, 133, 135, 136, 138–140, 160–168, 189, 206
Sri Lanka Dilemma 167
Srikanth Kondapalli 3, 11
String of Pearls 161, 163
SWRD Bandaranaike 160

T.V. Paul 106
Taiwan 123
Tajikistan 47, 217
Taliban 13, 213
TAR 186, 188, 189, 190
Thailand 64, 80
Tibet 44, 45, 47, 134
TPP 1
Trump 104, 208

Ujjwal Upadhyay 5, 84
UK 67
UN 47, 60, 173, 188
US 2, 6, 14, 20, 21, 28, 34, 36, 48, 51, 63, 67, 75, 76, 79, 86–88, 103–108, 111, 115, 118, 121, 122, 124, 127, 139, 144, 154, 161, 171, 173, 185, 187–189, 193, 194, 199, 204, 208, 211, 213, 218, 219

Vietnam 129, 204

Wen Jiabao 200
West Asia 31, 163
World Bank 54, 63, 111, 200, 206, 207
World Order 102
WTO 49, 51, 122, 123
Wuhan 76, 211
Wuhan meeting 34

Xi Jinping 11, 16, 34, 35, 41, 42, 49, 52, 53, 58, 62, 67, 86, 87, 98, 134, 171, 176, 188, 201, 202, 203, 217

Y.Yagama Reddy 4, 58
Yongjin Zhang 44

Zhu Rongji 174
Zia 175

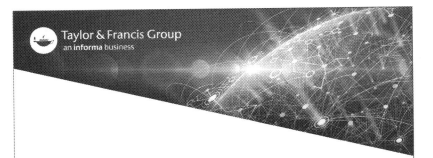

Printed in the United States
by Baker & Taylor Publisher Services